University of St. Francis
GEN 172.42 L128
F

W9-AFC-275
3 0301 00055838 3

1989

Ethics and Strategic Defense

American Philosophers Debate Star Wars and the Future of Nuclear Deterrence

Douglas P. Lackey

Baruch College and The Graduate Center
City University of New York

Wadsworth Publishing Company
Belmont, California
A Division of Wadsworth, Inc.

Philosophy Editor: Kenneth King
Editorial Assistant: Cheri Peterson
Production: Cece Munson, The Cooper Company
Print Buyer: Randy Hurst
Copy Editor: Meredy Amyx
Cover: John Edeen
Compositor: TCSystems, Inc., Shippensburg, Pennsylvania

© 1989 by Wadsworth, Inc. All rights reserved. No part of this book may
be reproduced, stored in a retrieval system, or transcribed, in any form or
by any means, electronic, mechanical, photocopying, recording, or
otherwise, without the prior written permission of the publisher,
Wadsworth Publishing Company, Belmont, California 94002, a division of
Wadsworth, Inc.

Printed in the United States of America
1 2 3 4 5 6 7 8 9 10——93 92 91 90 89

Library of Congress Cataloging-in-Publication Data

Ethics and strategic defense: American philosophers debate Star Wars and
   the future of nuclear deterrence / edited by Douglas P. Lackey.
   p.   cm.
   ISBN 0-534-09588-7
   1. Strategic Defense Initiative—Moral and ethical aspects.
2. Deterrence (Strategy)—Moral and ethical aspects.   I. Lackey, Douglas
   P.
UG743.E73 1988
172'.42—dc19   88-9632
                                                  CIP

Preface

172.42
L128

From the 1950s through the 1970s American nuclear weapons policy was shaped by the idea of nuclear deterrence. In 1983, President Reagan became the first president to question the strategic primacy of deterrence, suggesting that strategic defenses—a "Star Wars" system—might be a morally superior alternative. Since 1983, over $13 billion has been spent exploring the possibilities of strategic defense, and it is certain that the Strategic Defense Initiative will survive the Reagan presidency and continue into the 1990s.

Most discussions of strategic defense since 1983 have concentrated on the technical problems of Star Wars systems. This is the first collection of essays devoted to the *moral* issues raised by President Reagan in 1983. Are strategic defenses morally superior to nuclear deterrence? Are they superior to some forms of nuclear deterrence, or to all forms? Are there hidden moral defects in the policy of strategic defense? Are there any policies that are morally superior to *both* nuclear deterrence and strategic defense?

Answers to these questions require knowledge of the ethical concepts, not just technical information. The contributors to this volume, most of them professionally trained in the history of ethics and moral theory, demonstrate by example how the techniques of moral evaluation can be extended from the sphere of private life to one of the most important public issues of our time. In the contributions by professional philosophers I have sought to include papers that exhibit a grasp of the relevant details together with the philosopher's special virtues: logical consistency, analytic precision, and strict impartiality.

If anthologies could have dedications, I would dedicate this volume to Professor Marshall Cohen, the first and only editor of *Philosophy and Public Affairs,* whose Olympian standards for that journal have established and legitimatized the field of applied ethics, and made possible volumes such as the one assembled here.

Douglas P. Lackey
Baruch College and the Graduate Center
City University of New York

133,658

iii

Contents

Part I. Introduction: The Moral Comparison of Deterrence and Defense

Douglas P. Lackey

T hose who had the interest or fortitude to tune in to President Reagan's address of 23 March 1983 on the military budget had little warning that they were in for something historic. For fifteen minutes the speech proceeded along familiar lines, describing a growing Soviet threat and calling for increased defense spending. But then the president suddenly switched gears, catching even the Pentagon by surprise. "Since the advent of nuclear weapons," the president said,

> steps have been increasingly directed toward deterrence of aggression through the promise of retaliation. . . . [But] I have become more and more deeply convinced that the human spirit must be capable of rising above dealing with other nations and human beings by threatening their existence. . . .
>
> If the Soviet Union will join with us in our effort to achieve major [arms] reduction, we will have succeeded in stabilizing the nuclear balance.
>
> Nevertheless, it will still be necessary to rely on the specter of retaliation, on mutual threat. And that's a sad commentary on the human condition. Wouldn't it be better to save lives than to avenge them? . . .
>
> What if free people could live secure in the knowledge that their security did not rest on the threat of instant U. S. retaliation to deter a Soviet attack, that we could intercept and destroy strategic ballistic missiles before they reached our own soil or that of our allies? . . .
>
> With these considerations firmly in mind, I call upon the scientific community in our country, those who gave us nuclear weapons, to turn their great talents now to the cause of mankind and world peace, to give us the means of rendering these nuclear weapons impotent and obsolete.

Perhaps the most remarkable feature of this "Star Wars" speech is its straightforward appeal to moral considerations. When the president asks, "Wouldn't it be better to save lives than to avenge them?" he doesn't mean merely that it is better to save *American* lives than to avenge them but that it is better to save *human* lives than to avenge them, and this appeal has the universal character we associate with moral principles. The "better" the president seeks is the *morally* better, perhaps not in the sense that what we are doing now is wicked, but rather in the sense that what we are doing now would be wicked if we could find some better alternative. The call to the scientists at the end of the speech is a summons to create this morally better option.

The argument that a system of strategic defense would be morally superior to the prevailing system of nuclear deterrence is of course not new. The challenge "Wouldn't it be better to save lives than to avenge them?" echoes Donald Brennan's remark, "We should prefer live Americans to dead Russians," which dates from the antiballistic missile (ABM) debate of 1969.[1] Nevertheless, the moral element in the new debate about strategic defense does seem more prominent than it was during the ABM controversy in the late 1960s. When the president describes strategic defenses as the means "to free mankind from the prison of mutual terror,"[2] such language makes movement away from nuclear deterrence a task of overriding moral urgency.

The moral argument developed by the president and by many contemporary supporters of strategic defense has two steps. First, the present system of nuclear deterrence is characterized as a system of Mutual Assured Destruction (MAD), and MAD is alleged to contain moral defects. Second, a system of effective or even partially effective strategic defenses is alleged to be free of the moral defects of MAD.

The moral defect in MAD that seems to trouble the president most is that the system threatens innocent people all around the world. "Today," the president remarked in 1985, vis-à-vis his understanding of MAD,

> our war deterrent is based on [this]: they have missiles, we have missiles, and if they fire their missiles and kill millions of our people, we will fire ours and kill millions of theirs. That's no way to go. How long can the American people stand for a strategy that threatens so many innocent lives?[3]

President Reagan's first secretary of defense also views strategic defenses as "more idealistic, moral, and practical than . . . mutual assured destruction."[4] But for Secretary Weinberger the moral defect in MAD is not that it threatens innocent people but that it denies Americans their right to self-defense:

> I've never believed in the idea that somehow we enhanced our security by giving up any attempt to defend ourselves. I've always thought it far more effective and far more moral and noble . . . to try and destroy weapons rather than people.[5]

The purpose of this volume is to evaluate these moral claims and others like them. Is the current system of nuclear deterrence morally condemnable? If it is

---

[1]Donald Brennan, "The Case for Population Defense," in Johan Holst and Jurgen Schneider, *Why ABM?* (New York: Pergamon Press, 1969), pp. 336–337. The full quote reads, "We should rather prefer live Americans to dead Russians, and we should not choose to live forever under a nuclear sword of Damocles."

[2]Ronald Reagan, State of the Union address, 4 February 1985.

[3]Ronald Reagan, speech in Milwaukee, 15 October 1985, quoted in *Star Wars Quotes* (Washington, DC: Arms Control Association, 1986), p. 46.

[4]Ibid., p. 47.

[5]Caspar Weinberger, Washington *Times* (28 March 1984).

condemnable, do strategic defenses provide a morally superior alternative? Does a commitment to a nuclear second strike—that is, a commitment to strike back with nuclear weapons if struck by them—violate the right of innocent people worldwide? Are strategic defenses justifiable on the grounds of self-defense?

. . .

As is true of most things, the moral comparison of nuclear deterrence and strategic defense is more complicated than it looks at first sight. If by "Mutual Assured Destruction" we mean any policy that attempts to deter unwanted behavior of opponents by threatening them with nuclear attack, then in fact there are many versions of MAD.[6] At a minimum it is necessary, before passing moral judgment, to distinguish between (a) a system of nuclear deterrence in which nuclear weapons are used only in response to nuclear attack on ourselves and (b) a system of nuclear deterrence in which nuclear weapons are used in response to other forms of unwanted behavior, including attacks on our allies. According to many moral analysts, there are also significant moral differences among (c) deterrent policies that make cities as such the assigned targets of nuclear missiles, (d) deterrent policies that do not target cities as such but target military installations within cities, and (e) deterrent policies that do not target cities or anything within them. There also seem to be significant moral differences between (f) policies that program nuclear strikes against cities in response to any kind of nuclear attack and (g) those that program nuclear strikes against cities only in response to nuclear strikes against cities.[7]

To complicate matters further, there are many types of strategic defense. It is essential for moral analysts to distinguish (a) strategic defenses that are capable of defending urban areas from (b) strategic defenses that are capable only of defending strategic weapons. For those who think that any use of nuclear weapons constitutes a special moral problem, there is a moral difference between (c) strategic defenses that utilize nuclear explosions, such as X-ray lasers, and (d) strategic defenses that do not utilize nuclear explosions. For those concerned with the militarization of space, there is a moral difference between (e) ground-based strategic defense and (f) space-based strategic defense.

---

[6]Given the frequency with which MAD is denounced, surprisingly little effort has gone into defining what the critics mean by "MAD." Sometimes it seems that "MAD" denotes any policy that programs a strategic nuclear response (of any kind) to a nuclear attack on the United States or its allies. At other times, it seems to refer to a policy that programs a massive nuclear attack targeted explicitly on cities in response to *any* strategic nuclear strike on the United States or its allies. The first definition is rather vague; the second is at variance with the actual war-fighting plans of the United States. See Desmond Ball and Jeffrey Richelson, eds., *Strategic Nuclear Targeting* (Ithaca, NY: Cornell University Press, 1986).

[7]The Reagan administration argued for the moral significance of these targeting distinctions when contesting the position of the American National Conference of Catholic Bishops in 1982. See the letter of National Security Advisor William Clark in *Origins* 12:20 (18 November 1982). For arguments that the moral significance of the distinction between targeting cities and targeting within cities is exaggerated, see Douglas Lackey, "The Moral Irrelevance of the Counterforce/Countervalue Distinction," *The Monist,* June 1987.

Still worse, in contemporary philosophical ethics there are numerous articulated systems of morality, each of which commands its devoted supporters. Among them are these:

- *utilitarian theories,* which maintain that the right policy is the one that does the most good for all concerned and, according to which moral action should concern itself exclusively with maximizing future good;

- *natural-rights theories,* which maintain that peoples and nations have rights that must not be violated, even to serve the common good, rights that peoples and nations are entitled to defend with force, even when such defenses do not promote the common good;

- *theories of justice,* which maintain that peoples and nations should be treated according to their just deserts, as determined by their prior behavior, and which often stress the obligation to cooperate with those who seek to cooperate, but which also stress the absence of obligations toward those who fail to seek to cooperate;

- *duty-based theories,* which maintain that right action consists in discharging duties entailed by one's social role, and which concern themselves with articulating how a good parent, citizen, soldier, or political leader, as such, should act;

- *virtue-based theories,* which concern themselves with the motives and capacities of moral agents, and which connect the assessment of motives with some theory of human flourishing.

Faced with these competing theories, all defended by philosophers and endorsed by various constituencies of American citizens, the policy analyst has no choice but to be eclectic—to accept *all* major moral theories as relevant to the moral judgment of policy. Instead of being a utilitarian, the analyst must accept "utilitarian considerations"; instead of endorsing natural-rights theory, the analyst must accept "rights considerations"; and so forth, determining the different weights assigned to these considerations according to what Aristotle called practical wisdom, but which the uncharitable might call the "seat of one's pants."

In arguments about strategic defenses, utilitarian considerations motivate those who believe that strategic defenses will increase—or decrease—the risk of nuclear war. Rights-based considerations are advanced by those who feel that the American right to self-defense entitles the United States to strategic defenses, and also by those who feel that the risks of extending the arms race into space impinge upon the rights of third parties who wish to enjoy a world, and a space, free of superpower conflicts. Justice-based considerations are invoked by those who cite the Soviet refusal to cooperate in arms control and to accept the system of stable deterrence, as well as by those who feel that the move toward strategic defenses blocks attempts at international cooperation by provoking offensive increases rather than step-by-step reductions in strategic arms. Duty-based considerations seem to have prompted President Reagan to find some better means to "preserve, protect, and defend" the American people than a system that provides, in his view, the empty consolation that in any nuclear war more than just Americans will die. Those concerned with virtue and motive in both the individual and national spheres will evaluate whether those who support strategic defenses are interested in a safer world or interested in a world in which the United States recovers military dominance through threats of nuclear attack, made newly credible by strategic defenses that block a Soviet response. The moral analyst must survey such considerations and weigh them all.

It may turn out that *every* system of morality will judge that every type of strategic defense is morally superior to each and every type of nuclear deterrance. It may turn out that *every* system of morality will judge every type of nuclear deterrence morally superior to every type of strategic defense. If so, the moral comparison of deterrence and defense will be relatively easy. But there are many other ways things might turn out. It is possible that all principal systems of morality will find *some* types of strategic defense morally superior to *some* types of nuclear deterrence and some types of deterrence superior to some types of strategic defense. It is also possible, even likely, that different moral codes will make different judgments when presented with particular comparisons between deterrent and defensive systems. As if this were not complex enough, there is the consideration that different strategic systems respond differently to different provocations. A system that prescribes a morally superior response to one provocation (such as a limited counterforce attack against American ICBMs) may provide a morally inferior response to another provocation (such as a massive countervalue strike against American cities). One system may be morally superior before war begins and another may be morally superior after deterrence fails.

Then there is the possibility of ties. True, with some systems of morality—for example, the systems maintaining that the morally obligatory policy is the one that creates the most good for all concerned—it is extremely unlikely that there will be ties. But with other moral systems, systems that pay less attention to detailed actual consequences and more attention to the kinds of actions the policy prescribes, the possibility of ties is quite likely. If we have a moral system that evaluates a policy as "obligatory," "permissible," or "condemned" by measuring actions prescribed by the policy against a list of moral rights, then it will often happen that two competing policies are *both* rated as morally permissible, or both rated as morally obligatory, or both morally condemned.[8]

In the great contest between defense and deterrence, partisans on each side praise their own approach and condemn the alternative. The possibility of moral ties is rarely considered. But if deterrence and defense are both morally permissible, and neither is obligatory, then they are morally equal and the choice between them can be made only on nonmoral grounds. And should it turn out that they are both morally condemned, then some third option, such as unilateral nuclear disarmament, might emerge as morally obligatory. Students of strategy will find this inference unlikely, since they consider unilateral nuclear disarm-

---

[8]If a moral system rates two incompatible actions as both obligatory then it is impossible for an individual—or a nation state—to do the morally right thing. Some theorists argue that such tragic dilemmas are an irreducible part of morality. I believe such results show that the moral system is inconsistent.

ament politically unrealizable. But ethics cannot dismiss any option that can be realized by an act of will, and nuclear disarmament is within the reach of the will.

Other logical snares lie in wait for policy analysts who try to play the philosophers' game of moral assessment. One common fallacy is to confuse a moral *feature* with the overall moral *character* of a policy, which is the true object of moral assessment. Each policy has many moral features, some positive, some negative, and it is tempting for supporters of a policy to seize upon a few positive features and from them to leap to the judgment that the policy is obligatory. But when one is comparing Policy A with Policy B, the presence of a positive moral feature in A will support the judgment that A is morally superior to B only if the sole difference between A and B is that A possesses the feature and B does not. It rarely happens that two policies differ in only one feature; usually, each policy exhibits a mixed bag of virtues and vices. Now, one cannot choose between two such mixed bags simply by preferring the bag with the greater excess of virtues over vices, because some features are morally much more important than others. What the ethicist must do is set up and justify a ranking of virtues and vices and then use this ranking to arrange policies in order of moral superiority, just as the rank order of letters in the alphabet can be used to establish alphabetical order among words. Unfortunately, there is no consensus among students of ethics on what constitutes the proper ranking of virtues and vices. Since there are many competing moral theories, there is not even a consensus about what is a virtue and what is a vice, and a policy of restraint that exhibits the virtue of rational self-control to nuclear pacifists like Helen Caldicott will exhibit craven self-abnegation to air force generals like Daniel Graham.

It might appear that the vexing problem of moral ranking is simplified in the case of nuclear weapons policy because of the overriding importance of preventing nuclear war. Naturally, a policy that will cause a nuclear war *for sure* is morally inferior to nearly everything else. But we never deliberate about policies that will cause nuclear war for sure. Invariably we are faced with policies each of which generates a *probability,* itself difficult to estimate, that nuclear war will occur.[9] The entrance of probability into the process of moral estimation complicates matters immensely. Even if philosophers agreed that prevention of nuclear war is the highest moral value, they would not agree that the policy that generates the least chance of nuclear war is invariably morally best. If Policy A generates a 20 percent chance of nuclear war (say, over fifty years) and Policy B generates a 15 percent chance, but Policy B is markedly inferior to A when we look at other moral values, some may judge that B is morally inferior overall, even though A is more likely to cause nuclear war than B, and A and B are all we have.

The presence of all these variables makes the moral comparison of deterrence and defense dismayingly difficult. If nuclear deterrence—any system of deterrence—is immoral, its immorality is no simple matter, and the judgment that deterrence is immoral does not immediately point to the moral superiority of a certain system of strategic defense. Nevertheless, the task of moral analysis must

---

[9]Even unilateral nuclear disarmament generates a probability that nuclear war will occur, since the policy still permits the occurrence of nuclear war—for example, a nuclear war between China and Russia.

be undertaken, if for no other reason than that the supporters of strategic defense have raised the issue in moral terms. The papers that follow show professional philosophers and the philosophically minded coming to grips with the moral issues, struggling to determine which moral principles are relevant and how they should be applied.

But in one respect this book will be simpler than many of the current analyses of strategic defenses. There is little discussion in these essays of the physical details of strategic defenses, of laser beams and electronic railguns, of the chances that defenses will locate their targets in the allotted time, of the countermeasures that the opponent might develop against them, and so forth. This is a task for specialists, and it has been well surveyed in other places, so far as the present state of scientific research permits.[10] Philosophers as such are not equipped to judge whether a given system will perform effectively. But they can consider these questions: (a) *if* the system performs effectively, what will be the moral result? and (b) *if* the system does *not* perform effectively, what will be the moral result? By considering each possibility in turn, reasoning hypothetically about technical results, philosophers leave scientific matters to the scientists and confine themselves to their traditional tools: logic and their moral sense. In the past these have served them well.

Since the introduction of ICBMs in the early 1960s, American strategic policy has been dominated by offense and the strategy of deterrence. The Strategic Defense Initiative created in the wake of the March 23, 1983, speech represents the strongest effort by any administration to break this pattern. Whether the new approach—if it proves technically feasible—is morally superior to the present system remains to be determined. But the contributors to this volume all agree on one thing: if strategic defenses *are* morally superior, they ought to be constructed. If they are morally inferior, perhaps even the research should stop. Morality cannot be *one* element of national policy: national policy must conform to it. There is no conflict between the true national interest and moral concerns, since nations must be moral if they deserve to exist. One doubts that the Founding Fathers would have wanted it any other way.

---

[10]One good starting point on the empirical questions is *Ballistic Missile Defense Technologies,* published in 1985 by the U. S. Congress Office of Technology Assessment.

Part II. Nuclear Strategy and Proposals for Strategic Defense

Douglas P. Lackey

The analysis of strategic defense has traditionally been undertaken by military strategists, who have probed proposals for strategic defenses from the standpoint of national security. Obviously, moral critics should be familiar with this strategic context before rushing to moral analysis. The following historical sketch is provided by the editor for readers with an interest in nuclear ethics but little background in the history of nuclear weapons policy.

I n 1958, when I was a boy growing up in Wayne, New Jersey, a gas main broke in the nearby town of Riverdale. The gas ignited, and the roar of the fire could be heard for miles around. My brother and I left the dinner table and ran outside. Up and down the street, people were running out of their houses, looking up into the sky. "Is it the Russians?" the woman across the street yelled to us. "I don't know," I said, and the man next door went inside to see if the TV was still on.

The people on my street were experiencing something new for Americans: the sensation of vulnerability to devastating foreign attack. The continental United States had last been attacked by foreigners in 1812, and all enemies since had kept respectfully to the other side of the sea. But the Soviets had exploded a hydrogen bomb in 1953 and had put a satellite in orbit in 1957. It was obvious to all of us that if the Soviets could put a satellite over our heads they could put an atomic bomb in our backyards. Most of us were convinced that the Soviets wanted to bury us. We all felt threatened; we all wanted some kind of protection.

The Eisenhower administration had taken a few protective steps and had thought about others. In 1954, the president had considered and then tabled a recommendation from a committee of the Joint Chiefs of Staff to launch a surprise nuclear attack on the Soviet Union, destroying Soviet thermonuclear capacity in its cradle.[1] The precise reasons why Eisenhower rejected the 1954 call for preventative war are unknown. General Matthew Ridgeway had argued that such sneak attacks were immoral, and there was always the risk that one Soviet nuclear bomber would survive the surprise attack and return to destroy Washington or

---

[1]David Alan Rosenberg, "The Origins of Overkill," *International Security* 7:4 (Spring 1983).

New York. At any rate, after Sputnik, preventive war was a dead option, especially given the exaggerated estimates of Soviet ICBM capacity taken as gospel in the late 1950s.

Matthew Ridgeway was right; preventive nuclear war is a bad idea, in 1954 or any other year. But once the option of preventive war had been scrapped, the Soviet nuclear threat was here to stay. The question was what was to be done to contain it. Strategy provides a limited repertoire of options in dealing with dangerous enemies. The most agreeable option—converting the enemy into a friend—was not pressed in the 1950s, despite the opportunity provided by the death of Stalin in 1953. Soviet insistence on hegemony in Eastern Europe, reaffirmed in East Germany in 1953 and in Hungary in 1956, was too tough a sticking point, and on the domestic scene the view that the Communists "understand only force" was an axiom of politics. This left the options of deterrence and defense.

The bulk of military expenditures in those years, as in the years since, went for deterrence: the attempt to influence behavior through threats of reprisal. Fitted with hydrogen bombs, the Strategic Air Command fleet of B-47 and B-52 bombers grew and grew, providing the main demonstration that the United States was prepared to respond to unwanted Soviet initiatives "massively, at times and at places of our own choosing," as Secretary of State Dulles had explained in 1954. The Strategic Air Command plans for a nuclear attack on the Soviet Union in 1954, if enacted, would have killed about seventy million people;[2] the Single Integrated Operational Plan (SIOP) for 1960 would have killed about four hundred million people in the Soviet Union and China, by the Joint Chiefs' own estimates.[3] This form of deterrence, which threatens a single sort of reprisal for any and all untoward actions, was named, appropriately enough, *Massive Retaliation*.

The reprisals threatened by the policy of Massive Retaliation were so large that it is at first sight difficult to conceive that they might be ineffective. Nevertheless, it was widely recognized that they might fail to deter, either because the opponent might believe that the reprisal was not forthcoming or because the opponent might believe that a given goal was worth the risk. One problem with deterrence is that it works only if the opponent is impressed by the threat, and there was no way for *us* to know how impressed *they* were. Surely our American minds were impressed by the threat of nuclear reprisal, but we could not be sure if communist minds were similarly awed, since we were convinced that communist minds were different from our own.

Alongside deterrence, then, the Eisenhower administration sought to provide defenses; that is, measures that would neutralize a Soviet nuclear attack, should one occur.[4] By 1954, the administration had initiated a variety of passive defense

---

[2]David Alan Rosenberg, "A Smoking Radiating Ruin at the End of Two Hours: American Plans for Nuclear War with the Soviet Union: 1954–55," *International Security* 6:3 (Winter 1981–82).

[3]Desmond Ball, *Targeting for Strategic Deterrence* (London: Institute for Strategic Studies, 1983).

[4]The line between deterrent measures and defensive measures is not easily drawn. If defensive measures are defined as those that neutralize an attack, then if one is convinced

programs, designating fallout shelters, stockpiling biscuits, and conducting "duck and cover" exercises in the public schools. On the active side, the administration began the construction of early-warning radar systems and the army deployed a surface-to-air missile, the Nike-Ajax—later superseded by the Nike-Hercules—to shoot down incoming Soviet Bear and Bison bombers. When it became clear in the early 1950s that the Soviets were developing long-range rockets, research began on the third Nike, the Nike-Zeus, specifically designed to shoot down incoming ballistic missiles.

With the U.S. air force and navy effectively in control of strategic nuclear deterrence, the army claimed the less glamorous role of homeland nuclear defense, insisting on its importance for national security.[5] Arguing for a balance of offensive (deterrent) and defensive measures, General Maxwell Taylor testified in 1957:

> It had been easy to fall back on the line of reasoning that the best defense is a good offense. But the fact is that, under a national policy of abstention from initiating an atomic attack on our enemies, we are obliged to develop an air defense capacity as an indispensable component of our overall general war deterrent force. Otherwise, we will invite attack and expose our people as well as our offensive forces to destruction.[6]

Representatives of the air force exhibited little confidence in the army's antimissile missile. In November 1957, one month after Sputnik, the air force presented the Joint Chiefs with four arguments, subsequently leaked to the *New York Times,* against the army's Nike-Zeus. The arguments, which prefigure the Star Wars controversies by more than twenty-five years, were that offense in a nuclear age necessarily dominates defense, that the Nike-Zeus could not discriminate enemy missiles from decoys, that the Soviets could easily overpower the system by deploying more offensive missiles, and that confidence in defenses fosters a dangerous "Maginot Line" state of mind.[7] This sort of interservice warfare over ballistic missile defense (BMD) diminished somewhat when the research component of the Nike-Zeus program was taken over by the Defense Advanced Research Projects Agency (DARPA), newly formed in 1958.[8] Indepen-

---

that an attack is imminent, a preemptive strike against enemy airfields and silos counts as "defensive." To be on the safe side, I will consider as defensive only measures that help to neutralize an attack *in progress.*

[5]Given the introduction of battlefield nuclear weapons to NATO forces in 1953, the army was and still is involved in nuclear deterrence overseas.

[6]Maxwell Taylor, testimony before the Senate Committee on Appropriations, 1957, quoted in Ernest J. Yanarella, *The Missile Defense Controversy* (Lexington: University of Kentucky, 1977), p. 32.

[7]Jack Raymond, "Air Force Urges Joint Chiefs Ban Army Missile Bid," *New York Times,* 21 November 1957.

[8]The concentration of BMD projects in DARPA had mixed effects over the years. On the one hand, moving BMD to the independent sector of the Pentagon has subdued partisan

dent studies in the Pentagon, however, seemed to confirm the air force's case that the Nike-Zeus could be overwhelmed by incoming missiles with multiple warheads.[9]

If air force criticisms of the Nike-Zeus were sound, then all that was left for the United States was deterrence. Nevertheless, in the late 1950s debate raged concerning the strategic effectiveness and moral permissibility of nuclear deterrence, at least in its massive retaliation form.

Effectiveness was the main concern of the nuclear strategists. It was hard to believe that the United States would kill four hundred million people for any cause, and impossible to believe that the United States would kill four hundred million people for small or intermediate provocations, especially if the result of killing the four hundred million could only be a retaliatory strike that would destroy whatever was left of the United States. Massive Retaliation was simply incredible, and if it was incredible, it would fail to deter.[10]

Moral questions regarding Massive Retaliation were raised by a small but articulate group of philosophers and religious thinkers. Many of them saw in Massive Retaliation a return to the terror bombing of World War II, a policy that they viewed as immoral, regardless of the justice of the cause. To be sure, Dulles had not yet bombed anybody, but he and the United States fully intended to use nuclear weapons against Soviet and Chinese cities if Soviet actions failed to pass muster. The philosophers reasoned that if it was immoral to carry out that intention, it was immoral to form the intention in the first place. The intention to commit mass murder is a murderous intention; deterrence requires murderous intentions; therefore deterrence is a kind of murder.[11] None of the critics of nuclear deterrence, however, raised objections to the development of active or passive defenses against nuclear attack.

When the Kennedy team arrived in 1961, Secretary of Defense McNamara and his aides from the RAND corporation "Think Tank" reviewed strategic policies, taking the larger offensive systems first, and only then moving on to defense. They

---

support of BMD proposals by particular military services. On the other hand, concentration in DARPA and related organizations such as the Strategic Defense Initiative Organization has removed a powerful source of criticism and has generated a bias in favor of the complex and glamorous over the pedestrian but effective.

[9]The Pentagon studies, by the Reentry Body identification group, headed by William F. Bradley, concluded that incoming multiple-warhead missiles "demand such a high rate of fire from an active defense system . . . that the expense of required equipment may be prohibitive." Quoted in Fred Kaplan, *The Wizards of Armageddon* (New York: Simon & Schuster, 1983).

[10]These lines of thought were most famously pursued in Henry Kissinger's *Nuclear Weapons and Foreign Policy* (New York: Harper & Row, 1957) and Bernard Brodie's *Strategy in the Missile Age* (Princeton, NJ: Princeton University Press, 1959).

[11]This argument was pressed on the Catholic side in the United States by Father John C. Ford in "The Hydrogen Bombing of Cities," in W. J. Nagle, ed., *Morality and Modern War* (Baltimore: Helicon, 1960) and in England by G. E. M. Anscombe and her coauthors in Walter Stein, ed., *Nuclear Weapons: A Catholic Response* (London: Merlin, 1961). On the Protestant side the argument was pressed at length by Paul Ramsey in *War and the Christian Conscience* (Durham, NC: Duke University Press, 1961).

replaced the single massive retaliatory strike of the Eisenhower years with a five-step sequence of graduated offensive options, guided by the rule that Soviet cities should not be struck if American cities had not been struck. As McNamara explained things at Ann Arbor in 1962, the new options were designed to make the main focus of nuclear attack the enemy's military forces, not its civilian population. Although each stage of what was called "SIOP-63" called for a substantial nuclear attack, McNamara and his aides felt that the flexible character of the new plan resolved most of the criticisms directed at Massive Retaliation. On the strategic side, the new plan provided "small" responses to small provocations, rendering deterrence credible, and it provided reasons to the enemy for not striking American cities, rendering deterrence nonsuicidal. On the moral side, by directing nuclear weapons at military forces and not the civilian population, the new plan looked less murderous than the old.[12] At least one of the most trenchant moral critics of Massive Retaliation gave the new strategy of "Flexible Response" his blessing.[13] Recalcitrant critics who argued that the new plan was no more morally acceptable than the old soon found themselves an isolated minority, especially after the Nuclear Test Ban Treaty knocked the pins out from under the American antinuclear peace movement in August 1963.[14]

With offensive systems sporting new strategic and moral credentials, the problem of what to do if deterrence failed seemed relatively less urgent. At first McNamara pressed for an expanded program of civil defense, but public hysteria followed by public protest against fallout shelters soon put passive defense on the nation's back burner. The American public's reaction to fallout shelter proposals in 1961 and 1962 involved an emotional disgust with the idea of hiding in the ground, a realistic assessment of the enticements of the postnuclear world, and a political critique that demanded that the administration spend less time preparing for war and more time preparing for peace. The political critique of fallout shelters suggested, for the first time, that defense as well as deterrence might contain moral flaws.[15]

---

[12]For review of the changes introduced by McNamara, Kaufmann, et al., see Desmond Ball, *Politics and Force Levels: The Strategic Missile Program of the Kennedy Administration* (Berkeley: University of California Press, 1980) and Fred Kaplan, *The Wizards of Armageddon* (New York: Simon & Schuster, 1983).

[13]Paul Ramsey's miscellaneous arguments that Flexible Response successfully discriminates soldiers from civilians are collected in *The Just War* (New York: Scribner's, 1968). Nonphilosophers were less impressed with the soldier/civilian distinction and more impressed by the argument that Flexible Response would lead to fewer deaths overall, should nuclear war come. See Richard Fryklund, *100 Million Lives* (New York: Macmillan, 1962).

[14]The critics of Flexible Response argued that the number of innocent civilians who would be killed in even the smallest of McNamara's planned nuclear attacks would be enormous, and that such a slaughter of the innocent would be murderous even if American missiles were aimed at military targets rather than city halls. See, for example, Anthony Kenny, "Counterforce and Countervalue," *Clergy Review* (1962), reprinted in Walter Stein, ed., *Nuclear Weapons: A Catholic Response,* 2nd ed. (London: Merlin, 1965).

[15]Passionate arguments for fallout shelters are given in Herman Kahn, *On Thermonuclear War* (Princeton, NJ: Princeton University Press, 1960). For the national mood concerning

McNamara's enthusiasm for fallout shelters did not carry over into enthusiasm for the Nike-Zeus. While publicly agreeing with army ABM supporters that some defenses are better than none, McNamara worried that the Nike-Zeus could be fooled by decoys, destroyed by direct attack, or saturated by cheap ICBMs. He supported funding for research and development but denied funding for production and deployment. He was not impressed when a Nike-Zeus shot down at Atlas ICBM over the Pacific in July 1962. Furthermore, analysis of ABM systems within the Defense Department turned up a new and serious flaw in the basic concept of ballistic missile defense. Any deployment of defenses would be likely to stimulate developments in offenses on the other side, and the development of new offenses would destabilize any strategic equilibrium the two superpowers might achieve.[16] By 1963, the Nike-Zeus was dead and research was initiated on a new system, the Nike-X.

The Nike-X system consisted originally of the Nike-Zeus intermediate-range interceptors and a short-range fast-accelerating terminal-phase interceptor called Sprint. The Nike-Zeus component developed in 1965 into the Spartan missile, designed to disable enemy missiles in midcourse in space. Once again, the army and the Joint Chiefs pressed for deployment, while McNamara held out for continued research. Pressure for deployment escalated when McNamara announced in 1966 that the Soviets had begun to deploy an ABM system around Moscow. In early 1967 the Joint Chiefs argued that an ABM system would *stabilize* deterrence by assuring the Soviets that the United States was not solely "first-strike minded."[17] To defuse movement toward a massive and perhaps unworkable ABM system, McNamara announced in September 1967 that the United States would deploy a limited version of the Nike-X system, now called Sentinel, to defend against Chinese nuclear attacks and small or accidental launches by the Soviets.[18]

The Sentinel decision set the stage for the debate of 1968, in which those who wanted a bigger ABM fought it out with those who wanted no ABM at all. The opening salvo was Hans Bethe and Richard Garwin's article "Anti-Ballistic Missile Systems," published in the March 1968 *Scientific American*. Bethe and Garwin argued that the Sentinel system could be confused by decoys and blinded by the electromagnetic pulses released by high-altitude nuclear explosions. They argued that it would cost an enemy less to deploy additional warheads than it

---

shelters, see "Fallout Shelters," *Life,* 15 September 1961 (positive) and "Survival: Are Shelters the Answer?" *Newsweek,* 6 November 1961 (negative). For McNamara's support of shelters, see Benson Adams, "McNamara's ABM Policy, 1961–67," *Orbis* 12 (Spring 1968), 200–225.

[16]The claim that the argument that strategic defenses are "destabilizing" originated in 1962 DOD studies is attributed by Yanarella, *The Missile Defense Controversy,* p. 84, to James Trainor in "DOD Says AICBM Is Feasible," *Missiles and Rockets,* 24 December 1962.

[17]Yanarella, *The Missile Defense Controversy,* p. 136.

[18]For the tortured argument that the United States needed an anti-Chinese but not anti-Soviet ABM, see Robert McNamara, *The Essence of Security* (New York: Harper & Row, 1968), Appendix.

would cost the United States to knock them down. Above all, they argued that the system was unnecessary because each superpower had the ability to destroy its opponent, even after suffering a full-scale nuclear attack. Since nuclear attack was suicidal, neither side would undertake to attack the other, a condition Garwin described as "the present rather comforting situation of mutual assured destruction." The construction of an effective antiballistic missile system, Garwin noted, was one of the prime threats to this continuing strategic stalemate.

Critics of the Bethe-Garwin article argued that assured destruction provided a deterrent against large nuclear attacks but not against small ones, and it was in fact a small-scale nuclear attack that Sentinel was designed to neutralize. For sure, the critics argued, the United States was not going to destroy Soviet cities while American cities were still standing. "Would we," GE Missile and Space Division executive Daniel Fink wrote to the *Scientific American*, "respond [to a limited nuclear attack] by an overwhelming attack against their cities, knowing full well that counterresponse would lead to our own destruction?"[19]

Fink's letter to the *Scientific American* in effect repeated the charge that had been leveled against Dulles's Massive Retaliation policy and that had been laid to rest—so it was thought—by the introduction of SIOP-63 in 1963. The most widely publicized feature of that plan was that it was designed to spare cities if American cities had been spared. That plan was still in effect virtually unchanged in 1968. Nevertheless, Fink was one of the many to suggest that American strategic plans left the president with a "suicide or surrender" dilemma in the face of a limited nuclear attack.[20]

McNamara more than anyone else was responsible for the impression that American nuclear war plans had changed. By 1964, it was clear that the attempt to target and destroy Soviet strategic weapons in the face of new Soviet efforts to protect them led to serious technical difficulties that even massive expenditures might not overcome. To prevent the air force from obtaining an endless line of credit for an impossible counterforce mission, McNamara stopped talking about sparing cities and began talking in 1965 about maintaining an "Assured Destruction" capacity that would enable the United States to destroy the Soviet Union "as a viable society" even after a Soviet first strike.[21] In subsequent years, McNamara repeatedly described an Assured Destruction capacity as the ability to destroy a quarter of the Soviet people and half of Soviet industry in a second strike. Since the attack that would provoke such a response was left undescribed,

---

[19]Daniel J. Fink, letter, *Scientific American,* June 1968.

[20]Cf. Richard M. Nixon, "Should the President, in the event of a nuclear attack, be left with the single option of ordering the mass destruction of enemy civilians, in the face of the certainty that it would be followed by the mass slaughter of Americans?" *U. S. Foreign Policy for the 1970s: A New Strategy for Peace* (Washington, DC: Office of the White House, 18 February 1970).

[21]U. S. Congress. House Committee on Appropriations, *Department of Defense Appropriations for Fiscal 1966, Hearings before a Subcommittee on Appropriations,* 89th Cong. 1st Sess. 34–36.

it is not surprising that many people by 1968 believed that the United States was prepared to launch such attacks in response to provocations of any size and any type.

Furthermore, the critics who in 1968 equated Assured Destruction with Massive Retaliation might have written better than they knew. Although SIOP-63 provided the president with five graduated attack options, the *smallest* attack plan called for launching more than 2000 megatons of nuclear weapons at the Soviet Union. Given the placement of numerous Soviet ICBM fields in the more densely populated sections of European Russia, even the smallest counterforce nuclear attack on the Soviet Union was likely to cause such destruction that a Soviet retaliatory strike against American cities was probable if not certain. Thus, when Garwin defended Assured Destruction in 1968, he cautioned that a retaliatory strike should be issued only in response to a massive attack. Smaller attacks, apparently, were to be handled by conventional means: "[Assured Destruction] serves only to preserve a nation from complete destruction. More conventional military forces are needed to fill the more conventional military role."

By late spring of 1968 a group of senators led by John Cooper of Kentucky had formed an anti-ABM coalition, and every move toward Sentinel deployment provoked acrimonious Senate debate. The anti-ABM group in the Congress received unexpected support from citizens' groups living near designated Sentinel sites, who perceived the ABM not as a shield but as a lightening rod that would attract nuclear fire in their direction. As with fallout shelters, many people found that things that were supposed to make them safe only made them feel less secure.

The anti-ABM senators were extensively briefed by Garwin, Bethe, Jerome Wiesner, Herbert York, George Kistiakowsky, and other scientists who had been involved in or close to ABM research almost from the start. One scientist, George Rathjens, was particularly concerned about the relation between the deployment of an ABM system and the deployment of MIRVs—multiple independently targeted reentry vehicles placed on top of Minuteman and Poseidon missiles. Whereas the earlier Pentagon studies had warned that the ABM might be "destabilizing" in the sense of provoking an arms race, Rathjens argued that the ABM was destabilizing in a more serious manner: it created pressure to launch a first strike in a crisis, with MIRVs catching enemy strategic forces on the ground and the ABM picking off the rest of the retaliatory second strike. "With both MIRV and an ABM system," Rathjens wrote,

> such a preemptive attack would not seem as unlikely as it does now. It might not appear irrational to some, for example, if an uncontrollable nuclear exchange seemed almost certain, and if by striking first one could limit damage to a significantly lower level than if the adversary were to strike the first blow. In short, if one or both of the two superpowers had such capabilities, the world would be a much more unstable place than it is now.[22]

---

[22]George Rathjens, "The Dynamics of the Arms Race," *Scientific American,* April 1969. Rathjens argued that both systems should be banned but that, if only one were banned, the ABM should go and MIRV should stay.

The combination of protest and argument won the day in Congress, and by spring 1969 the Sentinel plan was dead.[23]

Despite growing domestic opposition, the Nixon administration still wanted an ABM, provided that it could be built cheaply and provided that it was intended to stop Russian missiles, not just Chinese ones. The Pentagon R&D division reported to the president that a cheaper ABM system could be constructed only on the condition that it defend ICBM missile sites, not American cities. In March 1969, President Nixon announced that the Sentinel system would be dropped and that a new Nike-X derivative, called Safeguard, would be constructed to defend American missile fields.

The switch from defending cities to defending missile fields mitigated many of the criticisms directed at the Sentinel system. To defend a city, every incoming ballistic missile must be struck down. To defend a missile field, the ABM system need only strike down enough incoming warheads that some missiles in the field survive, since only a few surviving missiles will suffice to inflict devastating retaliation against the opponent. Furthermore, defense of missile fields implies that one's missiles will be in the ground when enemy missiles arrive, and this provision signals to the opponent a commitment to a second strike. Finally, there are fewer ICBM fields than there are cities, and the fields are located in sparsely populated states, like North Dakota and Alabama, not noted for political protests directed at military installations.

Despite these improvements, the Safeguard proposal provoked a debate that continued through the summer of 1970.[24] For the first time, scientists outside the Pentagon were called before congressional committees to testify about the merits and demerits of a strategic system. Many scientists testified that Safeguard was physically akin to the Sentinel and the Nike-X and that all the vulnerabilities of the Nike-X were still vulnerabilities in Safeguard. Furthermore, the Safeguard was intended to defend American ICBM fields, and the question could be raised whether ICBM fields needed defending in the first place.

American Minuteman ICBMs were buried underground in reinforced concrete silos that could withstand everything but a direct hit or a near miss by a nuclear warhead. So long as the Soviets had substantially fewer warheads than the United States had Minutemen, the Minutemen alone constituted a powerful second-strike force. But by 1969, the Soviets had begun to deploy multiple warheads on top of their SS-9 missiles, and if each warhead could be targeted on a Minuteman silo,[25]

---

[23]The anti-Sentinel coalition won the war even though it lost every vote. Democracy can be a strange business.

[24]The case for Safeguard can be surveyed in Jurgen Holst and William Schneider, Jr., eds., *Why ABM?* (Elmsford Park, NY: Pergamon Press, 1969), especially the chapters by Albert Wohlstetter and Herman Kahn. For the case against Safeguard, see Abram Chayes and Jerome Weiner, eds., *ABM: An Evaluation of the Decision to Deploy an Anti-Ballistic Missile System* (New York: Harper & Row, 1969).

[25]Although the Soviets deployed multiple warheads in 1969, they were not independently targetable warheads and shared the inaccuracy of the carrying missile. In 1969 the Soviets had no independently targetable warheads at all, and deployed none until 1975.

it appeared that the Minuteman force, undefended by the ABM, might be vulnerable to a preemptive strike.

So it was argued by Albert Wohlstetter, a former RAND strategist of considerable influence in strategic circles. A number of anti-ABM scientists took issue with Wohlstetter's contentions, and there ensued a Byzantine debate about how many Minutemen might survive various attacks that the Soviets might launch. Eventually, Wohlstetter succeeded in showing that 500 MIRVed SS-9s could destroy 83 percent of the Minuteman missile force, a proof that pro-ABM senators chose to view with alarm.

The debate about Minuteman vulnerability, which sputtered on until squelched by the Scowcroft Report in 1983, proved to be a considerable distraction from the real issues. The real question in 1969 was not whether the Minuteman was becoming vulnerable but whether the ABM was a solution to this or any other vulnerability problem. If the Soviets increased MIRVed SS-9 production, the Minutemen would become vulnerable. But if the Soviets increased MIRVed SS-9 production, Safeguard became ineffective as well. Surely, if the Soviets wanted to put Minutemen at risk by building enough SS-9s to crack the silos, they would build enough SS-9s to overwhelm Safeguard defenses. Indeed, the radars needed to operate Safeguard seemed considerably more vulnerable than the missile silos they were supposed to protect. The argument that the offense could outrun the defense still seemed to apply.

On 5 August 1969 the Senate split fifty-fifty on Safeguard funding, with Vice-President Agnew casting his tie-breaking vote in favor of deploying Safeguard around two ICBM fields in North Dakota and Montana. But the battle was not over. In February 1970, the Pentagon asked for funds for five more Safeguard sites, and four of those five sites proved to be near cities, including the nation's capital. The warnings of ABM critics that Sentinel and Safeguard were first steps toward deployment of a wide-scale Nike-X area defense seemed to be confirmed. All the old anti-Sentinel arguments about crisis instability were revived. Nevertheless, the anti-ABM forces lost again (47–52) in August of 1970.

The victory of 1970 was a Pyrrhic victory for Safeguard. Nixon himself ended up accepting the case of the scientists that Safeguard could not protect cities: "Although every instinct motivates me to provide the American people with complete protection against a major nuclear attack, it is not now within our power to do so." More interesting, Nixon had come to accept the argument that the ABM was destabilizing: "It might look to an opponent like a prelude to an offensive strategy threatening the Soviet deterrent."[26] Increasingly Nixon and National Security Advisor Kissinger looked on Safeguard not as a viable strategic system but as a bargaining chip to be traded away in Strategic Arms Limitation Talks (SALT) negotiations with the Soviets, which had begun in November 1969. Indeed, a letter from chief negotiator Gerald Smith to the effect that the Safeguard was a crucial bargaining chip appears to have swayed senatorial votes in the pro-Safeguard vote in 1970.

If the American ABM was destabilizing, then a Soviet ABM was destabilizing, at

---

[26]U. S. Arms Control and Disarmament Agency. *Documents on Disarmament 1969* (Washington, DC: GPO, 1969).

least to the degree that it was effective. The Soviets had exhibited Galosh antiballistic missiles in Red Square as early as 1964, and by 1966 they had begun adding to the air defenses around Moscow. It was generally agreed that the Galosh posed no impediment to an American second strike, but the deployment of Galosh manifested a Soviet commitment to area defense, and it was inevitable that Galosh would get better in time.

Persuading the Soviets that antiballistic missiles were a bad idea took considerable ingenuity. The Soviets had never developed a theory of nuclear deterrence, much less a theory of second-strike nuclear deterrence, and their nuclear strategy was an appendage of a military strategy oriented toward repulsing incoming attacks and then defeating the opponent in all-out war.[27] The ABM was a logical consequence of the primary imperative of repulsing attack. At a London press conference in 1967, Soviet Premier Kosygin had defended Galosh by arguing, "An anti-missile system may cost more than an offensive one, but it is intended not for killing people but for saving lives."[28] When Kosygin met with Secretary McNamara at Glassboro, New Jersey, in June 1967, he responded to McNamara's arguments about the ABM and stability by remarking, "When I have trouble sleeping, it's because of your offensive missiles, not your defensive missiles."[29]

It took three years, but the Soviets were finally persuaded to give up their commitment to area defense. The Treaty on the Limitation of Anti-Ballistic Missile Systems, signed in Moscow on 26 May 1972, permitted retention of the Galosh system around Moscow and the Safeguard site at Grand Forks, North Dakota, but it permitted each superpower only one additional ground-based ABM site [Article III] and required the United States and the U.S.S.R. "not to develop, test, or deploy ABM systems or components which are sea-based, air-based, space-based, or mobile land based" [Article V]. Each superpower pledged to forswear ABM systems "for the defense of the territory of its country" [Article I] and promised not to deploy radars of the sort that could be used for a nationwide ABM defense [Article VI].

Garwin, Rathjens, and others who were particularly concerned with the stability of mutual deterrence saw in the ABM treaty a repudiation of the general idea of defensive systems. Persons more sympathetic to defensive systems read the treaty simply as a repudiation of defensive systems like Galosh and Safeguard; that is, of antimissile missiles. The treaty itself said: "For purposes of this Treaty an ABM system is a system to counter strategic ballistic missiles or their elements in flight trajectory, currently consisting of (a) ABM interceptor missiles . . . , (b) ABM launchers . . . , and (c) ABM radars . . ." [Article II]. At first sight, this article seems to limit the treaty to antimissile missiles. However, the article defines "ABM systems" as systems "currently consisting of . . ." and the word *currently* implies that ABM systems at other times may employ more than just

---

[27]Cf. General Nikolai Talensky, "Missile Defense: A Response to Aggression," *Bulletin of the Atomic Scientists,* February 1965.

[28]Alexei Kosygin, quoted in Z. Brzezinski et al., eds., *Promise or Peril: The Strategic Defense Initiative* (Washington, DC: Ethics and Public Policy Center, 1986), p. 219.

[29]Kaplan, *The Wizards of Armageddon,* p. 346.

interceptor missiles. The essential idea of an ABM system so far as the treaty is concerned seems to be that an ABM system is anything that "counters" ballistic missiles in flight.

The United States signed the ABM treaty because Nixon and Kissinger were convinced that in the nuclear age security must rest primarily on deterrence. Endorsing a line of thought stretching back at least to 1963,[30] the president and his national security advisor decided that defenses either would not work or would work only well enough to destabilize nuclear crises. But why did the Soviets, who had no tradition of basing national security on deterrence, sign the ABM treaty? Perhaps a clue can be found in General Nikolai Talensky's argument, published in 1965, in defense of the Soviet ABM. Talensky argued:

> The creation of an effective anti-missile defense merely serves to build up the security of a peaceable, non-aggressive state. . . . On the other hand, if the effective anti-missile system is built by the side that adheres to an aggressive policy, a policy from positions of strength, this may well intensify the danger of an outbreak of war.[31]

In short, Talensky felt that a Soviet ABM would help the Soviet Union defend itself but that an American ABM would increase the chances of nuclear attack on Russia. If Talensky's thinking influenced the decision to sign the ABM treaty, the Soviets in 1972 sacrificed a defense they felt was useful, reasoning that the risks increased by permitting Safeguard were larger than the risks reduced by extending Galosh.

The signing of the ABM treaty took antiballistic missiles off the center stage of national debate. The single American ABM installation at Grand Forks was decommissioned, without protest, in 1976 on the prosaic ground that its limited effectiveness failed to justify its costs. All the strategic changes of the 1970s and early 1980s—the mass deployment of American MIRVs on Minuteman and Poseidon missiles, the introduction of Limited Nuclear Options into American nuclear war-fighting plans, the deployment of MIRVs on Soviet long-range missiles, the development of third-generation nuclear weapons such as the neutron bomb, the modernization of Soviet intermediate-range ballistic missiles in Europe, the NATO decision to reintroduce ground-launched cruise missiles and intermediate-range ballistic missiles into Europe, the retargeting of American strategic weapons toward Soviet military command and control centers, the American preparations for fighting and prevailing in an extended nuclear war— addressed real or alleged requirements of deterrence, not the general balance of offense and defense. During the interminable search for a survivable basing mode for the new MX missile, no prominent MX advocate suggested that the ABM treaty be abrogated and that Safeguard be reactivated to defend the MX. The

---

[30]Yanarella, *The Missile Defense Controversy,* p. 181, traces the idea of "deterrence without defense" back to discussions of the partial test ban treaty debate of 1963. (Note that a ban on nuclear testing in the atmosphere banned in-flight testing of the Nike-X.)

[31]Talensky, "Missile Defense," p. 215.

army, traditional supporter of missile defense, kept its hand in the strategic weapons game by sponsoring the deployment in Europe of its Pershing II, an offensive missile par excellence.

Nevertheless, through the seventies and early eighties there were rumbles of discontent on the strategic right and left:

• People hoping for some kind of victory in the Cold War viewed the post-1972 situation as an indefinite and dissatisfying stalemate.

• Those who saw the East–West competition as a zero-sum game felt that anything the Soviets approved, such as the ABM agreement, must necessarily be bad for the West.

• Philosophers and peace activists with ethical qualms about nuclear deterrence were unhappy with an arrangement that seemed to perpetuate the immoral condition of mutual assured destruction.[32]

• Some of those who accepted mutual deterrence in the short run felt that in the long run the scheme would collapse in catastrophe.[33]

• People who had been impressed by the argument that banning defensive systems would lead to curtailments in offensive weapons were disheartened and alarmed by the explosion in deployed warheads in the late 1970s.

• The Soviet construction of a phased-array radar complex deep within the Soviet Union at Krasnoyarsk clearly violated the ABM treaty, Article VI.

• The Soviets in the late 1970s were rumored to be investing heavily in ABM research.

• Various technical advances in computers and electronics seemed to solve a number of technical problems that had bedeviled the Safeguard system.

By the early 1980s, a number of strategists were reviewing the arguments in the ABM debate in the light of what they took to be the negative lessons of the seventies.[34]

The opening round of the new ABM debate was an article in the Spring 1981 *Strategic Review* by retired air force general Daniel O. Graham entitled "Toward a New U. S. Strategy: Bold Strokes Rather than Increments." Graham's article repudiated mutual assured destruction and called for a national security posture focused on neutralizing attacks rather than retaliating after they occur. For the first time, however, attack neutralizing was to be an air force mission, accomplished through a space-based missile defense. With support from the con-

---

[32]Cf. Douglas Lackey, "Ethics and Nuclear Deterrence," in James Rachels, ed., *Moral Problems* (New York: Harper & Row, 1975).

[33]Fred Ikle, "Can Mutual Deterrence Last Out the Century?," *Foreign Affairs*, January 1973.

[34]Cf. Colin Gray, "The Missile Defense Debate in the Early 1970's," *Survival*, March/April 1981.

20   Douglas P. Lackey

servative Heritage Foundation, Graham and his associates in 1982 expanded the 1981 article into a full-fledged strategic and technical doctrine called the *High Frontier*.[35]

High Frontier advocates argue that the United States in the 1970s fell behind the Soviet Union in space research, in strategic forces, in conventional forces, and in world influence, so much so that "Soviet success now threatens the continuing availability of raw materials which are critical to the industrialized West."[36]

The cause of this decline, according to the High Frontier view, is the doctrine of Mutual Assured Destruction, consummated by the ABM treaty:

> A U.S. strategy which relied at its core on the capability to annihilate civilians and denied the soldier his traditional role of defending his fellow citizens has had a deleterious effect on the traditional American military ethic and on the relationship between the soldier and the normally highly supportive public.[37]

The remedy for this military decay of the United States is to replace the doctrine of Assured Destruction with a doctrine of Assured Survival, founded on an effective defense against nuclear attack. The remedy for the decline in world influence—the route to ultimate victory in the Cold War—is for the United States to seize the initiative in the development of space resources:

> An investment during the next 5 to 20 years in space can provide access to the entire solar system—not just for the United States but for the whole world. If the U. S. does not take the lead, those resources may well be developed by others, notably the USSR, with far less willingness to share access.[38]

The High Frontier proposals for defense against ballistic missiles called for a layered defense, with space-based satellites interrupting Soviet ICBMs at the end of the boost phase, and ground-based defenses picking off reentry vehicles in the terminal phase. Neither layer of active defense required nuclear explosions; enemy missiles and warheads were to be destroyed by direct collision with solid objects.[39] Since no defense against nuclear attack can presume to be perfect,

---

[35]The term *High Frontier*, coined by Princeton physicist G. K. O'Neill to denote his (nonmilitary) proposal for human colonies in space, was appropriated by Graham and his associates, causing considerable consternation among many pro-space citizens' groups.

[36]Daniel O. Graham, *The Non-Nuclear Defense of Cities: The High Frontier Space-Based Defense Against ICBM Attack* (Cambridge, MA: Abt Books, 1983), p. 2.

[37]Ibid., p. 14.

[38]Ibid., p. 77.

[39]For details of High Frontier defense, see Graham, *The Non-Nuclear Defense of Cities*, pp. 98–109. Few specialists have taken the High Frontier proposals seriously, and Robert M. Bowman, in *Star Wars: An Insider's Case Against the Strategic Defense Initiative* (Los Angeles: Jeremy Tarcher, 1985, pp. 154–158), argues that the proposals will work only if the intercepting objects are fired *53 seconds before the Soviet ICBM is even launched.*

these active defenses are to be supplemented with a system of civil defense involving relocation of people away from cities and protection in self-help fallout shelters. Although High Frontier publications claimed that these suggestions are consistent with the ABM treaty, it is fair to assume that under these arrangements, the ABM treaty would necessarily be abrogated, a development that High Frontier advocates could hardly view with regret.

The High Frontier publications claimed that these defenses required only "off-the-shelf" technology; the terminal-point defenses were allegedly deployable in three years, the space-borne defense deployable in six. Clearly, the High Frontier advocates wanted to avoid the Nike-X syndrome of maximal research and minimal deployment. Nevertheless, their 1982 report included upbeat accounts of high-tech missile defense possibilities involving particle beams, high-energy lasers, and high-power microwaves.

Despite pessimistic assessments of the usefulness of these technologies by specialists at MIT,[40] a number of people were looking seriously at high-tech defenses in the early 1980s, including the eminent physicist Edward Teller. Teller, a strong supporter of the ABM,[41] visited President Reagan in the fall of 1982. Teller focused the president's attention on the contrast between defense and deterrence and told the president that a number of radical scientific discoveries, including the X-ray laser,[42] vastly improved the chances for effective strategic defense.

Teller's visit to the president coincided with a high level of domestic agitation about nuclear weapons policy. Reagan had arrived in the White House with what he took to be a mandate for restoring American military strength, but the belligerent language of Reagan aides in 1981 and 1982, and their frequent remarks about fighting, winning, or at least prevailing in nuclear wars, had terrified the public and revived the domestic antinuclear movement. By the end of 1982, the president, the half-million peace demonstrators that had filled New York's Central

---

[40]See Kosta Tsipis and John Parmentola, "Particle Beam Weapons," *Scientific American,* April 1977, and Kosta Tsipis, "Laser Weapons," *Scientific American,* December 1981.

[41]Teller had publicly opposed the Partial Test Ban Treaty of 1963 because it made testing the Nike-X impossible. See U. S. Congress, Senate, *Report of the Committee of Foreign Relations: The Nuclear Test Ban Treaty,* Executive Report 3, (1963), pp. 437–440, and "Not Only Effective but Truly Humane," *U. S. News and World Report,* 26 May 1969, p. 87. His views in the fall of 1982 are expressed in "Dangerous Myths about Nuclear Arms," *Reader's Digest,* November 1982.

[42]For Teller's interactions with Reagan and his support for the X-ray laser, see David Pearlman, "Top Secret Plan for Laser Weapon," *San Francisco Chronicle,* 25 September 1982; "Teller Said to Urge Development of X-Ray Laser," *Aerospace Daily,* 1 December 1982; and "Space Based X-Ray Laser Backed by Teller," *Defense Daily,* 27 January 1983.
The X-ray laser is a self-destructing weapon triggered by a thermonuclear explosion. It is not clear that the president understood that the new super-laser was in fact a nuclear weapon and by definition a device that could not be used to make nuclear weapons "impotent and obsolete." By 1985 the confusion had been cleared up and the Strategic Defense Initiative Organization reported to Congress that its "principal emphasis was placed on technologies involving non-nuclear kill concepts" (U. S. Department of Defense, Strategic Defense Initiative Organization, *Report to Congress* [1985], p. 3). Work on the X-ray laser is funded largely by the U. S. Department of Energy.

Park in April, and the National Council of Catholic Bishops could all agree on one thing: that nuclear deterrence was not a good long-term solution to the world's nuclear problem.[43]

Reagan kept his conversion to strategic defense largely to himself, and his Star Wars speech of 23 March 1983 constituted an end run around the usual policy-making process. "The human spirit must be capable of rising above dealing with other nations and human beings by threatening their existence," the president said toward the end of what had been announced as a speech on the military budget.

> If the Soviet Union will join us in our efforts to achieve major [arms] reduction, we will have succeeded in stabilizing the nuclear balance.
>
> Nevertheless, it will still be necessary to rely on the specter of retaliation, on mutual threat. . . .
>
> What if . . . we could intercept and destroy strategic ballistic missiles before they reached our soil? . . . Current technology has attained a level of sophistication where it is reasonable for us to begin this effort. . . . Tonight . . . I am directing a comprehensive and intensive effort to define a long-term research and development program to begin to achieve our ultimate goal of eliminating the threat posed by strategic nuclear missiles.

The consternation both within and without the government caused by the announcement of the Strategic Defense Initiative (SDI) was compounded the following week when the president suggested to reporters that fully effective strategic defenses were so conducive to peace that it would benefit the United States to share defensive technologies with the Soviets—an idea reiterated in his televised debate with Walter Mondale in 1984:

> My idea would be that with a defensive weapon, that we would sit down with them and say, 'Now, are you willing to join? . . . If you are willing to join us in getting rid of all the weapons in the world, then we can give you this one.[44]

In the Star Wars speech and in many subsequent presentations, the president envisaged strategic defense as a nationwide area defense that would replace mutual assured destruction with "mutual assured security" based on a nationwide system of leak-proof strategic defenses.[45] Four days after the Star Wars speech,

---

[43]For rejections of deterrence from the nuclear left, see Dan Smith, ed., *Protest and Survive* (New York: Monthly Review Press, 1981); Jonathan Schell, *The Fate of the Earth* (New York: Knopf, 1982); and Douglas Lackey, "Missiles and Morals," *Philosophy and Public Affairs,* Summer 1982. The National Council of Catholic Bishops gave a "strictly conditioned moral endorsement" of deterrence in the fall of 1982, the condition being that the nation make real progress to something other than deterrence. See the ad hoc committee report, "The Challenge of Peace," *Origins* 12:20 (28 November 1982).

[44]Transcript of debate in the *New York Times,* 22 October 1984.

[45]"Mutual assured security" is a phrase that appears in an interview with the president in the *New York Times,* 11 February 1985. The commitment to area defense appears in his

Secretary Weinberger described the Reagan plan as "removing the fear of just threats of retaliation by developing a system of defenses that will ensure that no missile get through."[46]

Nevertheless, very few defense specialists in the administration shared the president's hopes for a leak-proof defense. Less than a month after the Star Wars speech, the president's national science advisor, George Keyworth, told *U. S. News and World Report* that the president's "objective is to have a system that would convince an adversary that an offensive attack would not be successful."[47] Likewise, the White House's own Future Security Strategy Study, set up in the wake of the Star Wars speech and reporting in October 1983, scarcely mentioned *replacing* deterrence but concluded mildly that intermediate defense capabilities "would reduce the confidence of Soviet planners in their ability to destroy high-priority military targets," while a fully deployed ballistic missile defense "could significantly reduce the military utility of Soviet preemptive attacks, thereby potentially increasing both deterrence and strategic stability."[48]

Critics were quick to point out that the difference between a system that will neutralize an attack once launched and a system that will psychologically impress an opponent so that he will not attack at all is precisely the difference between strategic defense and deterrence. Like the shift from Sentinel to Safeguard, the Reagan initiative in the hands of specialists had become another version of nuclear deterrence. For those who felt that the problem with Assured Destruction was not simply that it relies on deterrence but that it relies on deterrence via punishment, the proposed switch to a system of "deterrence by denial" represented a significant change in defense posture.[49] For those who believed that "deterrence by denial" would consist of blocking attempts to destroy American strategic weapons, which would then be launched back at the Soviet Union, the distinction between deterrence by punishment and deterrence by denial was practically meaningless.

Working alongside the Future Security Strategy Study in 1983 was the Defense Technology Study Team, headed by James Fletcher, formerly and currently the head of NASA. "What has happened to justify another evaluation of ballistic

---

second inaugural address (21 January 1985) and in the State of the Union address (4 February 1986), which describes the Star Wars program as working toward "a security shield [that] can one day render nuclear weapons obsolete and free mankind from the prison of nuclear terror." Some strategic defense advocates (Ben Bova, Jerry Pournelle) prefer "mutual assured survival."

[46]Caspar Weinberger on NBC's "Meet the Press," 27 March 1983.

[47]*U. S. News and World Report,* 11 April 1983.

[48]"Defense against Ballistic Missiles: An Assessment of Technologies and Policy Implications," issued by the U. S. Department of Defense, April 1984, p. 3.

[49]The distinction between "deterrence via punishment" and "deterrence via denial" dates at least from Glenn Synder's *Deterrence and Defense* (Princeton, NJ: Princeton University Press, 1961).

missile defense as a basis for a major change in strategy?" the Fletcher team asked. "Advances in defensive technologies warrant such a reevaluation."[50] The report ran through the full repertoire of BMD techniques, noted that the chances of destroying the Soviet missiles on their way up, not just on their way down, had substantially improved since 1970, and concluded that "the technical challenges of a strategic defense initiative are great but not insurmountable." Like the Future Security Study, the Fletcher report spent little time on the notion of a national space shield, but focused its near and middle-range hopes on the defense of American ICBMs. At the suggestion of the Fletcher report, in January 1984 a new entity, the Strategic Defense Initiative Organization (SDIO), was established in the Pentagon to coordinate existing BMD research programs and to develop new ones.

As 1984 progressed, the SDIO spent about $1.5 billion, distributed among the projects in the following categories:

radar discrimination	communication hardening
optical discrimination	space-based laser concepts
radar imaging	ground-based laser concepts
laser imaging	space-based particle-beam concepts
infrared sensing	in-atmosphere collision technology
boost surveillance	above-atmosphere collision technology
space surveillance	hypervelocity railgun technology
optical surveillance	hypervelocity launcher development
terminal imaging	battle management command, control, and communications
space-based imaging	survivability studies

Perhaps the high point of the early phase of SDI research was the successful test of a high-energy laser beam against a (stationary) ICBM in 1985.

As in the ABM debate of 1967–1969, much of the discussion of the Strategic Defense Initiative turned on questions of technical feasibility. Many of the protagonists of the ABM debate returned to the fray, arguing that the new directed-energy and kinetic-kill technologies were susceptible to countermeasures and surmountable by increased offense. Furthermore, since the new "boost-phase intercept" defenses would be constantly moving over and beyond the Soviet Union, the number of satellites needed to track and destroy rising ICBMs

133,658

---

[50]U. S. Department of Defense, *Defensive Technologies Study* (unclassified summary), April 1984, p. 2.

would be enormous. Worse still, the satellites and space weapons would themselves be open to attack, and defenses would be needed to defend the defenses.[51]

In a restaging of the Wohlstetter–Rathjens collision of 1969, space scientist Robert Jastrow claimed that the anti-ABM scientists had grossly exaggerated the number of satellites needed for boost-phase intercept. A numerical debate ensued in which the anti-SDI scientists conceded that the original number might have been too large but that the real number was still too big for a practical system.[52]

The technical case against the SDI received a strong boost in April 1984 when a Congressional Office of Technology Assessment Report, *Directed-Energy Missile Defense in Space,*[53] confirmed many of the arguments of the anti-SDI scientists. Written by Ashton Carter, a young and politically neutral specialist, the report argued (1) that perfect or near-perfect defenses are too remote to serve as a policy goal, (2) that less-than-perfect defenses may hurt security more than help it, (3) that the strategic goals of the SDI program are shifting or undefined, and (4) that the directed-energy weapons needed for boost-phase intercept have not been demonstrated, even in the laboratory. Three years later, the American Physical Society undertook an eighteen-month study of directed-energy weapons and concluded that the energies needed for effective defense were at least two orders of magnitude greater than had been produced in laboratory tests of the lasers and particle beams under study in the SDI.[54]

For those already converted to strategic defense, Ashton Carter's arguments simply produced a call for more research money. But obviously the problems of strategic defense were not purely technical. Nor were all the arguments of the middle eighties simply repetitions of the ABM debate. One factor present in the SDI debate that was absent in 1969 was the ABM treaty itself. The repeated claims that the SDI was "just research," and therefore fully consistent with the ABM treaty met with considerable skepticism.[55] The purpose of the Strategic

---

[51]For technical anti-SDI arguments in 1984, see Hans Bethe, Richard Garwin, Kurt Gottfried, and Henry Kendall, "Space-Based Ballistic Missile Defense," *Scientific American,* October 1984; John Tirman, ed., *The Fallacy of Star Wars* (New York: Random House, 1984); and Sidney Drell and Wolfgang Panofsky, "The Case against the Strategic Defense Initiative," *Issues in Science and Technology,* Fall 1984.

[52]See Robert Jastrow, "Reagan vs. the Scientists," *Commentary* January 1984, "The War against Star Wars," *Commentary,* December 1984, and "The Technical Feasibility of Ballistic Missile Defense," *Journal of International Affairs,* Summer 1985. For rebuttal, see "How Many Lasers for Boost Phase Intercept?," *Nature,* 23 May 1985.

[53]Ashton Carter, *Directed-Energy Missile Defense in Space* (Cambridge, MA: MIT Press, 1984).

[54]See C. K. Patel and N. Bloembergen, "Strategic Defense and Directed Energy Weapons," *Scientific American,* September 1987.

[55]For administration claims that the SDI is consistent with the ABM treaty, see *The President's Strategic Defense Initiative* (Washington, DC: The White House, January 1985) and *The Strategic Defense Initiative* (Washington, DC: U. S. Department of State, Special Report 129, June 1985). For a legal analysis of when research (permitted) crosses into

Defense Initiative was to find effective defenses; if those were found, they would be deployed, and if they were deployed, the ABM treaty would go by the boards, and with it, the skeptics charged, would go the whole process of superpower arms control.[56] By 1985, the administration had shifted its ground, arguing that the ABM treaty was so frequently violated by the Soviets that it could hardly be consider morally binding on the United States. "Do we want a treaty," the secretary of defense had remarked as early as 1984, "which the Soviets are not observing and have violated, to stand in the way of our ability to develop a thoroughly reliable system of defenses which can render nuclear missiles impotent?"[57] Finally, in 1986, the State Department tried to reconcile the SDI with the ABM treaty by arguing that the treaty applied only to interceptor *missiles,* and hence that even deployment of laser, particle-beam, or kinetic-kill defenses would not violate U. S. treaty obligations.

A second new element in the arguments about strategic defenses is the participation of computer scientists. The Nike-X, Sentinel, and Safeguard systems required computers for their operation, but the computational problems in the strategic defenses envisioned in the Reagan program differ by several orders of magnitude. A video game may involve computer programs several hundred lines long. The computer programs for strategic defenses will require programs several million lines long. The challenge of building hardware and writing software for systems that large was recognized early on, and the problem was taken up not by the SDIO but by DARPA's Strategic Computing Program, inaugurated in 1983. For the new strategic defenses, and for weapons and battlefield management in the twenty-first century, DARPA is counting not on the old-style sequential processing but on parallel processing and artificial intelligence, as indicated by the title of their report: *Strategic Computing, New Generation Computer Technology: A Strategic Plan for Its Development and Application to Critical Problems in Defense.*

But many computer specialists feel that the proposed task is simply impossible. The claims of "artificial intelligence" in computers are themselves controversial. But the problem described by anti-SDI computer specialists is more mundane: the system will not run until the programs are debugged, and the programs cannot be debugged because the system cannot be tested in the field. The process of trial and error, in which unanticipated results are generated by the program in response to

---

development (forbidden), see Milton Smith, "The Legal Implications of Missile Defense," *California Western International Law Journal* 15:1 (Winter 1985).

[56]McGeorge Bundy, George Kennan, Robert McNamara, and Gerard Smith, "The President's Choice: Star Wars or Arms Control," *Foreign Affairs,* Winter 1984–85; Sidney Drell and David Holloway, *The Reagan Strategic Defense Initiative: A Technical, Political, and Arms Control Assessment* (Stanford, CA: Stanford University Center for International Security and Arms Control, 1984); Alan B. Sherr, *Legal Issues of the Star Wars Defense Program* (Boston, MA: Lawyers Alliance for Nuclear Arms Control, June 1984); and Thomas K. Longstreth, John E. Pike, and John B. Rhinelander, *The Impact of U. S. and Soviet Ballistic Missile Defense Programs on the ABM Treaty* (Washington, DC: National Campaign to Save the ABM Treaty, March 1985).

[57]Caspar Weinberger, on "The Real Star Wars," (NBC-TV, 8 September 1984).

unanticipated inputs, and then removed by careful reprogramming, cannot occur: the system must work the very first time it is challenged.[58]

The system, then, seems bound to be unreliable. What is worse, the system seems to require that human beings be prevented from correcting its errors. The task of intercepting up to thirty thousand warheads in less than thirty minutes is a problem so complex, requiring such speed of execution, that computers involved in strategic defense must necessarily function automatically, without the distractions of human intervention.[59] The DARPA report takes this as an advantage:

> In contrast with previous computers, the new generation will exhibit human-like "intelligent" capabilities for planning and reasoning. . . . Using this new technology, machines will perform complex tasks with little human intervention, or even with complete autonomy. . . . Our leaders will employ intelligent computers as active assistants in the management of complex enterprises.[60]

What DARPA takes to be an advantage, many consider a liability. Computers in the NORAD warning system frequently sound attack alarms that human supervisors have (thus far) successfully diagnosed as false.[61] Removal of the human supervisors from the control of strategic defenses would raise the chance of unintended nuclear war.[62]

The new proposals for strategic defenses raise questions about American military space policy that were not relevant in the ABM debate. Ever since the 1950s there has been a division between those who feel that space should be reserved for civilian purposes and those who feel that space can and should be used for military purposes as well.[63] For space-purists, the orbiting battle stations of the new strategic defenses are the last word in the militarization of space. For space-militarists, space has always been militarized and the new defenses

---

[58]See Jonathan Jacky, "The 'Star Wars Defense' Won't Compute," *The Atlantic,* June 1985; Herbert Lin, "The Development of Software for Ballistic Missile Defense," *Scientific American,* December 1985; and David Parnas, "Why I Quit Star Wars," *Common Cause Magazine,* May/June 1986.

[59]Fletcher panel member Edward Gerry is quoted in the IEEE *Spectrum,* September 1985, as saying, "There is no time for man in the loop."

[60]Jacky, "The 'Star Wars' Defense Won't Compute," p. 20.

[61]The best public account of these problems is Dan Ford, *The Button* (New York: Simon & Schuster, 1985).

[62]Alex Dely, "Star Wars, False Alarms, and Unintended Nuclear War," *Peace Research Reviews* 10:4 (May 1986).

[63]For a general history, see Walter A. McDougall, *The Heavens and the Earth* (New York: Basic Books, 1985). For discussion more focused on military space policy, see Colin Gray, *American Military Space Policy* (Cambridge, MA: Abt Books, 1982); Jack Manno, *Arming the Heavens: The Hidden Military Agenda for Space* (New York: Dodd, Mead, 1984); and Paul Stares, *The Militarization of Space: U. S. Policy 1945–84* (Ithaca, NY: Cornell University Press, 1985).

represent no radical change in the American use of space.[64] After all, it is through space that ICBMs travel on their way to their targets.

The foundation of outer space law, the Treaty on Principles Governing the Activities of States in the Exploration and Use of Outer Space, Including the Moon and Other Celestial Bodies, ratified by the United States in 1967, specifies that "States Parties to the Treaty undertake not to place in orbit around the earth any objects carrying nuclear weapons or any other kinds of weapons of mass destruction, install such weapons on celestial bodies, or station such weapons in outer space in any other manner" (Article IV, par. 1). All the proposed strategic defenses, with the exception of the X-ray laser, are consistent with this paragraph of Article IV. The article goes on to affirm: "The moon and other celestial bodies shall be used by all States Parties to the treaty exclusively for peaceful purposes" (Article IV, par. 2). If the intent of the treaty was to prevent military action in space—that is, if "peaceful purposes" means "nonmilitary purposes"—then the new space-based missile defenses are contrary to the treaty. However, if "peaceful purposes" means "nonaggressive purposes," then the use of strategic defenses in space against an aggressive launch of ICBMs is consistent with the treaty. Many of those who support the Strategic Defense Initiative argue that deploying the defenses is consistent with the Outer Space Treaty. The High Frontier advocates of strategic defenses go further; they argue that the militarization of space is a good thing, since (they argue) military control and economic development historically have gone hand in hand.

Consistent with High Frontier suggestions, the president in 1982 formed a unified Aerospace Command, which some view as a step toward extension of routine air force operations into outer space.[65] One type of military operation that would be consistent with military control of outer space is antisatellite (ASAT) warfare. The Soviet Union currently has a moderate ASAT capability; the United States is developing a serious ASAT capability. Although the U. S. ASAT program is not part of the Strategic Defense Initiative, it is clear that if the United States develops space-based strategic defenses, these defenses will have the ability to destroy satellites as well as strategic weapons. Those who are opposed to antisatellite weapons, on the grounds that the best guarantee of peace is for each side to show the other's spy satellites that it is up to no harm, are accordingly opposed to strategic defense as well.[66]

The ABM treaty, the software issue, and the purity-of-space concept are new elements in the thirty-year controversy about strategic defense. But in the end, the old problems may prove to be the more important ones. It is still not clear to many technicians that the new systems will work. It is still not clear to many

---

[64]Colin Gray, "Space Is Not a Sanctuary," *Survival* (September/October 1983).

[65]For air force aspirations to space, see Thomas Karas, *The New High Ground* (New York: Simon & Schuster, 1983).

[66]See Robert Bowman, *Star Wars: A Defense Expert's Case Against the Strategic Defense Initiative*, pp. 48–53, for a draft of a treaty that would ban antisatellite weapons and that seems to have considerable Soviet support.

strategists that strategic defenses would be a good thing even if they did work.[67] The problem of countermeasures, the problem of system saturation, and, above all, the survivability of the system, all raised in the ABM debate, must be resolved by the new systems as well. As Paul Nitze, a strong supporter of the strategic defense initiative, explained:

> The technologies must produce defensive systems that are survivable; if not, the defenses themselves would be tempting targets for a first strike. . . . New defensive systems must be cost effective at the margin, that is, it must be cheap enough to add additional offensive capability so that the other side had no incentive to add additional capability to overcome the defense. If this criterion is not met, the defensive systems could encourage a proliferation of countermeasures and additional defensive weapons. . . .[68]

It was clear that Nitze felt that nothing on the boards could meet these standards when he made these remarks in 1985, and administration officials later denied that these standards represent official policy.[69] Policy or not, many critics feel that the Nitze standards express simple common sense and that no system yet considered, the Nike-Hercules, the Nike-X, Spartan, Sprint, Sentinel, Safeguard, or the modern space-based systems, shows any promise of immediately meeting them.

Between 1984 and 1988, Strategic Defense Initiative programs had spent about $7.3 billion, with $5.2 billion requested for fiscal 1988. Interest in more advanced technology for strategic defense seems on the wane, and interest in the more old-fashioned "kinetic kill" systems seems on the rise. Although the program has funded research in more than 500 for-profit corporations, 100 universities, and 100 nonprofit organizations,[70] most SDI projects remain in the experimental stage, and few are likely to emerge from the laboratory within this century. Four large-scale projects will be initiated in 1988:

1.   a national test facility, which will employ supercomputers to simulate nuclear attack, enabling scientists to "test" how defensive systems might work;

2.   a free-electron laser system, to be constructed at White Sands Missile Range, New Mexico;

3.   a kinetic-energy weapons system to be developed by Rockwell by 1992;

4.   a space-based surveillance system to detect missiles immediately after launch, to be developed by Lockheed and Grumman.

---

[67]See Charles Glaser, "Why Even Good Defenses Might Be Bad," *International Security,* Fall 1984.

[68]Paul Nitze, "On the Road to a More Stable Peace," in Craig Snyder, ed., *The Strategic Defense Debate* (Philadelphia: University of Pennsylvania Press, 1986), p. 223.

[69]Secretary of Defense Caspar Weinberger, testimony before the Senate Foreign Relations Committee, *New York Times,* 15 December 1985.

[70]Herb Brody, "Where the Money's Going," *High Technology Business,* December 1987.

The budget for the test facility exceeds $1 billion; the three other projects will cost several hundred million each, excluding overruns. With work on this scale, it seems likely that the Strategic Defense Initiative will live on, even without the continuing support of Ronald Reagan as president.[71] Nevertheless, this defense program, more than most, is sensitive to political pressure and ethical criticism. Sooner or later, the American people must decide if strategic defense is a morally good thing.

---

[71]For a rather jaunty picture of the penetration of SDI funds into American science at large, see Malcolm W. Browne, "The Star Wars Spinoff," *The New York Times Magazine,* 24 August 1986. The budget request for spending on SDI by the SDIO and the Department of Energy for 1989 is nearly $7 billion.

Part III. The Moral Case for Strategic Defense

1

The Non-Nuclear Defense of Cities: Proposed Statement of U.S. Policy

Gen. Daniel O. Graham

Through the 1970s the discussion of strategic defense was confined to specialists. But the change of administrations in 1980 led several strategists to rethink prevailing assumptions about strategic defense. Of these, the most prominent was Daniel O. Graham, whose 1981 article "Towards a New U. S. Strategy: Bold Strokes Rather than Increments" (*Strategic Review*, Spring 1981) introduced the notion of space-based missile defense into debates about nuclear strategy.

For Graham, the creation of strategic defenses was not merely a technical change in nuclear weapons policy. Space-based missile defense was a move toward the revitalization of the United States, which Graham viewed as gripped by malaise and paralyzed by self-doubt. Graham's "High Frontier" proposals called for defense of the United States from space and for control of space by the United States, arguing that through the dominance of space the United States could recover its dominant position on the world stage.

Graham argued that a reliance on MAD violated military ethics by taking civilians as targets and by denying soldiers the right to defend their countrymen. To these traditional arguments, Graham added the new argument that the move into space was morally required because

This reading is a selection from Daniel O. Graham's *The Non-Nuclear Defense of Cities* (Cambridge, MA: Abt Books, 1983). Used with permission of Abt Books Inc.

the moral values represented by the United States will prevail only if Americans seize the initiative the historical moment provides.

The United States and its allies now have the combined technological, economic, and moral means to overcome many of the ills that beset our civilization. We need not pass on to our children the horrendous legacy of "Mutual Assured Destruction," a perpetual balance of terror that can but favor those most inclined to use terror to bring down our free societies. We need not succumb to ever gloomier predictions of diminishing energy, raw materials, and food supplies. We need not resign ourselves to a constant retreat of free economic and political systems in the face of totalitarian aggressions. The peoples of the Free World can once again take charge of their destinies, if they but muster the will to do so.

In April of 1981, the Space Shuttle Columbia made its dramatic maiden voyage into space and back safely to Earth. This event was not merely another admirable feat of American space technology. It marked the advent of a new era of human activity on the High Frontier of space. The Space Shuttle is a development even more momentous for the future of mankind than was the completion of the transcontinental railway, the Suez and Panama Canals, or the first flight of the Wright brothers. It can be viewed as a "railroad into space" over which will move the men and materials necessary to open broad new fields of human endeavor in space and to free us from the brooding menace of nuclear attack.

This is an historic opportunity—history is driving us to seize it.

A few thousand years ago, man's activities—his work, his commerce, his communications, all of his activities, including armed conflict—were confined to the land.

Eventually man's technology and daring thrust his activities off the land areas of the continents and into the coastal seas. His work, commerce, communications, and military capabilities moved strongly into this new arena of human activity. Those nations that had either the wit or the luck to establish the strongest military and commercial capabilities in the new arena reaped enormous strategic advantages. For example, the Vikings, although never a very numerous people, became such masters of the coastal seas that their power spread from their homes in Scandinavia over all the coasts of Europe and into the Mediterranean Sea, up to the very gates of Byzantium.

At the beginning of the 16th century, after the epic voyages of men like Magellan and Columbus, human activity surged onto the high seas. Once again, the nations that mastered this new arena of human activity reaped enormous strategic rewards. First Spain and Portugal utilized their sea power to found colonies and to solidify their strength in Europe. Later, Great Britain, with an unsurpassed fleet of merchantmen and fighting ships, established a century of relative peace which we remember as Pax Britannica.

In the lifetime of many of us, man's activity moved strongly into yet another arena, the coastal seas of space—the air. And once again the nations which quickly and effectively made use of this new arena for commerce and defense

The Non-Nuclear Defense of Cities 33

gained great advantages. As Americans we can take pride that the greatest commercial and military successes in aviation have been achieved by our nation.

But today, following the epic voyages of our astronauts to the Moon and our unmanned explorer satellites to the rings of Saturn and beyond, we find man's activities moving strongly into yet another new arena—the high seas of space. Already the United States and other major nations, including the Soviet Union, are making huge investments in space. Much of our communications, intelligence, weather forecasting, and navigation capabilities are now heavily dependent on space satellites. And, as history teaches us well, those nations or groups of nations that become preeminent in space will gain the decisive advantage of this strategic "high ground."

We must be determined that these advantages shall accrue to the peoples of the Free World; not to any totalitarian power. We can improve the Shuttle, our railway into space, placing space stations at its terminals and sharply reducing the cost-per-pound of material put into space. We can thus open the doors of opportunity to develop entire new space based industries, promising new products and new jobs for our people on Earth. We can eventually create the means to bring back to Earth the minerals and the inexhaustible solar energy available in space. By doing so, we can confound the gloomy predictions of diminishing energy and material resources available here on Earth. This will not only enhance the prosperity of the advanced, industrialized nations of our Free World, but will also provide the means to solve many of the hitherto intractable problems of the developing countries.

Further, we can place into space the means to defend these peaceful endeavors from interference or attack by any hostile power. We can deploy in space a purely defensive system of satellites using nonnuclear weapons which will deny any hostile power a rational option for attacking our current and future space vehicles or for delivering a militarily effective first strike with its strategic ballistic missiles on our country or on the territory of our allies. Such a global ballistic missile defense system is well within our present technological capabilities and can be deployed in space in this decade, at less cost than other options that might be available to us to redress the strategic balance.

We need not abrogate current treaties to pursue these defensive options. A United Nations Treaty prohibits the emplacement of weapons of mass destruction in space, but does not prohibit defensive space weapons. The ABM Treaty requires discussion among Soviet and U. S. representatives of any decision to proceed with defensive systems "based on other principles" such as space systems. We should initiate such discussions and propose revisions, if necessary, in the ABM Treaty which is scheduled for review in 1982.

Essentially, this is a decision to provide an effective defense against nuclear attack for our country and our allies. It represents a long overdue concrete rejection by this country of the "Mutual Assured Destruction" theory which held that the only effective deterrent to nuclear war was a permanent threat by the United States and the Soviet Union to heap nuclear devastation on the cities and populations of each other. The inescapable corollary of this theory of MAD (perhaps the most apt acronym ever devised in Washington) was that civilian populations should *not* be defended, as they were to be considered hostages in this monstrous balance of terror doctrine. The MAD doctrine, which holds that attempting to defend ourselves would be "destabilizing" and "provocative," has resulted not only in the neglect of our active military and strategic defenses and our civil defense, it has also resulted in the near total dismantlement of such strategic defenses as we once had.

For years, many of our top military men have decried the devastating effect the MAD theory has had on the nation's security. In fact, our military leaders have, over the years, denied its validity and tried within the limits of their prerogatives to offset its ill effects. But those effects are readily evident. The only response permitted under MAD to increased nuclear threats to the United States or to its allies was to match these threats with increased nuclear threats against the Soviet Union. Further, a U. S. strategy which relied at its core on the capability to annihilate civilians and denied the soldier his traditional role of defending his fellow citizens has had a deleterious effect on the traditional American military ethic, and on the relationship between the soldier and the normally highly supportive public.

This legacy of MAD lies at the heart of many current problems of U. S. and allied security. We should abandon this immoral and militarily bankrupt theory of MAD and move from "Mutual Assured Destruction" to "Assured Survival." Should the Soviet Union wish to join in this endeavor—to make Assured Survival a mutual endeavor—we would, of course, not object. We have an abiding and vital interest in assuring the survival of our nation and our allies. We have no interest in the nuclear devastation of the Soviet Union.

If both East and West can free themselves from the threat of disarming nuclear first strikes, both sides will have little compulsion to amass ever larger arsenals of nuclear weapons. This would almost certainly produce a more peaceful and stable world than the one we now inhabit. And it would allow us to avoid leaving to future generations the horrendous legacy of a perpetual balance of terror.

What we propose is not a panacea which solves all the problems of our national security. Spaceborne defense does not mean that our nuclear retaliatory capabilities can be abandoned or neglected. The United States would still maintain strategic offensive forces capable of retaliation in case of attack. The Soviets, while losing their advantage in first strike capabilities, would still be able to retaliate in case of attack. Nor does our approach to the strategic nuclear balance eliminate the need to build and maintain strong conventional capabilities.

We Americans have always been successful on the frontiers; we will be successful on the new High Frontier of space. We need only be as bold and resourceful as our forefathers.

The Non-Nuclear Defense of Cities   35

2

Excerpts from a Speech on Military Spending and a New Defense

Ronald Reagan

On 11 February 1983, at his monthly meeting with the Joint Chiefs of Staff, President Reagan was presented with five different strategic options for the future of the United States. Of the five, which, according to Gregg Herken ("The Earthly Origins of Star Wars," *Bulletin of the Atomic Scientists,* October 1987), included increasing conventional forces and shifting from land-based strategic forces, the president selected increased strategic defense. Three senior air force staff officers were commissioned to draft the public announcement of the change in nuclear strategy, but the final wording seems to have been in part the work of the president himself.

Unlike Graham's paper above, the president's speech does not characterize the current strategic posture of the United States as immoral. Instead it argues that the present situation could be morally improved by strategic defenses, should they prove feasible. Nevertheless, the speech does convey a moral revulsion for nuclear weapons in general and nuclear deterrence in particular. Even though the proposed strategic defenses are at best defenses against ballistic missiles only, the president called upon the scientific community to create the means to render nuclear *weapons* "impotent and obsolete."

The speech is noncommittal on the direction of future research. It neither endorses nor rejects the use of chemical lasers, supported by Boeing, X-ray lasers, proposed by Teller and the Livermore staff, or kinetic-kill weapons, sponsored by the High Frontier. But clearly the president seeks a technological breakthrough and not a revival of the Nike-X style of defense.

The president read the speech on national television on 23 March 1983.

In his speech, the president calls on American scientists to "give us the means of rendering these nuclear weapons impotent and obsolete." The cautious reader should note that the "nuclear weapons" to which the president refers here are only nuclear *missiles,* and that there is nothing in the proposals for strategic defense discussed in his speech or in this book that will stop the delivery of nuclear weapons by bombers, cruise missiles, PT boats, or by other more clandestine means. Defusing the nuclear threat *in toto* will be a long process.

· · ·

M y predecessors in the Oval Office have appeared before you on other occasions to describe the threat posed by Soviet power and have proposed steps to address that threat. But since the advent of nuclear weapons, those steps have been increasingly directed toward deterrence of aggression through the promise of retaliation. This approach to stability through offensive threat has worked. We and our allies have succeeded in preventing nuclear war for more than three decades.

In recent months, however, my advisors, including in particular the Joint Chiefs of Staff, have underscored the necessity to break out of a future that relies solely on offensive retaliation for our security. Over the course of these discussions, I have become more and more deeply convinced that the human spirit must be capable of rising above dealing with other nations and human beings by threatening their existence. Feeling this way, I believe we must thoroughly examine every opportunity for reducing tensions, and for introducing greater stability into the strategic calculus on both sides.

One of the most important contributions we can make is, of course, to lower the level of all arms, and particularly nuclear arms. We are engaged right now in several negotiations with the Soviet Union to bring about a mutual reduction of weapons. . . .

I am totally committed to this course. If the Soviet Union will join with us in our effort to achieve major reduction, we will have succeeded in stabilizing the nuclear balance.

Nevertheless, it will still be necessary to rely on the specter of retaliation, on mutual threat. And that is a sad commentary on the human condition. Wouldn't it be better to save lives than to avenge them? Are we not capable of demonstrating our peaceful intentions by applying all our abilities and our ingenuity to achieving a truly lasting stability?

I think we are. Indeed, we must. After careful consultation with my advisors, including the Joint Chiefs of Staff, I believe there is a way. Let me share with you a vision of the future which offers hope. It is that we embark on a program to counter the awesome Soviet missile threat with measures that are defensive. Let us turn to the very strengths in technology that spawned our great industrial base, and that have given us the quality of life we enjoy today.

What if free people could live secure in the knowledge that their security did not rest upon the threat of instant U. S. retaliation to deter a Soviet attack, that we could intercept and destroy strategic ballistic missiles before they reached our own soil or that of our allies?

I know this is a formidable technical task, one that may not be accomplished before the end of this century. Yet current technology has attained a level of sophistication where it is reasonable for us to begin this effort. It will take years, probably decades, of effort on many fronts. There will be failures and setbacks, just as there will be successes and breakthroughs. And as we proceed, we must remain constant in preserving the nuclear deterrent and maintaining a solid capability for flexible response.

But isn't it worth every investment necessary to free the world from the threat of nuclear war? We know it is. In the meantime, we will continue to pursue real reductions in nuclear arms, negotiating from a position of strength that can be assured only by modernizing our strategic forces.

At the same time, we must take steps to reduce the risk of a conventional military conflict escalating to nuclear war by improving our non-nuclear capabilities. America does possess—now—the technologies to attain very significant improvements in the effectiveness of our conventional, non-nuclear forces. Proceeding boldly with these new technologies, we can significantly reduce any incentive that the Soviet Union may have to threaten attack against the United States or its allies.

As we pursue our goal of defensive technologies, we recognize that our allies rely upon our strategic offensive power to deter attacks against them. Their vital interests and ours are inextricably linked. Their safety and ours are one. And no change in technology can or will alter that reality. We must and shall continue to honor our commitments.

I clearly recognize that defensive systems have limitations and raise certain problems and ambiguities. If paired with offensive systems, they can be viewed as fostering an aggressive policy, and no one wants that.

But with these considerations firmly in mind, I call upon the scientific community in our country, those who gave us the nuclear weapons, to turn their great talents now to the cause of mankind and world peace, to give us the means of rendering these nuclear weapons impotent and obsolete.

Tonight, consistent with our obligations of the ABM Treaty and recognizing the need for closer consultation with our allies, I'm taking an important first step. I am directing a comprehensive and intensive effort to define a long-term research and development program to begin to achieve our ultimate goal of eliminating the threat posed by strategic nuclear missiles. This could pave the way for arms control measures to eliminate the weapons themselves. We seek neither military superiority nor political advantage. Our only purpose—one all people share—is to search for ways to reduce the danger of nuclear war.

My fellow Americans, tonight we're launching an effort that holds the promise of changing the course of human history. There will be risks, and results take time. But I believe we can do it. As we cross this threshold, I ask for your prayers and your support. Thank you. Good night. And God bless you.

3

The Moral Case for the
Strategic Defense Initiative

Capt. Kenneth Kemp

**Kemp compares strategic defense with two alternatives: disarmament
and deterrence. Disarmament, even mutual disarmament, is morally
problematic because it makes nuclear weapons more valuable, not less,
to those who illicitly possess them. Deterrence is morally problematic,
not because it embodies immoral intentions but because of the great
damage that even inadvertent nuclear war would cause. Strategic
defense, then, emerges as the morally superior alternative for a world
in which nations out of prudence must retain nuclear arms.**

T he whole human race faces a moment of supreme crisis on its advance
towards maturity.[1] So warned the Fathers of Vatican II in opening their
discussion of the problem of war in the modern world. How did we get to
this moment of supreme crisis?

The roots of the crisis can be traced at least as far back as Eighteenth Century
France where, within a space of a few years, there occurred two events which laid
the foundations for the problem we now face. The first was the Montgolfier
balloon ascent, which began man's conquest of the air; the second was conscrip-
tion into the Republican armies, which began the nationalization of war. The
century and a half that followed these events saw a radical transformation in the
nature of war. The population-as-national-resource of the French revolutionaries
was soon transformed into the population-as-target. But as long as wars were

---

Air force captain Kenneth Kemp published this essay while he was a member of the
Department of Philosophy and Fine Arts at the United States Air Force Academy.

This essay was first published in *Catholicism in Crisis* (June 1985). Used with permission
of *Crisis*, The Journal of Lay Catholic Opinion, published by the Brownson Institute, Inc.,
Notre Dame, IL 46556.

[1]*Gaudium et Spes,* paragraph 77.

fought on the ground, actual attacks on the enemy population were, by and large, first impossible (because the enemy army stood in the way) and then unnecessary (because once the army in the field was defeated, the population at home saw that there was no alternative to surrender).

The conquest of the air changed all that. Air power made it possible to attack the home population as a means to winning the war. Although the strategy was tried during World War I, technology at that early date was still too primitive and the strategy had no effect on the outcome of the war. But the horrors of the protracted trench warfare that was World War I made the development of air power look like an attractive alternative—a quick blow to the enemy homeland should end a war at relatively low cost, or so the strategists thought. It did not, of course, but the targetting of civilian populations nevertheless, and in spite of military opposition, came into its own. The technology used through most of the Second War was inefficient (it took a 1,000-plane raid which lasted three days to destroy Dresden), but effective. But World War II made its contribution to technology as well as to strategy, for the war saw the development both of the ballistic missile and of the nuclear bomb. It was the combination of these two inventions—an invulnerable delivery system and a weapon small enough to be carried, but large enough to be "useful"—in a moral context which tolerated the destruction of enemy cities that created the current predicament, the "supreme crisis" of the opening passage.

It did not have to be this way, of course. Immediately after the war, the United States, which had a monopoly on the possession of nuclear weapons, offered to give them up through the Baruch Plan. But this offer was rejected by the Soviet Union. Immediately after the war, the United States demobilized the largest army the world had ever seen, but the Soviet Union, in Czechoslovakia, in Berlin, and in Korea, to cite just the most salient incidents, made it clear that, though the Nazi menace had been destroyed, the threat to the free world was not in the least diminished. More recent events, in Czechoslovakia (again), in Poland, and in Afghanistan, make it clear that the threat is still before us.

The response we chose, reliance on nuclear weapons, was an economy move—nuclear weapons were cheaper, and more convenient, than maintaining a large conventional army. But the choice we made created a new danger, for the very weapons on which we relied for our defense came to pose a danger of their own. The American Bishops, in their recent pastoral letter, summarized the situation as follows:

> we perceive two dimensions of the contemporary dilemma of deterrence. One dimension is the danger of nuclear war, with its human and moral costs. . . . The other dimension is the independence and freedom of nations and entire peoples, including the need to protect smaller nations from threats to their independence and integrity.[2]

---

[2] *The Challenge of Peace: God's Promise and Our Response,* para. 174.

This reliance on the specter of retaliation to secure basic human values is, in President Reagan's words, "a sad commentary on the human condition."[3] What can we do about it? Three general lines of policy are available, each with variations.

The first is disarmament: we could get rid of nuclear weapons. Two variations of the disarmament policy are available—unilateral and multilateral. The first ignores the fact that the current situation is not just a bad one, it is a *dilemma*. The Bishops rightly insist that

> The moral duty today is to prevent nuclear war from ever occurring *and* to protect and preserve those key values of justice, freedom, and independence which are necessary for personal dignity and national integrity.[4]

Unilateral disarmament may avoid one of the horns of the dilemma, but only at the risk of impaling us all on the second.

The second variation of the disarmament policy is multilateral disarmament. Surely if both sides agreed to give up all nuclear weapons, then deterrence could be achieved, as it once was, conventionally, by our ability to deny the enemy success on the field of battle, rather than by threat of unacceptable retaliatory losses. And if deterrence should fail, at least there would be no chance that the war which ensued would destroy the whole planet. The problem here is not over whether a nuclear-free world would be a good thing—everyone agrees that it would. The question is rather over whether we can get there, and if so, how? For there are significant, perhaps insuperable, obstacles which stand between us and a nuclear-free world, at least along any of the most commonly proposed roads to that end.

Disarmament would only provide security if we could be sure that the other side actually did disarm. And verification of arms control agreements is a tricky business. At the current relatively high levels of armament, the tolerable margin of error is within our technological capabilities—if we miscount by 10 missiles, or perhaps even by 100, it is a matter of little strategic significance. But in a disarmed—or nearly disarmed—world even such a small difference in arsenal size would give decisive strategic advantage to the nation that had it. The incentives for cheating on arms control would be great and would only be magnified by the fear that the other side might be cheating as well.

A related danger is that the small arsenals, whether achieved via gradual reductions on the way to disarmament or via cheating on an agreement to disarm completely, are highly unstable. This instability arises from each nation's perception that the only way to survive the crisis is to destroy the other nation's nuclear forces in a preemptive strike. The prospect of achieving a successful pre-emptive strike on a nation with a strategic arsenal of a thousand warheads,

---

[3]Speech on Defense Spending and Defensive Technology, March 23, 1983.

[4]Ibid, para. 175. Emphasis in original.

The Moral Case for the Strategic Defense Initiative   **41**

properly deployed, is fairly small. There is no point in attacking unless one can assure that the victim of the pre-emptive strike has no significant retaliatory capability, and gaining that kind of assurance is no easy matter. But the probability of success in destroying an arsenal of only 10 weapons is much greater. That is why small nuclear arsenals are relatively unstable. The Bishops rightly emphasize the importance of considering stability when discussing the criteria to be used in evaluating new weapons systems.[5]

Complete nuclear disarmament, then, makes cheating too rewarding; even approaching it is dangerously destabilizing.

A second policy alternative is to stick with the current strategy of deterrence by threat of nuclear retaliation, or some variation of it. The variations on this policy pertain to the nature of the retaliatory threat. The history of U. S. nuclear policy seems to be a rather uneasy vacillation between general threats to destroy Soviet society and more focused threats on particular aspects of Soviet power (pre-eminently, but not exclusively, on its military forces). This strategy of deterrence by threat of punishment has kept "peace of a sort" for some forty years now, but it is, for numerous reasons, less than ideal. First, execution of certain threats would clearly be immoral.

> Any act of war aimed indiscriminately at the destruction of entire cities or of extensive areas along with their populations is a crime against God and against man himself. It merits unequivocal and unhesitating condemnation.[6]

In an earlier letter[7] the American Bishops argued that even threats against enemy population centers were immoral, since they required a conditional intention to do what was immoral. But the moral principle on which they relied, that intention to do what is immoral is itself immoral, seems to me not to apply to the kind of self-frustrating intention which characterizes deterrent threats. For an intention to do something immoral is objectionable just because it is the last step the agent takes on the way to performance of an immoral action. The intention to retaliate which characterizes the nuclear deterrent strategy, however, is conditioned on an event (a Soviet attack) which, it is believed, the very adoption of the intention makes unlikely. Thus, far from being anyone's last step on the way to perfor-mance of the act of retaliation, it is designed, among other things, precisely to make the act of retaliation unnecessary. In any case the point is moot, for several recent statements of official U. S. policy have explicitly stated that "for moral and political reasons, the United States does not target the Soviet civilian population as such."[8]

---

[5]Ibid., para. 189. Indeed their failure to recognize that their emphasis on the good of disarmament and their concern for avoiding instability run in somewhat different directions is one of the unresolved tensions of the pastoral.

[6]*Gaudium et Spes*, para. 80.

[7]*To Live in Christ Jesus* (1976).

[8]Letter from Mr. William Clark, then national security advisor, to Cardinal Bernardin, January 15, 1983. See also, Secretary of Defense Caspar Weinberger's *Annual Report to the Congress*, February 1, 1983, p. 55.

Second, even with the most scrupulous attention to the moral principle of non-combatant immunity, retaliatory threats raise both self-interested and moral worries. The very existence of the weapons raises the possibility, however remote, of accidents. Further, if deterrence should fail, there is always some danger that war would escalate to nuclear war and nuclear war to massive nuclear exchanges. And despite the technological advances which increase the accuracy of nuclear delivery vehicles, the co-location of military targets and civilian populations keeps alive the prospect of widespread collateral damage.

Nuclear deterrence, whether implemented through reliance on a policy of mutually assured destruction or on a policy of flexible response, may be the best of the currently available options, but it is just what the Bishops declare it to be, inadequate as a long-term basis for peace.[9] In saying this, they were echoing sentiments which had been expressed by Pope John Paul II the year before. In a message to the U. N. he had said:

> In current conditions, "deterrence" based on balance, certainly not as an end in itself, but as a step on a way toward progressive disarmament, may still be judged morally acceptable. Nonetheless, in order to assure peace, it is indispensable not to be satisfied with this minimum which is always susceptible to the real danger of explosion.[10]

The dissatisfaction with nuclear deterrence is not, of course, confined to the clergy. In a recent conversation, President Reagan expressed his dissatisfaction with the present state of affairs:

> Think of it. You're sitting at that desk. The word comes that they [the missiles] are on their way. And you sit here knowing that there is no way, at present, of stopping them. So they're going to blow up how much of this country we can only guess at, and your response can be to push the button before they get here so that even though you're all going to die, they're going to die too. . . . There's something so immoral about it.[11]

The Bishops urge that we "move . . . in a new direction, toward a national policy and an international system which more adequately reflect the values and vision of the kingdom of God."[12] The President put the same point as follows: "The human spirit must be capable of rising above dealing with other nations and human beings by threatening their existence."[13]

---

[9]Op. cit., para. 186.

[10]Message, U. N. Special Session, 1982.

[11]Hugh Sidey, "The Presidency," *Time,* January 28, 1985, p. 29.

[12]Op. cit., para. 134.

[13]Speech of March 23, 1983.

These remarks lead us into the third policy option which might be adopted in response to the nuclear dilemma—strategic defense. In the opening paragraph of my essay, I argued that the dilemma we face was created by the coupling of an invulnerable delivery vehicle—the ballistic missile—and a devastating warhead. A policy of strategic defense would be designed to make the delivery vehicle vulnerable.

Such a policy would not be a panacea. It would not solve the problems of poverty or racism. It would not even *solve* the problem of national security, but it would nevertheless solve one particularly intractable aspect of that last problem in a way preferable to the current policy for reasons both of morality and of self-interest.

The advantages of a defensive over a retaliatory policy seem clear. Defense against nuclear weapons raises no problems of intending (in any sense) what it would be immoral to do. Defense against nuclear weapons raises no problems of what to do if deterrence should fail. Defense against nuclear weapons does not leave us vulnerable to accidents. And perhaps most importantly, the ability to defend oneself against nuclear weapons opens the road to nuclear disarmament, by removing the instability of small arsenals and by removing the incentive to cheat on disarmament agreements. These are, of course, precisely the kinds of advantages cited by President Reagan in proposing that we look into strategic defense. At one point he asked, "Would it not be better to save lives than to avenge them?" and at another he points out that strategic defense could "pave the way for arms control measures to eliminate the weapons themselves."

Does strategic defense have disadvantages? Two are commonly cited.

First, critics object that it undermines the only really successful nuclear arms control treaty we have ever achieved. It is true that, though research into the possibility of strategic defense would not violate any provision of SALT I, deployment of such a system, at least on the scale being discussed here, would do so. But it is not clear that it is for that reason bad. Arms control treaties are, after all, not ends in themselves; they are means to preserving national security and international peace, as they themselves make clear.[14] They should remain in force only so long as they help to achieve the end for which they were established. But SALT I makes sense only in the context of a strategy of mutually assured destruction, of vulnerable populations and invulnerable retaliatory forces. And that, as we have seen in a policy which Bishops, Pope, and President all agree is acceptable only as an interim strategy!

Second, critics object that implementation of strategic defense would open a dangerous window of instability, a period in which the Soviet Union would see itself as having one last shot at the American nuclear arsenal before it became forever out of reach, protected by the strategic defensive shield. This is, of

---

[14]Cf. "Basic Principles of Relations between the United States and the Union of Soviet Socialist Republics," *Department of State Bulletin,* June 26, 1972, pp. 898–899, signed by President Nixon and General Secretary Brezhnev at the 1972 Moscow Summit which accompanied signature of the SALT I accord. This document states in part that "The USA and USSR regard as the ultimate objective of their efforts the achievement of general and complete disarmament and the establishment of an effective system of international security."

course, a danger. Careful co-ordination with our adversaries would be necessary to assure that we, and they, deploy strategic defensive systems in such a way that no such window of instability is opened. And the Reagan administration is explicit about the fact that the Strategic Defense Initiative should be "a cooperative effort with the Soviet Union, hopefully leading to an agreed transition toward effective non-nuclear defenses."[15] But the problem, though real, does not seem insuperable.

The real question seems to be, not whether strategic defense would be morally superior to deterrence by threat of nuclear retaliaton, but whether it would work, and whether we can afford it. Both questions, however, seem premature. Strategic defense is not, at present, a possibility. President Reagan's Strategic Defense Initiative proposes only that we initiate "a long-range research and development program," to see just what the possibilities are. The research will itself, of course, not be free, but as President Reagan asks, "is it not worth every investment necessary to free the world from the threat of nuclear war?" To which we might add, given what we have said about the moral superiority of this strategy over the alternatives, would it be morally permissible to ignore what may be the only road to the elimination of nuclear weapons?

---

[15]Mr. Paul Nitze, "On the Road to a More Stable Peace," a speech before the Philadelphia World Affairs Council, February 20, 1985.

4

Nuclear Strategy: Can There Be a Happy Ending?

Fred Charles Iklé

While Fred Iklé was director of the Arms Control and Disarmament Agency in the Nixon and Ford administrations, he published in the January 1973 issue of *Foreign Affairs* a remarkable article entitled "Can Nuclear Deterrence Last Out the Century?," one of the first attacks on the long-term acceptability of American strategic arrangements published *after* the ABM treaty of 1972. In this article Iklé argued that the mutual vulnerability formalized by the ABM treaty created an unstable system that threatened world safety in the long run. Furthermore, even in the short run, the system was morally unacceptable:

The jargon of American strategic analysis works like a narcotic. It dulls our sense of moral outrage about the tragic confrontation of nuclear arsenals, primed and constantly perfected to unleash widespread genocide. It fosters the current smug complacence about the soundness and stability of mutual deterrence. It blinds us to the fact that our method for preventing nuclear war rests on a form of warfare universally condemned since the dark ages—the mass killing of hostages.

The remedy vaguely suggested by Iklé in his 1973 article was increasing emphasis on precision, so that nuclear attacks could be directed toward more traditional military targets without collateral mass destruction. Since 1983, however, Iklé has become convinced that the remedy for the problems of deterrence requires replacing deterrence with strategic defense.

Fred Iklé was Deputy Director of Defense for Policy from 1981 to 1988.

This selection is excerpted from "Nuclear Strategy: Can There Be a Happy Ending?," first published in *Foreign Affairs* 63:4 (Spring 1985).

Today's opponents of strategic defense argue that their concept—"two sides" agreeing to a stable relationship of consensual vulnerability—reflects not a choice of doctrine but an inescapable technological fact. The mutual threat of assured destruction as the guarantor of peace, they say, is unchangeable because nuclear weapons cannot be disinvented.

Although nuclear weapons cannot be disinvented, other things are being invented. To say that the immense destructiveness of nuclear weapons makes the nuclear era unique is but a partial truth. As we look back in human history, to be sure, nuclear arms represent a unique change in the meaning of war and peace. For the future, however, we must expect other changes of perhaps comparable scope and consequence. Technology does not stand still, nor stay put in a few countries. And no heavenly law operates in this world to constrict the results of technological advances to "two sides."

It is important, therefore, to separate technological facts from doctrinal fictions. It is a fact that modern technology provides means that could be used to destroy people, wealth and even parts of nature with a totally unprecedented speed, intensity and magnitude. It is fiction, however, that the nuclear arsenals of the two superpowers are the only such means we need to be concerned about. It is a fact that other devices for mass destruction, existing or yet to be invented, could be delivered to an intended target in ways that are difficult, or perhaps too costly, to prevent. To conclude, however, that the only practical way to protect against destruction is to threaten retaliation in kind reflects not a permanent fact of technology but a choice of doctrine.

The sequence in which science presents governments with possibilities for new devices of destruction or new means to counter them is a vagary of history. Imagine that early in this century the development of science had taken a different turn. Biology and genetic engineering might have made dramatic advances, instead of the great progress in physics that then occurred. As a result, a different "Manhattan Project" in World War II could have produced a radically new biological weapon, exploiting the destructive potential of genetic engineering that people have begun to worry about today. Such a weapon could be far more efficient for causing mass destruction than the biological agents that the United States eliminated in the early 1970s, in compliance with the biological weapons treaty. That treaty, we recall, permits defensive measures but prohibits testing and stockpiling of offensive biological weapons—the reverse logic of the Anti-Ballistic Missile (ABM) Treaty.

Today's opponents of ballistic missile defenses often argue that such defenses are useless, since the "other side" could always smuggle nuclear bombs into our cities—the suitcase bomb. Hence, they conclude, we must rely exclusively on our ability to retaliate. None of these opponents of defense, surely, would choose to ban defenses and rely only on retaliation in kind if the "other side" developed powerful new biological weapons—whether or not these could be delivered in suitcases.

Yes, ballistic missile defenses could be circumvented. There are many ways to sneak a nuclear explosive into a city. Some day such an act might be attempted by a terrorist organization, or by a nuclear power that pursues irrational terrorist ends. A U. S.–Soviet relationship of consensual vulnerability would afford absolutely no protection against such a disaster. On the contrary, it might make it more likely or even aggravate its consequences.

Thus, it is not the destructiveness of a particular technology, but vagaries of both technological development and of American strategic thought, that have led to the excessive emphasis on retaliation and to the neglect of defenses in the current strategic posture of the United States. The notion of a stable strategic relationship based on the acceptance of mutual vulnerability reflects not a state of nature but a state of mind. . . .

The strategic world does not consist of "two sides," each willing to be locked into a symmetry of utter vulnerability. Even though we tried to conform to this dogma, the "other side," that is to say the real Soviet leaders and their real military advisers, did not. These men made every effort to reduce the vulnerability of their country—and especially of themselves. They ordered the construction of a great many hardened command posts, located well away from cities, for military commanders and officials at all levels of the government and Communist Party. They maintained a vigorous effort to improve their air defenses and develop missile defenses. And, above all, they deployed missiles increasingly capable of destroying our nuclear forces, thus equipping themselves to eliminate the cause, the very source, of their own vulnerability.

Why didn't the Soviet leaders act in accordance with our theory? Perhaps they did not want to entrust forever the future of Soviet communism and the Soviet empire to the rationality of American leadership. Perhaps they did not want to rely on the discipline and technology of the American military forever to prevent a cataclysmic accident. Perhaps, in their eyes, American policy seemed incoherent—and, hence, made them skeptical of our intent—since it combined the American doctrine of "stable" mutual vulnerability with the NATO deterrence policy that includes the threat of using nuclear weapons first in response to a massive conventional attack. But it is also possible that they saw in the absence of U. S. ballistic missile defense an invitation to acquire the missilery capable of destroying the U. S. land-based deterrent.

Those who remain opposed to strategic defense argue that missile defenses would merely stimulate the "action-reaction cycle of the arms race." The Soviet leaders, they maintain, would feel compelled to thwart our active defenses. Up to a point, to be sure, this may be a valid prediction. For a while, yes, the Soviet leaders undoubtedly would try to thwart our active defenses, much as they are trying to thwart passive defenses such as hardening and mobility that protect our deterrent today. By increasing the numbers, accuracy and destructive power of their missile warheads, they aim to overwhelm our hardened missile silos; by expanding their air defenses, they try to counter the survivability of our bombers; by stepping up their anti-submarine program, they try to negate the protective mobility and quietness of our nuclear missile submarines.

Here is a classic action-reaction cycle in armaments. Ought the United States to desist from improving these protective measures for its deterrent forces? Would anyone advocate such U. S. self-restraint—say, a halt in the hardening of our missile silos or in maintaining the protective elusiveness of our submarines—"to slow down the arms race"? In this country, most opponents of strategic defenses would not endorse such an idea. On the contrary, they postulate a stubborn determination on each side to protect its retaliatory forces. Yet their dogma excludes the possibility that one side might have, as well, a stubborn determination to protect its homeland. . . .

Unable to achieve a stable equilibrium of vulnerability between us and the Soviet Union in the past, are we likely to achieve such a strategic order in the future? Compelling reasons make this a most improbable outcome.

If we put the flesh and bones of real governments on the abstraction of "two sides," and if we recognize that these governments must function in the real world of many powers—of allies, of captive nations, of friends and foes—then we can readily see why such a two-sided equilibrium of mutual vulnerability is a relationship that cannot remain stable.

To begin with, the makers of Soviet foreign policy take a long-term view. Even if they were prepared to trust the U. S. government always to play the role of the reliable partner in such an equilibrium, they would feel it essential to take account of other nuclear powers, present or future. The planners in Moscow surely recognize that, despite the astonishingly successful American–Soviet cooperation in curbing the spread of nuclear weapons, the capacity to manufacture nuclear explosives will continue to spread to additional countries. They must be aware, for example, that they once helped China to acquire a nuclear capability and are now facing a slowly expanding strategic nuclear force across the world's longest border.

But, quite apart from the fact that the arena of nuclear powers does not consist of only two sides, there is a more fundamental reason why we should not expect the Soviet leadership to settle for the strategic order of consensual vulnerability. Like oil and water, the two ingredients in this order will always separate: the accord on a stable equilibrium of mutual restraint is psychologically incompatible with the constant threat of reciprocal annihilation. The first ingredient of this mixture represents the best in international relations: a continued willingness to cooperate in restraining one's own military power, coupled with a serene reliance on the opponent's prudence and his common sense. The second ingredient of the mixture represents the worst in international relations: an endless effort to maintain forces that are constantly ready to annihilate the opponent, coupled with an unremitting determination to deny him escape from this grip of terror.

The believers in the dogma of a stable, mutually agreed vulnerability fail to appreciate the dynamic of this incompatibility. Their vaunted strategic order is unstable at its very core. We cannot keep the balance of mutual threats of mass destruction from ceaselessly tilting. Yes, we can try to adjust this quivering balance, year after year, augmenting our offensive nuclear forces, substituting more effective or more survivable nuclear arms for older ones, in order to defeat the inevitable Soviet attempts to reduce the magnitude of the American nuclear threat to themselves. This has been our policy in past decades.

Today's critics of strategic defense argue that the Soviet rulers would never accept a strategic order in which the United States and its allies were no longer vulnerable to nuclear mass destruction, even if these rulers could acquire a similarly effective defense of their own homeland. Yet the critics firmly believe that these same Soviet rulers, whom they view as hellbent on maintaining their threat of our destruction, will forever nestle down with us in an equilibrium of mutual vulnerability. By accepting such an equilibrium, the Soviet rulers would have to accept indefinitely a future where any American president, or (in their eyes) perhaps even "some American general," could unleash the engines that would destroy the Soviet Union. To the men in the Kremlin, such a world cannot look like a place of stability. It cannot be the chosen destination of Soviet policy. As Soviet Foreign Minister Andrei Gromyko put it in 1962: ". . . to base the policy of states on a feeling of universal fear would be tantamount to keeping the world in a permanent state of feverish tension and a hysteria anticipating war. In such an atmosphere, each state would fear that the other side would lose its nerve and fire the first shot." Contrary to Gromyko's protestations today, the 1972 ABM Treaty did not convert the Soviet government to a strategic order of consensual vulnerability; Soviet investments in offensive and defensive systems speak louder than current denials. . . .

The conclusions fall into place. We need to accomplish a long-term transformation of our nuclear strategy, the armaments serving it, and our arms control policy. To begin with, we must disenthrall ourselves of the dogma of consensual, mutual vulnerability—the notion that unrelieved vulnerability of the United States and the Soviet Union to each other's nuclear forces is essential for halting the competition in offensive arms, and is the best guarantee against the outbreak of nuclear war.

Such a relationship never obtained in the past and it is most unlikely to come into existence in the future. Moreover, an agreed balance of mutual vulnerability would be repugnant on moral grounds. And it could in no way reduce the consequences of an accidental nuclear attack. In the long run, reliance on a balance of mutual vulnerability would favor totalitarian regimes, with a demoralizing effect on democracies.

The key now for the needed transformation is technological development to make effective defensive systems possible for the United States and our allies. The priority requirement is non-nuclear missile defenses capable of negating the military utility of a Soviet missile attack and of diminishing its destructiveness. Depending on progress in arms reductions, the missile defenses might later be complemented with air defenses. As strategic defenses make it increasingly unlikely that Soviet offensive forces can accomplish their mission, the incentive for new Soviet investment in them is reduced. We thus enhance Soviet willingness to join us in deep reductions of offensive forces.

To this end, we ought to take two complementary approaches. We should energetically seek Soviet cooperation, since it would greatly ease and speed the transformation. But we must also be prepared to persist on the harder road, where the Soviet Union would try as long as possible to overcome our defenses, and would resist meaningful reductions in offensive forces. The better prepared we are and the more capable of prevailing on the hard road, the more likely it is that the Soviet Union will join us on the easy road.

Critics of missile defenses fear that defenses could not be made leak-proof against a massive attack, that a fraction of the missiles might penetrate, causing dreadful destruction, with whole cities lost. Usually this fear assumes that the Soviet leaders would expend the bulk of their missile force to destroy our cities. Yet if only a fraction of the attacking force were to reach some unpredictable targets, while missing most of the militarily important targets, to launch such an attack would accomplish no rational purpose. It would serve no strategic objective, and would be akin to a wanton terrorist act. It is precisely against such irrational acts that an exclusive reliance on deterrence would offer no protection at all.

We cannot know at this time whether the Soviet Union will join us and agree on major reductions in offensive nuclear arms, and whether it would abide by them. As one tries to promote arms control, Soviet failure to comply with past agreements is a bone in one's throat. But if the Soviet leaders are willing to cooperate on a purpose both East and West can share, that purpose surely cannot be the perpetual hostility that is inherent in unopposed forces constantly poised for mass destruction. It can however be a strategic order that will eventually eliminate Soviet vulnerability to massive nuclear destruction, even if this means in turn surrendering their capability to inflict mass destruction on Western Europe and the United States. Conversely, should the Soviet leaders choose to preserve their doomsday capability at any price, the prospects for arms control would be bleak indeed.

The more the offensive armaments can be reduced by agreement, the easier and cheaper the job of providing effective defenses. Yet, to be realistic about Soviet motivations, we must seek to develop and deploy systems that can provide effective defenses even without such reductions. The United States is now pursuing new technologies that hold promise for success on the "hard road" as well. Thus, we make it all the more probable that the Soviet leaders will join us some day on the easy road of cooperation.

Our thinking on nuclear strategy must reach far into the future. It is not enough that our strategy serve to prevent nuclear attack in this decade or the next. Nuclear armaments and defensive systems take ten years or more to design, develop and build; and once deployed they will last for a quarter-century or more. We are today constrained in the choices for our nuclear policy by strategic theories that thirty years ago began to influence the development of our present weapons systems. The time to start designing a safer nuclear strategy for the twenty-first century is now.

5

Whom the Gods Would Destroy, They First Make MAD

M. Stanton Evans

Evans traces the history of opposition to strategic defenses to
various civilian advisors and liberal intellectuals in the early 1960s.
Professional military officers, he argues, have never dismissed the
possibility or the usefulness of strategic defense. What liberals fear
most, according to Evans, is not that strategic defenses will not
work but that they *will*, ending the present military paralysis of the
West. Technical criticisms of Star Wars proposals are thin disguises
for a strategic attitude the American people would never accept if it
were explicitly stated.

hat makes the ABM accord so transcendently important is that it
enshrines in international law a totally revolutionary concept in the
history of nations: the idea that purely defensive weapons to protect
one's homeland from attack are "provocative" to the enemy—and
the corollary view that leaving one's civilian population exposed to possible
destruction is a step toward peace.

The viewpoint embodied in the ABM accord is known as "mutual assured
destruction," MAD for short. MAD is popularly fancied to be the creation of
Strangelovian militarists in the Pentagon; its true history is considerably more
complex. It begins with the now-bromidic concept of atomic stalemate, in which
the U. S. and USSR are deterred from attacking one another by the threat of
devastating retaliation, capable of being delivered in a matter of minutes by
long-range missiles armed with nuclear warheads. Such an exchange, we are

M. Stanton Evans is director of the National Journalism Center.

This selection is excerpted from "Whom the Gods Would Destroy, They First Make
MAD," first published in the *National Review* (14 March 1986). ©1986 by National Review,
Inc., 150 East 35th Street, New York, NY 10016. Reprinted with permission.

repeatedly informed, would be tantamount to mutual suicide, hence "unthinkable." So much is familiar to any denizen of the modern era within reach of a newspaper or TV set.

Less familiar is the paradoxical conclusion MAD theorists drew from this alarming situation. Pondering the matter among themselves in the early 1960s, a group of leftward intellectuals committed to nuclear disarmament decided that stalemate-*cum*-unthinkability was maybe not so awful, after all—that it could in fact be put to beneficial uses. For one thing, by precluding resort to atomic weapons, it creates a de-facto species of disarmament. For another, the pyschological and political pressures it generates can be employed to get de-jure agreements. From which it was deemed to follow that the "balance of terror" between the U. S. and USSR must be preserved and nourished.

Such thoughts were spelled out, in the early going, by theorists at the Institute for Defense Analyses and in a volume called *The Liberal Papers*. They were given their most influential expression, however, by Dr. Jerome Wiesner of the Massachusetts Institute of Technology, who broached the key particulars of MAD directly to the Soviets at a Moscow conference in 1960 and thereafter served as a disarmament maven for Presidents Kennedy and Johnson, opposing anti-missile defenses at every step along the road.

Wiesner phrased it this way at the Moscow conference: "While a system of mutual deterrence is less attractive in many ways than properly safeguarded total disarmament, it may be somewhat easier to achieve and could be regarded as a transient phase on the way toward the goal of total disarmament. . . . In this situation, an attack is deterred by the certain knowledge that it will be followed by a devastating reply. . . . If both sides in a military contest develop secure weapons, much of the incentive for an unlimited arms race disappears, even without controls."

Given these assumptions, measures to protect one's homeland with defensive weapons were considered highly undesirable. The nation that developed a successful anti-missile defense could avoid obliteration of its own cities, while being able to destroy those of the opposition. This would make nuclear war "thinkable" again, and upset the balance of terror that is so useful in the service of disarmament. By an inexorable process of deduction, we reach the conclusion that, precisely *because* an atomic war would be so horrible, we should have no defenses against it.

Once this position is arrived at, we are only a step away from the final surrealistic nuance of MAD theory: We should ensure that the Soviets' offensive weapons are fully capable of obliterating *our* civilian population, just as our weapons are capable of obliterating theirs. Or, as arms-control theorist Walter Millis put it in *The Liberal Papers,* "a genuinely deterrent policy would require the United States to cooperate with the Soviet Union in ensuring that their retaliatory force was as invulnerable as ours and that our population was equally exposed to attack with theirs."

Despite the breathtaking novelty of these opinions (Millis himself described them as "fantastic") they somehow managed, in relatively short order, to become official doctrine. It is doubtful that many military theorists have ever agreed with MAD in its more fervent modulations, or that strategic planners have accepted it in terms of targeting our weapons. Yet the most astonishing aspect of the

MAD theory—the idea of leaving our own civilian population deliberately defenseless—became, and to this day remains, the policy of the U. S. Government. . . .

Whatever else may be said about all this, it is conceptually the opposite of Reagan's SDI. As its genealogy and phrasing clearly suggest, the ABM accord is the very embodiment of MAD. SDI is its repudiation. When push comes to shove, whatever the quibble over new technology, one or the other must be abandoned.

If that issue were posed in straightforward fashion to the American people, there is little doubt what they would choose. Opinion polls suggest not only that the public like the idea of having anti-missile defenses, but that most people have assumed that we already have such weapons developed and in place. A 1982 survey by the Sindlinger organization, for example, found 66 per cent of those responding unaware that we didn't have defenses of this type; informed about the situation, better than 80 per cent of respondents favored their development.

So much, outside the realm of MAD conjecture, is only common sense. As a moral proposition, the idea of preserving the peace by saving tens of millions of lives rather than by threatening to destroy them has self-evident appeal. It has even more appeal when the lives to be saved include one's own. Most of us would like to be protected from nuclear incineration, and would look askance at the concept of being deliberately left hostage to the possibility of attack from Moscow. Phrased in these terms, MAD doctrine would be almost impossible to sell to the average person.

For that reason, the sponsors of MAD have taken considerable pains *not* to put the matter in these terms, except in rarefied discusssions that seldom get noticed by the public. In political debate, opposition to SDI, and to missile defenses generally, is usually phrased in guarded, bureaucratic fashion, stressing the technical or financial problems associated with ABMs. The idea of having a defense, it is suggested, is well and good, but simply isn't feasible. . . .

The problem, instead, is just the other way around. What really concerns MAD theorists is the possibility that SDI or some other defensive system, *would* work. Should that occur, and should the United States succeed in defending its civilian population from attack, the "balance of terror" would be upset. Mutual assured destruction, and the pressures it creates in favor of nuclear unthinkability, would be subverted.

The point is made by the ABM accord itself. If such defenses are so technically unfeasible, so easily fooled and overwhelmed, why do we need a solemn treaty, replete with elaborate definitions and provisos, in order to ban them? Likewise with Soviet, and other, efforts to get some kind of explicit agreement barring SDI. Why go to so much bother to prohibit something that is impossible?

This theme has been sounded repeatedly by MAD supporters in their more candid moments, speaking among themselves and to the Soviets. Thus Professor Wiesner at the 1960 gathering in Moscow: "It is important to note that a missile deterrent system would be unbalanced by the development of a *highly effective anti-missile system,* and *if it appears possible to develop one, the agreements should explicitly prohibit the development and deployment of such systems.*" (Emphasis added.) Thus also a British ABM opponent in a mid-Sixties conclave with the Soviets: "If one or the other side were to possess a *really effective anti-ballistic missile, that—ironic though it may seem—would be extremely*

dangerous, because it would upset the stability of the nuclear balance."
(Emphasis added.)

Such statements make it plain that the absence of defenses is a matter of doctrine, not technological kismet. So do the numerous actions we have taken in obedience to MAD theory—the common feature of which is that they *suppressed* technologies that were, and are, within our grasp. . . .

The MAD promoters understand this very well, which is why they are fighting SDI with every resource they can muster. They also understand that they don't need to abolish SDI outright to prevent it from taking effect. They simply need to contain it within the SALT-MAD framework, dragging it out as a futuristic, purely research-oriented project, and preventing deployment of those elements that would be useful to us in the near term (such as point defenses). In this respect, the ABM agreement is their trump card. As long as it remains in effect, SDI—or any other form of ABM deployment—will be impossible, and the MAD conception of planned defenselessness will continue to control our military posture.

In pursuit of this objective, recent literature from the MAD fraternity frequently stresses the supposed value of the ABM Treaty in and of itself—quite apart from the validity of the theory on which it is based, or the concrete results in terms of our security. Increasingly, the arguments in the treaty's behalf are neither technical nor strategic, but *political,* dwelling on its symbolic importance, centrality to the arms-control "process," and the like. The point of such discussion is to use the treaty as a kind of psychological totem, forestalling any thought of breakout, and thus forestalling SDI.

6

Why Offense Needs Defense

Caspar Weinberger

Whereas President Reagan in his Star Wars speech suggested that the United States should seek to *replace* offense with defense, Secretary Weinberger in these selections argues that an improved *mixture* of offense and defense is more likely to deter nuclear war than the present "offense only" arrangements. He contends such arrangements are more consistent with democratic values and that the United States cannot indefinitely sustain defense arrangements fundamentally at variance with its moral sense.

I.

lthough many contend that strategy does not apply to nuclear warfare in the same way it does to conventional warfare, recent history suggests that how one thinks about nuclear war decisively affects force deployments, force structure, weapons acquisition, and, above all, arms reduction agreements. The United States and the Soviet Union indeed have avoided war on the grand scale, even though preserving the peace has required a constant effort by the West to maintain its deterrent force and resolve. But no one can say with absolute certainty why these efforts have been successful thus far. Whatever the reason, America must continually search for better, more stable ways to keep the peace. This means thinking strategically. . . .

In the realm of U. S. defense strategy, it is necessary to move away from

Caspar Weinberger was secretary of defense from 1981 to 1987.

The first section of this selection consists of excerpts from "Why Offense Needs Defense," first published in *Foreign Policy* 68 (Fall 1987). Reprinted with permission from *Foreign Policy* 68 (Fall 1987). Copyright 1987 by the Carnegie Endowment for International Peace. The second section consists of excerpts from "The Vision of Strategic Defense," first published in *The Strategic Defense Debate,* edited by Craig Snyder (Philadelphia: University of Pennsylvania Press, 1986).

partisan politics and toward a serious evaluation of our strategy's basic tenets, especially since the advent of the idea of mutual assured destruction in the 1960s. For nearly 20 years the United States has narrowed its options significantly by always saying no to the possession of defensive systems.

It is time that America examine the results of that decision. Obviously, elements of that overall strategy, such as the basic U. S. commitment to nuclear deterrence and the NATO strategy of flexible response, retain proven value. But by examining its strategic principles in an intellectually honest manner, the United States can reaffirm those tenets that still apply and revise any that have become outdated. The notion that abandonment of defenses has been stabilizing is one that deserves particular attention. . . .

During the now famous encounter with then Soviet President Aleksei Kosygin at Glassboro, New Jersey, in June 1967, McNamara expressed frustration at not being able to convince Kosygin to take a similar view to America's and abandon the quest for a defense against nuclear missiles. Kosygin reportedly remarked: "We are defending Mother Russia—that's moral. You are increasing your offensive forces—that's immoral." Apparently, one of the most basic and ancient principles of strategy—the need for a mix of offensive and defensive capabilities to deter potential enemies—had been discarded in American strategic thinking then and replaced by concepts preached by the new American nuclear strategists.

Certainly, part of the logic that guided American policymakers reflected the problems associated with the development of technologies for defense against ballistic missiles. Given the lead that the United States possessed in nuclear weaponry, the inclination toward a purely offensive deterrent strategy can be understood. In hindsight, however, the consequences of abandoning the more traditional approach to strategy can be easily discerned.

On the one hand, the Soviet Union proceeded to explore and develop defensive technologies; on the other, the United States allowed what offensive advantage it possessed in nuclear technology to erode while making no attempt to acquire defensive technologies. It made little effort even to conduct research. McNamara, in full good faith, intentionally allowed this to happen. As early as January 1967, in testimony before a Senate committee, he justified his reasoning for not pursuing strategic defense:

> We believe the Soviet Union has essentially the same requirement for a deterrent or "Assured Destruction" force as the U. S. Therefore, deployment by the U. S. of an ABM [antiballistic missile] defense which would degrade the destruction capability of the Soviets' offensive force to an unacceptable level would lead to expansion of that force. This would leave us no better off than we were before.

Unfortunately, the Soviets approached their national security from an entirely different point of view, so McNamara found Soviet spending on "sievelike" defensive systems nearly incomprehensible. He called it "fanatical" and said it could be explained by "their strong emotional reaction to the need to defend Mother Russia." A better explanation is that Soviet deterrence doctrine has never conformed to a purely offensive approach. The United States made the familiar mistake of assuming that the Soviets were just like Americans and thought the same way.

Why Offense Needs Defense   **57**

In 1983, when President Ronald Reagan first announced his initiative to develop strategic missile defenses, the idea that active defense might play a constructive role in the strategic equation, and that it might lead to a more stable world, was greeted by many so-called defense experts as nothing less than heresy. Indeed, "strategic defense" was not part of the nuclear lexicon and therefore was immediately dismissed by some in Congress and others in the defense community at large. Today, however, the basic principle is rarely challenged except by those who believe that the conventional wisdom will never change. The debate in Congress is not whether the United States should work on strategic defense technologies, but how vigorously.

Curiously enough, in the early 1960s, as the debate over antiballistic missiles began to take shape, Nikolai Talensky, a retired Soviet general major who had been the editor of the military journals *Red Star* and *Military Thought,* expressed his views on ABMs in the October 1964 issue of the Soviet journal *International Affairs.* Talensky noted that "sooner or later, every new means of attack leads to the emergence of a means of defense." He cited such classic examples as the sword and shield and the shell and plate armor. According to Talensky, that same law exists in the age of nuclear rockets, despite the radical change in the nature of any possible armed struggle.

In noting the disastrous consequences of nuclear war, Talensky contended that effective ways must be sought to reduce the danger of nuclear rocket attack and, if possible, to neutralize it altogether: "I think that it is theoretically and technically quite possible to counterbalance the absolute weapons of attack with equally absolute weapons of defense." Clearly Talensky recognized the Western paradox of defense through offensive threat alone. He remarked, "Antimissile systems are defensive weapons in the full sense of the word: by their technical nature they go into action only when the rockets of the attacking side take to their flight paths, that is, when the act of aggression has been started."

Talensky's point of view reflects classical Soviet strategic thinking. In the past 10 years alone, the Soviet Union has spent 15 times as much on strategic defense as the United States. This effort has given the Kremlin today the advantage of the world's only deployed operational ABM system, the only operational antisatellite system, the most comprehensive, in-depth, and capable air defense system ever deployed, and an organization for passive defense of its leadership, population, and industrial assets—including hardened shelters for 175,000 Communist party and government leaders. In fact, these actions, along with extensive advanced research into new technologies for ballistic missile defense, belie current Soviet rhetoric. Indeed, as Soviet leader Mikhail Gorbachev lashes out at America's SDI research program, he ought to bear in mind Talensky's prophetic words: "Only the side which intends to use its means of attack for aggressive purposes can wish to slow down the creation and improvement of antimissile defense systems.". . .

History provides a fascinating parallel to the current controversy over whether defense should be considered part of U. S. nuclear strategy. In 1934 a British parliamentary debate, not unlike the present debate over the Strategic Defense Initiative (SDI), took place on the need for research in air defense technology. At that time, there was a growing concern about Nazi Germany's efforts to rearm itself. Many people believed that the potential destructiveness of bombing civilian populations from airplanes had been demonstrated clearly in World War I and that no defense ever could be built up to meet such an attack in the future. One proposed solution was to build a bomber force that would act as a deterrent by jeopardizing Germany's own population.

However, Winston Churchill, then a member of Parliament and later prime minister, spoke in favor of air defense, saying, "If anything can be discovered that will put the earth on better terms against this novel form of attack, this lamentable and hateful form of attack—attack by spreading terror throughout civil populations—anything that can give us relief or aid in this matter will be a blessing to us all." He went on to argue that until defenses were devised, deterrence would rest completely on Great Britain's ability to retaliate: "The fact remains that pending some new discovery, the only direct measure of defense upon a great scale is the certainty of being able to inflict simultaneously upon the enemy as great damage as he can inflict upon ourselves."

Churchill's remarks reflected a sense both of realism and of hope. He was acutely aware of the technological limitations of his time. Yet he recognized the merit in seeking a deterrent that did not rely solely on offensive retaliation. . . .

On March 23, 1983, Reagan challenged the scientific community to develop the technology that would allow the United Staes to move away from a policy of deterrence based solely upon the capability actually to defend the United States and its allies:

> What if free people could live secure in the knowledge that their security did not rest upon the threat of instant U. S. retaliation to deter a Soviet attack, that we could intercept and destroy strategic ballistic missiles before they reached our own soil or that of our allies?
>
> I know this is a formidable technical task. . . . But isn't it worth every investment necessary to free the world from the threat of nuclear war?

Like Churchill in the 1930s, Reagan challenged the so-called conventional wisdom of his time and was met with a great deal of skepticism and even ridicule. But there are lessons and, indeed, parallels to be drawn from the events surrounding the debate in the 1930s.

In 1932, there was a predominant assumption in Britain that the bomber would always get through; therefore, the idea of a British deterrent bomber force was considered credible and necessary. On the question of defense, many believed it was hopeless to try to defend against a fearful knockout blow from the air. As the German air threat became more real, British vulnerability to air attack became obvious. Consequently, in 1934 the Committee for the Scientific Study of Air Defense, known as the Tizard committee, was formed. A breakthrough in the early warning and detection technology led to the invention of radar. Britain also decided in 1936 to allocate more resources to fighter production, instead of bombers, to provide for a system of air defense.

This decision was almost too late. But because of the leadership and foresight of Churchill, and the indomitable national will he embodied, Britain survived. In time, barely in time, Britain had developed both offensive and defensive components in its strategy. The air defense decision had required great forethought and inventive genius, as well as the resolve to commit scarce resources.

II.

What we do in foreign and defense policy is closely connected with who we are and what we value. Naturally, we desire a realistic and moral deterrence policy that is responsive to the threat and reflects our democratic values. Our uneasiness with the strategic doctrine and programs developed in the 1960s is therefore perfectly consistent with our goals and principles. And with the Soviets clearly rejecting the concept of agreed mutual vulnerability, there is only one prudent course of action: change our own doctrine and programs. We must seek and secure a defensive capability that could ultimately lead to the end of nuclear missiles. This is not only prudent, it is far more in keeping with our democratic ideals than a mutual suicide pact.

In acknowledging the need to study the feasibility of a defense against Soviet missiles, we took a course radically different from that of the Soviet Union—we actually told the world what we are doing, and we invited the world to help us to achieve such a defense. We even briefed the Soviets on SDI in Geneva so they could understand our program and join us in discussing how we might fashion a stable transition away from deterrence based on offensive threats, if defensive technologies proved feasible.

In fact, we have explained to everyone our long-term goal, which is simply to study the potential of a transformation of the strategic order so that the threat of nuclear offensive forces and nuclear mass destruction can be drastically reduced—and eventually eliminated. We have learned that the dogma of agreed mutual vulnerability, over the long term, is not a safe guarantee against nuclear war, particularly when the Soviets do not accept it. Nor can it offer the world any hope of halting the ever-mounting stockpile of offensive arms. History has proven this.

But as we go forward with the needed transformation to a strategic order based on defense, we cannot, nor do we intend to, neglect our triad of deterrent offensive systems. Rather, for some time to come we must maintain and, indeed, modernize our deterrent forces and their communications systems. We do not yet know whether a thoroughly capable defense system can be established, so prudence demands that we not allow the dangerous gap between our triad and the growing Soviet nuclear force to widen. Nor do we wish to condemn ourselves to a future in which, as Churchill said, safety is "the sturdy child of terror." The survival of civilization must be built on a firmer foundation than the prospect of mutual terror.

We all recognized from the outset that if the research bears fruit, a complete system for strategic defenses could not be deployed overnight. We seek a stable transitional period when some defenses would be deployed and operating before others. Some have argued that this transition would be particularly dangerous, that it would upset the present deterrent system without putting an adequate substitute in its place.

The opposite is the case. If properly planned and phased, the transitional capabilities would actually strengthen our present deterrent capability. In fact, they could make a major contribution to the prevention of nuclear war, even before a fully effective system is deployed.

If the Soviet leaders ever contemplated initiating a nuclear attack, their purpose would be to destroy U. S. or Allied retaliatory capability and the military forces that would blunt Soviet aggression. Even partially effective defenses that could deny Soviet missiles their military objectives, or shake the Soviet's confidence in their ability to achieve such dire objectives, would discourage them from considering such an attack and would thus be a highly effective deterrent.

Recognition that a fully effective defensive system could not be deployed overnight must not dilute our efforts toward finding a thoroughly reliable, layered defense that would destroy Soviet missiles outside the Earth's atmosphere and at all phases of their flight. And let me stress that the choice is not between protecting military forces and protecting cities. The goal of our strategic defense research program, the vision and the hope of the President, is to stop Soviet missiles *before* they could destroy *any* targets, be they in the United States or anywhere else. The goal is noble and straightforward: to destroy weapons that kill people.

Thus, based on a realistic view of Soviet military planning, the transition to strategic defense would not be destabilizing. In fact, any initial defensive capabilities would offer many benefits. They would contribute to deterrence by denying Soviet attack goals, and should deterrence ever fail, they would save lives by reducing the scope of the destruction that would result from a Soviet attack. The more effective the defenses, the more effective this deterrence would be. This objective is far more idealistic, moral, and practical than the position taken by those who still embrace the mutual assured destruction (MAD) theory that defenses must be totally abandoned.

I know that some of our allies fear that our pursuit of the defense initiative would tend to "decouple" America from them. This is quite wrong. The security of the United States is inseparable from the security of our allies. In addition to strengthening our nuclear deterrent, such defenses would also enhance Europe's ability to deter Soviet aggression by reducing the ability of Soviet intermediate-range ballistic missiles—both conventional and nuclear—to put at risk either our allies or those facilities essential to conventional defense such as airfields, ports, depots, and communications networks. The same is true with respect to Japan and Korea. An effective defense against ballistic missiles would create great uncertainty in the mind of the aggressor, reduce the likelihood of a conventional attack on Western Europe, and thereby reduce the chance that the Soviet Union would contemplate such an attack in the first place.

If such a system can be developed, it will offer the Soviets a strong incentive to reduce their investment in offensive forces, and this is precisely what President Reagan is seeking. Even now we are asking the Soviets to join us in deep reductions in offensive weapons. But if we stop our work on strategic defense and give it away at the negotiating table, we will forever lose one of history's best chances to end the shadow and the fear of nuclear weapons.

Today we have but one choice if, by accident or design, deterrence fails—and that is retaliation with our offensive systems. Of course, we all hope deterrence will never fail. That is why all our efforts are designed to persuade any enemy that the cost of their aggression is too high.

The President's proposal at last offers us the first real opportunity to transform and enhance deterrence—the opportunity for us to make a major contribution to strengthening peace and preserving our liberty. But this hope exists only if we, in this generation, seize this matchless opportunity that is now given to us. We are, indeed, in Lincoln's words, "the last best hope of mankind." Let us then try the only hope we have of leading mankind away from the constant threat of nuclear holocaust.

7

The Principle of Proportionality and the Strategic Defense Initiative[1]

Capt. Kenneth Kemp

Most of the criticisms of the standard forms of nuclear deterrence concentrate on the fact that many innocent people will be killed by nuclear weapons used in a retaliatory strike. In this essay Captain Kemp focuses attention not on the innocence of persons who might be killed in a retaliatory strike but on the numbers: what in Just War Theory terms is referred to as the *Principle of Proportionality*. Kemp does not declare that deterrence violates the Principle of Proportionality, but he does argue that the principle requires us morally to seek a means of security less destructive than deterrence.

On March 23, 1983, President Reagan announced that he would launch a program to research the feasibility of replacing the current U. S. strategic policy of deterrence through threat of nuclear retaliation with a policy of defending the United States (and its allies) against missile attack. Since that speech, however, supporters of the Strategic Defense Initiative, both within and outside the administration, have developed the idea of strategic defense in diverse directions. This divergence in interpretation has arisen as a result of two questions.

First, should strategic defense be focused on defense of population or on defense of the means of retaliation? As initially conceived, and as still advocated by senior officials in the Reagan Administration, the Strategic Defense Initiative is

This essay has not been previously published. Copyright ©1989 Kenneth W. Kemp. Used by permission of the author.

[1]The opinions expressed in this paper are those of the author. They are not necessarily the opinions of the United States Air Force Academy, the Air Force, or the United States Government.

aimed at the former, technically more ambitious, project. It is strategic defense in this sense that I wish to defend in this paper.

The second question is whether strategic defense should make any use of nuclear technologies. Two particular uses of such technology have been proposed: the X-ray laser and nuclear-powered launch of heavy payloads. Neither of these proposals seems to me to violate the spirit of President Reagan's stated goal of abolishing nuclear weapons; nevertheless there is, in some quarters, a concern that *any* use of nuclear technology would leave us on the wrong side of the nuclear/nonnuclear firebreak. Although this is a legitimate concern that must be addressed, nothing I intend to say turns on how that issue is resolved.

Is the Strategic Defense Initiative a good idea? Evaluation of the policy is logically at least partially independent of the acceptability, moral or otherwise, of current U. S. strategic nuclear policy. One might well accept the argument that our present policy must be abandoned immediately and still hold that research into strategic defense would be a permissible, or even an obligatory, next step. I do not accept these arguments against current policy without major qualification, but since my interest in strategic defense stems at least in part from a moral critique of nuclear deterrence, I will have to say a word about the extent to which I think that deterrence is, and is not, acceptable.

But before I do that, I want to set out four distinct questions that might be asked about any proposed public policy. The four, in no particular order, are these:

- the technical question—Will the policy work?
- the economic question—Is it affordable?
- the political question—Is it politically possible?
- the moral question—Is it morally acceptable?

An acceptable policy would have to answer each of these questions in the affirmative. There are, of course, cases in which no morally acceptable policy would be politically possible. The question of how political leaders should respond to such situations (assuming, of course, that they are not in a position to make the politically impossible possible) is an interesting one, but not one that I plan to discuss here. We are not, I believe, in that kind of position—at least not at present. What I plan to focus on in this essay is precisely the moral question. How does it bear on the question of whether the current Strategic Defense Initiative should be pursued?

I suppose that the first step to be taken in any argument for a change from the status quo, particularly a change that involves spending money, is to show what is wrong with things the way they are. Why do we need any change in current policy?

My argument that some change in current policy is needed is basically a moral argument. I would like to use as the moral measure of our defense policy the just conduct criterion of the just war theory. One convenient taxonomy of the moral *ius in bello* distinguishes two central criteria against which we might test current U. S. strategic policy. These criteria are

1. discrimination. This criterion requires us to discriminate between legitimate and illegitimate military targets. In the words of the American Catholic Bishops, "the lives of innocent persons may never be taken directly, regardless of the purpose alleged for doing so."[2]

2. proportionality. This criterion requires, according to the Bishops, that we "take into account the probable harms that will result from [adopting a certain policy] and the justice of accepting them."[3]

In light of these criteria, I want to raise two questions. First, what implications does each of these criteria have for U. S. strategic policy? And second, would strategic defense pass muster?

Before answering the first question, it is important to make clear just what present U. S. policy is. Current U. S. policy is to deter any Soviet military attack on the U. S. or its allies by maintaining the capability to inflict, and leaving open the possibility of inflicting, unacceptably high retaliatory damage on the Soviet Union. Although the United States once inflicted such damage on essentially nonmilitary targets, current policy properly rules out the targeting of the civilian population of the Soviet Union.[4] This, I believe, makes it clear that U. S. nuclear policy does not fail the discrimination criterion.

Nevertheless, the policy does rest on the threat to use weapons that would cause high levels of collateral damage and have significant escalatory potential, even when aimed at military targets that are legitimate per se. This, of course, raises concerns about proportionality. These concerns are focused into two lines of moral criticism.

The first line of criticism makes the stronger claim. Here the charge is that the risk of nuclear war inherent in the very possession of these weapons far outweighs any benefits we receive by maintaining them. Whether the concern is with the possibility of a global "nuclear winter" or merely with the local effects of nuclear explosions, critics claim that the moral and physical risks are more than we are justified in permitting. If these critics were able to make their case, current policy, and perhaps even the very possession of nuclear weapons, would have to be abandoned immediately. Success in arguing this case would not, however, tell against pursuit of the Strategic Defense Initiative. Indeed, acceptance of, and action on, this argument only makes moot one of the central concerns of the *opponents* of strategic defense, namely, that strategic defense is destabilizing.[5]

---

[2]*The Challenge of Peace: God's Promise and Our Response*, §104.

[3]Ibid., §105.

[4]In a letter dated January 15, 1983, Mr. William Clark wrote to Joseph Cardinal Bernardin: "For moral, political, and military reasons, the United States does not target the Soviet civilian population as such." And Caspar Weinberger wrote in his *Annual Report to the Congress* (February 1, 1983, p. 55): "The Reagan Administration's policy is that under no circumstances may such weapons be used deliberately for the purpose of destroying populations." Both are quoted at §179, n. 81.

[5]Obviously a nation that disarmed immediately and then put up a strategic defense when it could would not appear to be threatening a first strike from behind a shield of invulnerability.

The Principle of Proportionality and the SDI

The second kind of moral criticism is more moderate. It can be seen in the statement of Pope John Paul II[6] to the effect that

> In current conditions "deterrence" based on balance, certainly not as an end in itself but as a step on the way toward a progressive disarmament, may still be judged morally acceptable. Nonetheless in order to ensure peace, it is indispensable not to be satisfied with this minimum which is always susceptible to the real danger of explosion.

On this interpretation of the moral status of deterrence, current policy need not be abandoned immediately; but it is nonetheless morally imperfect. To understand exactly how this position can be defended, let us take a closer look at the criterion of proportionality.

To begin, recall that the concept of proportionality has a larger context. Not only is it a criterion of just war theory but it plays a role in applying the principle of double effect as well. This, I believe, is essentially because it is just a central consideration in the resolution of any conflict of duties. For a monist—that is, for someone who believes that there is only one basic duty—proportionality is essentially unidimensional. Thus, for the utilitarian, perhaps the paradigmatic monist, the question of proportionality is reducible to a question of whether the good to be done by some proposed course of action outweighs the incidental concomitant harm. (Perhaps because of this same ethical theory all conflicts of duty are resolved by appeal to proportionality so construed, the approach has come in moral-theological circles to bear the name *proportionalism*.) But those of us who are pluralists, who believe, like W. D. Ross, that there is more than one basic duty, must not interpret the criterion of proportionality in this restrictive way. If there are a number of equally basic duties, then we can ask with respect to any conflicting pair roughly the same question that the utilitarian monist asks about conflicts between the duty to promote utility and the duty to avoid disutility; namely, which duty is the more stringent in this situation? For example, one might have to ask whether the good that could be achieved by breaking a promise were proportionate to the level of stringency that was conveyed to the promisee when the promise was made. This, I maintain, is a proportionality question, and not one that should be resolved merely by appeals to good and harms. The stringency of the promise is rather a function of certain features of the promise itself, and that is what must be taken into account in facing the criterion of proportionality.

Having said that, however, I nevertheless must confess that, in the particular context that I want to discuss in this essay, harm/benefit terminology seems to be the most natural way to make the points I am about to make. I suspect that this is just a consequence of the fact that it is conflicts between the duties of beneficence and of nonmaleficence that figure most prominently in this issue. Keeping in mind this limitation on how I am going to make my next points, let me suggest that proportionality can be violated in at least two ways.

The most straightforward way of going wrong with respect to proportionality is by permitting excessive collateral damage. Absolute judgments of disproportion-

---

[6]In his 1982 Message to the Special Session of the United Nations, §8.

ality are notoriously hard to make in any but the grossest cases. Indeed, some critics of the Just War Theory claim that this is a fatal flaw of the theory. I do not think the situation is as grim as that, though I wish someone could say more about how these calculations are to be made. One helpful suggestion was made by Prof. Joseph Boyle at the ACPA meeting in Pittsburgh two years ago. There he suggested that the test could be made by posing the question of whether the collateral damage would still be considered acceptable if one were faced with the prospect of suffering it rather than with the opportunity to inflict it. If 2000 of one's own civilians would be an unacceptably high price to pay, then 2000 casualties is too high a death toll among civilians *simpliciter,* no matter what their nationality. We must call this aspect of the proportionality criterion the *excessive damage clause*:

> One is not permitted to cause harmful side effects out of all proportion to the good one expects to gain.

I suppose that the first class of critics could be said to be making this objection against present policy.

But there are other ways of violating the criterion of proportionality. Imagine that, faced with two alternative courses of action, each of which would yield the same good, but which yielded markedly different side effects, one chose the course of action with the worse side effects. (Imagine, for example, that, assigned to destroy one enemy supply dump from a list of several possible targets, one chose to bomb a supply dump in a heavily populated area rather than a similar dump at a remote site.) Surely, such a choice is morally objectionable. I think it can fairly be subsumed under the proportionality criterion, but under a clause different from that to which appeal was made in the preceding paragraph. Let us call it the *unnecessary damage clause:*

> One may not do in a more costly way what could equally well be done in a less costly way.

This clause corresponds to the second line of criticism. What are its implications?

The unnecessary damage clause can be violated, it seems to me, not only by choosing one course of action when a less destructive one is available but by failing to seek out less destructive alternatives in advance, by putting oneself in a position where the only way of achieving one's objectives commits one to causing (or permitting) significant harmful side effects. Even if those executing the only option available could excuse themselves, which they might sometimes be able to do, those who made that option the only one available merit blame.

The Strategic Defense Initiative—that is, research into whether strategic defense is a viable option—seems to me to be required under this interpretation of the obligation to respect proportionality. I do not think that the present situation is so dangerous as to require immediate abandonment of nuclear weapons. And I do not believe that current policy violates any moral absolutes.[7] But it would be

---

[7] I defend this belief in "Nuclear Defense and the Morality of Intentions," *The Monist,* July 1987.

naïve to deny that it brings with it some finite risk of nuclear war. A defensive shield, unlike the present retaliatory arsenal, would not pose this threat. And, if deterrence fails, present policy may "require" us to use as our only available means of defense methods that entail significant collateral damage. Again, strategic defense, if it can be made to work, provides a morally less costly alternative.

My argument so far, then, is that anyone who accepts present nuclear policy is obliged to seek out safer alternatives, of which the SDI is currently the likeliest game in town. All the main lines of moral opposition to current policy (whether on the basis of discrimination or of proportionality) do not apply to SDI. Why, then, has the policy evoked so much opposition?

There seem to be a number of lines of criticism of the SDI. And, although each of these lines of criticism reflects a legitimate concern, I am not yet convinced that any of them weighs decisively against the initiative.

First, it is argued, the system will not work. This objection raises the technical question. It is hard to see how anyone can know the answer to this question in advance. It is somewhat distressing to note the high correlation between political views and technical views in this debate, with so many "hawks" sure that the system will work and so many "doves" sure that it will not. But in any case, the best solution seems to me to be to attempt to find out. And that means research.

Second, it is argued, strategic defense is too expensive. This objection appeals the economic criterion. Obviously, there are limits to what we can spend on national defense. But many of those who make this argument go on to talk about the importance of taking risks for peace, and so forth. But if SDI could indeed make nuclear weapons obsolete, would not the benefit be worth the cost? At present, no one really knows what such a system would cost to deploy. The present research costs seem to me to be worth the possible gain, but I do not know how to argue the point further.

The third criticism focuses on the political question. The Soviets, it is argued, will never go along with this system. If they do not, then (1) we will endanger our current relations with the Soviet Union as we research it, (2) we will destabilize superpower relations as we try to deploy it, and (3) we will incur ever-greater costs once it is in place as we try to overcome Soviet countermeasures. That would make it, essentially, politically impossible. This is a serious problem. But the situation may not be entirely without hope. After all, the Soviet Union has been working on a system of its own for a number of years. And initial public proposals do sometimes differ from what a nation can finally be persuaded to accept. But perhaps, in the final analysis, the system will not be politically feasible. Then we would be in the kind of situation mentioned at the beginning of the paper, in which the morally preferable option is politically impossible. I do not think we are in a position to know that now. At a minimum we are obliged to try to make the "politically impossible" politically possible. SDI research is a necessary part of that effort.

The soundness of the second part of this line of criticism—namely, that deployment of a strategic defense system is destabilizing—depends on the Soviets' attitude toward the system, not now but at the time of deployment. Whether it would be destabilizing depends on the nature of the system and the details of deployment. There is no reason why cooperative mutual deployment of such a system need be destabilizing. And that is what the initiative envisions.

Is the whole idea objectionable because deployment would violate the provisions of SALT I? Some defenders of the SDI respond to this fourth line of criticism by emphasizing that the Soviets have already violated this treaty. But the SALT objection to the SDI has always seemed odd to me for independent reasons. Treaties are not ends in themselves. They are means to the end of mutual security, as they themselves make clear. If SALT I served us well for the years that it has been in force, we should be glad. But the fact that it served us well then is not an argument that it must be a better policy for the future than the alternatives that are now being proposed. It must be defended on its own merits or be retired if and when better ideas come along.

The fifth line of criticism leveled against the SDI is that it is not as good an alternative as is simple and direct arms control. If the ultimate goal of the SDI is to render nuclear weapons obsolete, why not do it directly and spare the cost of SDI research and deployment? The defenders of SDI argue that direct disarmament is not a viable alternative; that SDI is the precondition of mutual disarmament. Here is why: Although many people seem to believe that, with respect to nuclear weapons, smaller arsenals (on both sides) are better, this does not seem necessarily to be the case. Any attempt to implement a comprehensive mutual nuclear disarmament would face the danger of increasing instability as the arsenals of each side approached zero. When each side has 1500 delivery vehicles, many of which have multiple warheads, preemptive disarming strikes are impractical. As the arsenal size decreases, these strikes require fewer hits and therefore their prospect of success increases. Moreover, the precision of the compliance monitoring effort becomes increasingly important as arsenals decrease in size. Overlooking a handful of missiles, which would have been tolerable at a relatively high level of armament, becomes serious at low levels. Concretely, overlooking five missiles out of a thousand is trivial; overlooking five out of ten is disastrous. The incentive to cheat is thus high. And the mutual fear that the other side is cheating creates crisis instability.[8] Significantly, these same small arsenals would not be unstable under strategic defense. Strategic defense would make disarming strikes technically impossible. Any assurance that the preemptive strike would indeed disarm the enemy would be lost. Strategic defense is not an alternative to arms control; it is a precondition of arms control's achieving its final objective. It would be nice if we could achieve the elimination of nuclear weapons without paying the cost of strategic defense, but this may not be possible to achieve, or even safe to try.

In conclusion, then, I believe that continued research into the possibility of strategic defense is morally required as part of a general effort to find a safer alternative to nuclear armaments. Perhaps the system will prove technically

---

[8]For a more detailed presentation of this argument, see Arthur Hockaday, "In Defense of Deterrence, " in Geoffrey Godwin, ed., *Ethics and Nuclear Deterrence* (St. Martin's, 1982). His work is a development of earlier work found in Albert Legault & George Lindsey, *The Dynamics of the Nuclear Balance* (Cornell, 1974).

unworkable, but we will not know until we have done more research. Perhaps the political problems that result from Soviet hostility to the idea will prove insurmountable; but we are not entitled to give up until we have made every effort to demonstrate to them that it is in our mutual interest. In the meantime, it is the job of the scientist to conduct the best research possible, and the job of all of us to pray that this, or at least some, viable alternative to deterrence by threat of retaliation can be found.

Part IV. The Moral Debate about Strategic Defense

The essays in this section are generally critical of strategic defense. I have included more "anti" essays in this section than "pro" essays in the preceding, but the balance is not unfair. The "pro" essays represent a coherent point of view: the superiority of strategic defense over Mutual Assured Destruction. The "anti" essays come from divergent points of view. Some of the authors think that nuclear deterrence is morally superior to strategic defense and seek to preserve deterrence from the Strategic Defense Initiative. Others believe that nuclear deterrence is immoral but that strategic defenses cannot supply a moral remedy. Some authors argue that strategic defenses cannot work at all; others believe that they will work well enough to provide a nuclear first-strike capacity to whomever has them. These positions exclude each other, and the underlying rationales cannot *all* be valid. The "pro" essays, then, are competing only against some fraction of the "anti" material.

1

Four Unsound Moral Arguments for Strategic Defense

Douglas P. Lackey

The editor reviews four arguments for the moral superiority of strategic defense: the argument that strategic defenses "save lives," the argument that strategic defenses are justified by the right to self-defense, the argument that deterrence is immoral because it treats the population of opposing states as hostages, and the argument that strategic defenses are the first step toward the revival of American influence through the control and exploitation of resources in space. The editor finds that at best these arguments show that strategic defenses are morally permissible, not that they are morally obligatory, or that strategic defenses are morally as justifiable as ordinary nuclear deterrence, not that they are morally superior to ordinary deterrence.

Most of the critics of the President's "Star Wars" proposal have concentrated on the technical difficulties of constructing a defense against incoming ballistic missiles. Few have taken a hard look at the *moral* aspects of strategic defense. This omission is surprising, since it is clear that the presumed moral superiority of strategic defense motivates the President and many of those who support his program. In the view of the President and his more eloquent supporters, like Fred Iklé, the Star Wars program is "both a military and a moral necessity,"[1] and the technical difficulties which

Douglas P. Lackey is professor of philosophy at Baruch College and The Graduate Center, City University of New York.

This essay was first published as "Moral Principles and Strategic Defense," in *The Philosophical Forum*, Volume XVIII, Number 1, Fall 1986. Used with permission of *The Philosophical Forum*.

[1]Presidential Foreword to *The President's Strategic Defense Initiative*, issued by the White House, January 1985.

now exist do not undercut this moral advantage. Values, they might say, cannot be inferred from facts or from factual difficulties. I have no doubt that many sincere people believe in the moral superiority of strategic defense; the problem for the philosopher is whether they have sound arguments to back up this view.

In the present discussion of strategic defense, I consider the basic comparison to be between a system of deterrence without defenses and a system of deterrence with defenses. I will not consider policies of defense-without-offense in which the United States gives up its arsenal of ballistic missiles and entrusts itself to a defensive shield. It is unlikely that such a shield could be constructed and utopian to think that the defense-without-offense policy would be adopted even if the shield could be constructed. It is politically most unlikely that the United States would give up all of its ballistic missiles considering its immense investment in them, and I think it quite probable that American political leaders would rationalize retention of ballistic missiles on the theory that a good nation like the United States would use them only to do good. Reduction in offensive arsenals is a consequence of arms control, not a consequence of strategic defense as such.

Let me begin with a few elementary moral points. First of all, since so much of the policy debate concerning strategic defense turns on questions of what is good or bad for the United States, I want simply to note for the record that what is good for the United States is not *necessarily* morally right and what is bad for the United States is not *necessarily* morally wrong. The Mexican Cession was a good thing for the United States, but the Mexican War was morally bad. Second, there is no *inherent* moral superiority in defense, or in strategic defense, or in a perfect strategic defense. A perfect defense for Auschwitz would not have been a morally good thing. Conversely, since I am not a pacifist, I believe that there is no inherent moral inferiority in offense: I believe that it was morally right for India to invade East Pakistan and help establish Bangladesh in 1971, and that it would have been morally proper for the United States to invade Cambodia in 1976 to forestall the massacres that were then in progress. My third elementary observation is that the fact that a policy in force has some moral faults does not provide a conclusive moral argument that the policy ought to be rejected, and the fact that some alternative policy has a few moral good points does not provide a conclusive moral argument that the policy ought to be accepted. What matters is the overall moral quality of the policy, compared with the alternatives. These points made, let us turn to the arguments supporters of deterrence-with-defenses present against the morality of deterrence-without-defenses.

The first argument is that strategic defenses would save American lives in the event of nuclear attack. Deterrence without defenses would forfeit those lives. Thus Donald Brennan wrote about the Safeguard ABM in 1969:

> Ballistic missile systems costing from $10 to $20 billion could reduce American fatalities [from 120 million] to between 10 and 40 million. . . . Thus, such a defense might change the postwar situation from one in which over half of the U.S. population was gone, to one in which 90% survived and economic recovery might be achieved within five to ten years. The difference would be enormous.[2]

---

[2]Donald G. Brennan, "The Case for Missile Defense," *Foreign Affairs* 43.2 (April 1969), p. 434.

Now, when Brennan says, "the difference would be enormous," he means morally enormous, not just economically enormous. This argument, the saving lives argument, is in all the pro-SDI books that I have encountered.

The repetition of an argument, however, does not make it sound. It is not clear to me that *if* a nuclear war occurs, it would be less destructive if the superpowers had constructed strategic defenses. On the contrary, the superpowers, if they come to blows, may feel compelled, given the opponents' defenses, to throw more bombs rather than fewer and to throw them at the most vulnerable targets—that is, at cities. As Leon Wieseltier writes, "[confronted with defenses] you can rain your ICBMs down upon your adversary's head and hope that some of them will get through, and maybe even land where you wanted them to land. *And that is MAD.*"[3]

Furthermore, Brennan's argument does not show that defenses will save lives, only that they *would* save lives in the event of an attack, assuming that the probability and severity of the attack is not affected by the installation of defenses. These are debatable assumptions, and even if they were true, we are still left merely with an argument that defenses *might* save some lives, not that defenses *will* save some lives. Furthermore, since most students of strategy agree that the chance of a nuclear attack on the United States without defenses but with second strike capacity is fairly small, the bottom line is that $20 billion for defenses might save some lives but probably won't save any.

How much moral weight should be given to the argument "if you spend $20 billion, you might save some lives but probably won't save any"? If I had $20 billion in federal funds to spend, and if my main moral imperative was to save American lives, I would choose options that *surely* would save lives, such as improvements in highway safety, rather than options that might save American lives but probably would not. Strategic defense is simply not a good moral buy.

The failure of the moral argument for defense here is similar, incidentally, to the failure of prudential arguments for civil defense. Suppose that you came to me with a plan for a foolproof fallout shelter: for $100,000 the shelter will save my life if there is a nuclear war. If I believe that the chance of nuclear war is less than one in ten thousand, I won't buy the shelter simply because as a reasonable person I judge that I will not need it. Without some argument that the chance of war under deterrence-without-defenses is high, Brennan has neither a moral or a prudential case.

The second argument is that deterrence-without-defenses involves a commitment, the formation of an intention, to kill many innocent people. Fred Iklé, the current Deputy Secretary of Defense for policy, wrote in 1973:

> The jargon of American strategic analysis works like a narcotic. It dulls our sense of moral outrage about the tragic confrontation of nuclear arsenals, primed and constantly perfected to unleash widespread genocide. It fosters the current smug complacence regarding the soundness and stability of mutual deterrence. It blinds

---

[3]Leon Wieseltier, "Madder than MAD," *The New Republic* 12 May 1986, p. 20.

us to the fact that our method for preventing nuclear war rests on a form of warfare universally condemned since the Dark Ages—the mass killing of hostages.[4]

Now many people besides Iklé have condemned deterrence on the grounds that it requires the formation of an intention to kill the innocent. But before we agree with Iklé's condemnation and before we believe that this condemnation leads us to the moral superiority of deterrence-with-defenses, we should note the following points: (1) The main motive behind nuclear deterrence is not to kill Russians but to protect Western Europeans and Americans; the operating plans for American strategic forces from 1963 on have not been designed to maximize casualties on the Soviet side: for all his sins Robert McNamara is not Curtis LeMay; (2) the formation of the intention to kill the innocent (in a second strike) is a separate act from the execution of that intention, and the immorality of forming the intention does not follow from the immorality of executing the intention; (3) the intention to kill innocent Russians in a second strike is a conditional intention, conditional upon receiving a first strike, and the very formation of the intention is motivated by the idea that if this conditional intention is credibly publicized the first strike may be permanently prevented; (4) not only is the intention to kill the innocent a conditional intention, it is a conditional intention to kill the innocent indirectly, insofar as the objects of retaliation are not civilians as such, but military facilities and the political leadership. The counterforce orientation of the American second strike, already dominant in 1973, became even more pronounced with the Schlesinger reforms of 1974, in which enemy cities and the highest command posts were placed on strategic withhold, exempted from American retaliation in at least the early stages of nuclear conflict. Of course, the civilian casualties from such counterforce attacks will run into the millions, but the difference between direct and indirect killing should matter morally for those who are trying to reach a moral judgment about deterrence-without-defenses through the moral assessment of the intentions behind this policy; (5) if we are considering deterrence-with-defenses rather than defense-without-offense, the United States retains the intention to strike back if struck: the change wrought by the installation of defenses is not the elimination of the intention but allegedly a decrease in the probability of its execution and allegedly a decrease in the severity of the retaliation, if the retaliation is matched to the damage caused by a Soviet attack blunted by a defensive shield.

In my view the most that can be derived from Iklé's eloquent article is not that deterrence-without-defenses is murderous, but that the development of this policy creates great risks to the innocent, and perfect-defense-plus-offense also creates great risks to the innocent. An interesting debate can develop as to which policy generates the smallest risks to the fewest innocent parties, but ethically, the risks are all of the same moral type.

---

[4]Fred C. Iklé, "Can Nuclear Deterrence Last Out the Century?" *Foreign Affairs* 51.2 (January 1973).

The third argument against deterrence-without-defenses is that such a system violates the right to self-defense. Thus Robert Jastrow, writing last year about the ABM treaty, said:

> Why did our government promise to keep its people naked before the threat of nuclear destruction? How could an American President sign away the right to self-defense of the American people?[5]

The trouble with this argument is that it confuses the possession of a right with the exercise of that right. The United States has the right to build reasonable defenses, and retains the right. But it promised in 1972 not to exercise that right, in return for benefits received. It is always morally legitimate to waive a right or to fail to exercise it. I have a driver's license that entitles me to drive, but if you approach me and offer me $1000 not to exercise my right today, I may give you my promise not to drive. It is not wicked of you to make the offer, and not wicked for me to accept it.

But of course what is really bothering Jastrow and most of the other advocates of strategic defense is that the present systems leave the American people vulnerable to Soviet attack, should they choose to attack. Those that have dark views about Soviet intentions can scarcely be comfortable with a system that makes Soviet first strikes psychologically difficult but physically possible. The trouble, of course, is that for such minds no shield can provide comfort, since there will be always the worry that the shield will break down. For such persons the only safety lies in the destruction of the Soviet System (an idea leaked by Daniel Pipes)—a big job that will probably require nuclear weapons, rather than making them impotent and obsolete.

The fourth argument appears in the President's Star Wars speech of March 23, 1983. If we retain deterrence-without-defenses, the President said:

> It will still be necessary to rely on the specter of retaliation . . . Wouldn't it be better to save lives than to avenge them?[6]

And Iklé, in his recent *Foreign Affairs* article,[7] repeatedly characterizes deterrence as involving "threats of revenge." If deterrence-without-defenses involves an element of vengeance, then this is indeed a moral flaw, since vengeance is mine, saith the Lord. But it is bizarre indeed to characterize the purpose of deterrence-without-defenses as vengeance: the primary purpose of deterrence-without-defenses is to prevent attack on the United States, that is, to

---

[5]Robert Jastrow, *How To Make Nuclear Weapons Obsolete* (Boston: Little, Brown and Company, 1985) p. 14.

[6]"President's Speech on Military Spending and a New Defense," *New York Times* 24 March 1983, p. A20.

[7]Fred C. Iklé, "Nuclear Strategy: Can There Be a Happy Ending?" *Foreign Affairs* 63.4 (Spring 1985) pp. 810–826.

save lives. And if a second strike should ever be launched under current arrangements, the reason for such a strike, in terms of the system, is that you can have credible, first-strike-preventing, life-saving deterrence only if you make a second strike a nearly inevitable response to the experience of a first strike. Once again, the proper moral contrast is not between life-saving defense and life-threatening offense but between two systems designed to prevent a first strike, each one of which raises risks of unknown size but of morally similar character.

The last argument against deterrence-without-defenses is different in character from the others, but it is important because I believe that it is a hidden force behind support for SDI and because it is one of the few arguments new on the scene and not thrashed out in the 60's during the ABM controversy. That is the argument from Manifest Destiny, the argument that space is the new high ground and that the nation, or system, that seizes the new high ground will control the destiny of future human generations. If so, then it is better, morally better, that the high ground be seized by the capitalist democracies than by the communist party dictatorships. Thus General Graham wrote in 1983:

> After the epic voyages of Columbus and Magellan, Spain and Portugal dominated the world through military and commercial control of the new area of human activity—the high seas. Later England and her powerful fleet of merchantmen and men-of-war established a century of Pax Brittanica. When the coastal seas of space—the air—became a new sphere of human activity, the United States gained great strategic advantages by acquiring the most effective military and civilian capability in aviation. Today, after epic manned and unmanned exploration of space, we shall see which nation puts the equivalent of the British merchantmen and men-of-war into space. We dare not let it be our adversary.[8]

Both Graham and Jerry Pournelle argue that exploration has traditionally been a joint military and commercial venture, and Colin Gray has echoed this attitude in his article, "Space Is Not a Sanctuary."[9] So what we have here is space exploration, strategic defense, and nationalism all inextricably tangled, and to give up the package is to abandon the epic human adventure and to abdicate from history.

What can a philosopher say about all this? Plenty, but I will say just five things. First of all, I assume with Aristotle that the acquisition of *theoretical* knowledge is the most important of human activities, that theoretical knowledge, including self-knowledge obtained through art, is an identification of the mind with the structure of objects, and that therefore domination—physical or political domination—is not a form of knowledge and not a high-grade level of human activity. Second, the change in relationships between human beings and natural objects brought about by moving human bodies from one spot to another has little theoretical interest; the problem is not to bring the object close but to make its

---

[8]Donald Graham, *The Nonnuclear Defense of Cities* (Cambridge, MA: Abt Books, 1983), p. 3.

[9]See Jerry Pournelle and Dean Ing, *Mutual Assured Survival* (New York: Baen Books, 1984), and Colin Gray, "Space Is Not a Sanctuary," *Survival* (Sept/Oct 1983).

structure apparent. Third, it follows that the "voyages of discovery" of the Columbus/Magellan/Neil Armstrong variety discover very little; they produce not theoretical knowledge but a little low-grade natural history at best. The epic human advances of the post-Medieval centuries were achieved not on the high seas but in little rooms in Cambridge or Königsberg by unathletic types like Isaac Newton and Immanuel Kant. Fourth, we should note that the Spanish/ Portuguese/British precedents cited by Graham might be less romantically interpreted by the victims of those imperialisms, who saw in the arrival of white men only the advent of pillage, slavery, disease, and death. Fifth, it can be argued that imperialism in many cases is an evil even for the ruling nation: the influx of gold from the Indies wrecked the Spanish economy and seems to have permanently disabled Spanish society. For all these reasons, it seems right, morally right, to repudiate the new space imperialism, to reject the idea of the physical conquest of space without abandoning the intellectual quest for the understanding of space, a quest that provides its own deep sense of adventure. To do so would not consign the United States to the dust bin of history, but would be a public acknowledgement to the world's older cultures that this younger American culture has begun to put away childish things. So to the extent that the President and the other advocates of SDI are influenced by the apostles of the High Frontier, my argument is that the President's vision is at fault, not just because it is a dream—but because, philosophically rated, it is as banal as it is unrealizable.

2

The Moral Vision of Strategic Defense

Steven Lee

Steven Lee argues that creating strategic defenses that are less than perfect is not different from directing missiles at the opponent's strategic weapons. Such a "counterforce" policy he finds unsatisfactory on the grounds that it is unstable in a crisis, creating pressure for a preemptive strike. Like counterforce systems, less-than-perfect strategic defenses are attempts to limit nuclear war after it begins, and the usual criticisms of "limited" nuclear war doctrines applies to strategic defenses as well.

T he proponents of the Strategic Defense Initiative (SDI) have made a move uncommon in the forty-year-old history of the debate over nuclear weapons policy: they have introduced morality as a significant factor in the public discussion. The SDI has, from its inception, been supported by a specific moral vision. One of the most prominent arguments publicly put forth in favor of the SDI, going back to President Reagan's initiation of the public debate in March of 1983, has been that it is morally preferable to achieve military security through defensive capability rather than through deterrent threats to innocent Soviet citizens. Assured defense is morally superior to assured destruction. This moral vision has led some to charge that Reagan has irresponsibly joined the group of naive idealists who reject nuclear deterrence, a group heretofore populated exclusively by those advocating nuclear disarmament. In any case, the opening of the public debate to moral argument gives philosophers their best opportunity in a long time: a chance through discourse in their area of expertise to have a real impact on the public understanding of a crucial policy issue.

The moral vision constitutes what I call the thesis of the moral novelty of the SDI: unlike most technological innovations in strategic systems proposed over the

Steven Lee is associate professor of philosophy at Hobart and William Smith Colleges.

This essay was first published in *The Philosophical Forum,* Volume XVIII, Number 1, Fall 1986. Used with permission of *The Philosophical Forum.*

past forty years, the SDI promises to make a fundamental difference in the moral status of strategic policy. The difference is this. Nuclear deterrence has always been based, at least ultimately, on the threat to destroy the opponent's population centers, so-called countervalue targets. However successful this policy has been at achieving deterrence, it has involved the conditional intention to attack noncombatants, an indiscriminate intention and morally unacceptable in terms of just war theory. The resulting moral paradox has been uncomfortable for many. Counterforce targetting, aiming nuclear weapons at military rather than at population targets, has been proposed as one way out of this paradox, and the shift in recent years to a more strongly counterforce policy has been applauded on moral grounds. The SDI, however, promises a much clearer escape from the paradox, a more radical moral break with our nuclear-policy past. The moral novelty of the SDI is its promise to make nuclear weapons obsolete. The technology promises that military security can be achieved without the intention to attack anyone.

Unfortunately, the thesis of the moral novelty of the SDI is false, and is seen as such even by most of the proponents of the program. To make nuclear weapons obsolete, the SDI would have to make nuclear deterrence unnecessary. But nuclear deterrence would be unnecessary only if the opponent's nuclear weapons posed no significant threat to one's nation, and this would be the case only if the opponent lacked the capability to explode any nuclear weapons on one's territory. The great destructive power of nuclear weapons makes utterly unacceptable any attack in which even a few nuclear warheads would get through. In fact, however, the SDI cannot create a "rainbow shield," a perfect leakproof defense against nuclear warheads. Some nuclear warheads would get through even the best defense envisioned. The assumption behind a layered set of defensive systems, central to the SDI concept, is that no one mode of defense will be sufficient to stop all warheads. But perfection cannot be achieved by layering imperfect systems: given the large numbers of Soviet nuclear warheads, some will get through. In addition, the SDI as currently envisioned is directed primarily against ballistic missile warheads, ignoring other existing modes of delivery, such as the cruise missile.

In the absence of a perfect defense, one's opponent must still be dissuaded from attacking, and for this a policy of deterrence would presumably still be required. Most proponents of the SDI now speak of its goal as being that of enhancing deterrence, not replacing it. But this is not just a matter of the goals that have in fact been adopted by those working on the SDI. It is part of the basic logic of the strategic situation: any strategic system deployed in a situation in which an attack cannot be perfectly defended against becomes by its very existence part of the effort to deter an attack.

Where does this leave the moral vision of strategic defense? The falsity of the moral novelty thesis makes the moral vision behind the SDI more mundane, but at the same time more problematic. This makes the moral assessment of the SDI less intrinsically interesting, but of greater practical importance. The moral vision behind the SDI is more mundane because it is now seen to be one of reducing the risk of nuclear war, through enhanced deterrence, rather than eliminating its possibility. The moral vision is more problematic because there are serious doubts about whether the SDI would reduce the risk of nuclear war. The moral vision behind the SDI partially merges with the moral vision behind counterforce policy:

each claims to reduce the risk of nuclear war through enhancing deterrence. But the SDI appears to provide a more effective way than does counterforce policy of reducing this risk, because it seems to provide a more effective way of limiting nuclear war. It is this understanding of the moral vision of the SDI that I will examine below.

Because the moral vision of the SDI partially merges with the moral vision of counterforce policy, it will be helpful to begin by considering the moral advantages that are claimed for counterforce policy. Counterforce policy is said to have two main kinds of moral advantage over countervalue (or assured destruction) policy. First, as mentioned just above, counterforce policy is said to lessen the risk of nuclear war by providing a more effective form of deterrence (one involving more credible retaliatory threats) than does countervalue policy. This is a form of utilitarian moral advantage which in fact happens to coincide with what is taken to be the strategic or prudential advantage of counterforce policy. Second, counterforce policy is said to have the more traditional moral advantage of satisfying just war theory's principle of discrimination. Unlike countervalue policy, counterforce policy does not involve the conditional intention to attack noncombatants; by the doctrine of double effect, the deaths of many noncombatants from a nuclear retaliation, though foreseen, are not intended. This is the way in which counterforce policy is said to resolve the moral paradox of nuclear deterrence referred to at the beginning.

The second of the moral advantages claimed for counterforce policy, however, is not relevant to assessing the moral vision behind the SDI. Given the falsity of the moral novelty thesis, the SDI cannot claim by itself to secure any advantage for strategic policy in terms of the principle of discrimination. Since the SDI would not make nuclear weapons obsolete, it would be deployed on top of an existing set of offensive weapons systems already designed to achieve deterrence. The addition of the defensive systems would not alter the status of the offensive systems in terms of the principle of discrimination. Hence, the SDI would make no moral difference in this regard. While I would argue that no system of offensive nuclear weapons, no matter how they are targetted, can satisfy the principle of discrimination, this issue is irrelevant to the moral assessment of the SDI itself.

The first moral advantage claimed for counterforce policy is, however, relevant to the moral assessment of the SDI, because it is claimed that the SDI, like counterforce targetting, would enhance deterrence. What is the argument that counterforce policy enhances deterrence, and so decreases the risk of nuclear war? For a threat to be effective, it must be credible. But the threat of countervalue retaliation is thought not to be credible, especially in the face of Soviet counterforce capability. If the U. S. had only countervalue capability, it is thought unlikely to retaliate for any aggression short of the destruction of its own cities, for countervalue retaliation in such circumstances would certainly bring on the destruction of these very cities by Soviet counterretaliation. If, however, the U. S. had counterforce capability, it is more likely to retaliate, since counterforce retaliation would not destroy Soviet cities, and so would be unlikely to bring about the destruction of U. S. cities in response. The more likely one is to carry out a retaliatory threat, the more credible the threat, and the greater its deterrent value.

Another way to put this argument is to say that counterforce policy is thought to make possible limited nuclear war. The threat to retaliate is the threat to engage in nuclear war, and this threat is credible only if engaging in nuclear war could be a rational act. Given the great destruction potential in nuclear weapons, nuclear war could be rational (i.e., could be an instrument to achieve some political purpose) only if such war were limited. Counterforce capability creates the possibility of limited nuclear war by making possible a nuclear war in which cities would not be destroyed. The actual mechanism by which a nuclear war would be kept limited requires a sufficiently strong counterforce capability to achieve what is called escalation dominance: one must be superior to one's opponent at every potential level of nuclear (and nonnuclear) conflict so that the opponent has a strong incentive not to escalate any conflict that arises.

Thus, the argument that counterforce policy enhances deterrence depends crucially on the possibility (or at least the perceived possibility) of limited nuclear war. Similarly, the SDI is conceived to enhance deterrence, for the SDI would provide another mechanism by which nuclear war could be kept limited. Moreover, the argument that the SDI would enhance deterrence seems to be even stronger than the argument that counterforce policy would do so, since the mechanism of limitation seems to be much more effective. Counterforce policy must rely on an exercise of human restraint to limit nuclear war: escalation dominance provides a kind of intra-war deterrence through which one hopes to encourage escalatory restraint on the part of one's opponent. But the SDI relies on a technological mechanism to limit nuclear war, *viz.*, our ability to destroy a high portion of incoming nuclear warheads. The technological mechanism seems to be a more effective form of limitation than human restraint. So, the SDI promises a greater enhancement of the effectiveness of deterrence: by increasing the likelihood that nuclear war could be kept limited beyond that resulting from counterforce policy, it would make retaliation seem an even more rational act, and hence more greatly increase the credibility of the retaliatory threat.

Does the SDI have the moral advantage of lessening the likelihood of nuclear war? It does not, and for the same reason that counterforce policy does not. The argument, just rehearsed, that the SDI and counterforce policy have this moral advantage rests on too narrow an understanding of how a strategic posture can lead to nuclear war. It is true that, other things being equal, the more credible a nuclear threat, the more likely it is to deter a nuclear attack. But a nuclear attack may occur in circumstances where the credibility of the retaliatory threat is not the most important factor in the attacker's deliberations, and in these circumstances the SDI and counterforce policy could increase the likelihood of nuclear war. To see this, consider two ways in which nuclear war might start: first, by a so-called bolt-from-the-blue; and second, by a pre-emptive attack in a crisis. A bolt-from-the-blue is a nuclear first-strike in a situation in which it is completely unexpected, when there is no crisis between the nuclear powers. The argument based on greater credibility does, presumably, speak to this case: the more certain one's opponent is that one will retaliate, and a defensive capability and a major counterforce capability give some greater certainty here, the less likely the opponent is to launch a surprise attack.

But things are very different regarding the likelihood of a pre-emptive attack in a crisis. A major counterforce capability as well as a strategic defense capability (when coupled with an offensive capability) significantly increase the risk that one's opponent will launch a pre-emptive attack in a crisis. (This is the argument that these strategic postures are crisis destabilizing.) A major counterforce capability makes it more advantageous for one to strike first, for in doing so one can destroy a large portion of the opponent's nuclear weapons. In a crisis, the opponent, recognizing this advantage (and perhaps also able to achieve this advantage itself through its own counterforce capability), and coming to think war inevitable in those circumstances, would be greatly tempted to launch what it would view as a pre-emptive attack. The incentive would be, as is said, to use the weapons or to lose them. The credibility of one's retaliatory threat obviously would play little role in such deliberations. The same strategic posture that gives greater credibility to one's retaliatory threat also makes a first strike to one's advantage. Whatever the gain in a lesser likelihood or a bolt-from-the-blue, a major counterforce capability would increase the overall risk of nuclear war due to a much greater likelihood of crisis pre-emption.

The same argument applies to a strategic defense capability, when this is coupled with a strategic offensive capability, as it would if the defenses were part of a deterrence policy. Since the defenses are not perfect, they do a better job against a smaller attack than against a larger; and the way to reduce the size of the attack is to destroy some of the opponent's weapons in a first strike. This is the first-strike advantage resulting from a strategic defense capability, and again, it gives the opponent a strong incentive to launch a pre-emptive attack in a crisis. Defenses in conjunction with offensive forces are themselves perceived as offensive. Ironically, the more effective the defensive systems, or more precisely, the more effective they are perceived to be, the greater the incentive they provide to the other side to attack pre-emptively. But this is just a consequence of the fact that the situation of least pre-emptive incentive is one where there is no defensive capability at all. The moral vision of strategic defenses is fundamentally flawed.

Finally, something should be said about the damage-limitation function of strategic defenses. It should be counted as a moral advantage of the SDI that it would limit the damage that would occur if deterrence fails. But again, this would decide the moral case in favor of the SDI only other things being equal. Other things are not equal: the nuclear war whose damage the SDI would limit would likely be a result of the very offensive/defensive posture of which the SDI would be a part. The value of the damage the SDI would avoid if there is a nuclear war is outweighed morally by the disvalue of the significantly greater risk of war consequent on such a strategic posture.

3

Morality of Offense Determines
Morality of Defense

Henry Shue

**Like Steven Lee, Henry Shue is worried about the destabilizing
effects of strategic defenses when such defenses are combined with
systems of offensive weapons like the MX missile. Nevertheless, he
argues that strategic defenses need not be destabilizing if they are
combined with the correct sorts and numbers of offensive weapons.
Although Shue looks more favorably on strategic defenses than many
contributors to this section, he does not argue that strategic defenses
are morally *obligatory*, merely that *at best* they are morally
permissible.**

M y first thesis is that the distinction between offensive weapons and
defensive weapons is not a distinction that can in itself carry any moral
weight. The offensive/defensive distinction itself carries no moral
weight for two reasons. First, weapons do not fall neatly into either
box. Is a tank an offensive weapon or a defensive weapon? Tanks can be used to
attack or to defend. What about depth charges? They can be used to attack or
defend. Even, say, radar can be used to detect an attack from the other side or to
guide an attack against the other side. A great many weapons, and a great many
pieces of equipment that are not exactly weapons, can be part of either an attack
or a defense. Don't look at the object—look at its function in a particular case.

But, secondly, even if you turn from weapons to their functions in a specific
instance, the distinction between attack and defense is still not a morally decisive
one by itself. Are the drug-dealers defending themselves against an attack by the
police? Is the resistance attacking an encampment of Nazis? A justified attack is

Henry Shue is senior research associate at the Center for Philosophy and Public Policy at the
University of Maryland.

This essay was first published in *The Philosophical Forum*, Volume XVIII, Number 1, Fall
1986. Used with permission of *The Philosophical Forum*.

presumably better than a defense by scoundrels. Is an invasion force which committed an aggression yesterday defending the seized territory today against counter-attack?

It would, therefore, be hopeless to debate the issue at the level of abstraction constituted by a question like: are defenses against nuclear missiles more moral than the nuclear missiles they defend against? The only way to arrive at an ethical assessment of missile defenses—that is, defenses against missiles—is to look at the function those defenses would serve and the role that this function serves in the overall plans, including the offensive plans, that we somewhat loosely tend to call nuclear strategies.

So, any initial question whether missile defenses can be ethically justified turns into the question: is there an overall strategy of nuclear deterrence in which missile defenses play an essential and positive role which can as a whole be ethically justified? This formulation has the disadvantage of enlarging the question, so that we now must discuss strategic *packages* of offense and defense. I see no alternative to doing this, however, even though I also see no way to do it adequately in brief compass. My solution is, for the most part, to lead you along a trail of highly controversial premises which do lead to a conclusion about missile defense but which themselves must go undefended.

In order to move quickly I begin from a pure but familiar abstraction, which is of course nowhere near actual policy: the theoretical policy of threatening assured destruction, meaning threatening retaliation—second-strike or later—targeted against the civilians on the other side. The policy of threatening assured destruction, I think, is morally irresponsible, because it includes no civilized plan about what to do if deterrence fails. Either it includes no plan at all or the plan is a barbaric one. A pure policy of assured destruction, which no country has ever actually had, contains no provision whatsoever for deterrence failure except to massacre the oppressed subjects of the government that had attacked. Politicians without even a single fall-back position in case their policy did not work perfectly and eternally would be morally irresponsible indeed.

We need not trouble ourselves, then, about the role that defenses would play under assured destruction. Their role would be to protect enough offensive missiles against counterforce attacks that destruction of the society ruled by the attacking government could indeed be assured. However, I do not think it is worth discussing a "policy" that consists of only these two steps: Step 1—threaten to slaughter the population of the adversary's society; Step 2—do it. Any nuclear policy that is going to have a prayer of being ethically justified needs some intermediate stage. The only candidates for this intermediate stage seem to be forms of armed resistance to an attack which has not been deterred. As a form of deterrence, the intermediate step is deterrence by threat of denial, not deterrence by threat of punishment. As a plan for the failure of deterrence—the failure of step 1—the next step is a form of fighting-back—if you like, war-fighting.

The fighting of a war after deterrence had failed could take one or more of three forms: 1. conventional, 2. ambitious nuclear counterforce, and 3. modest nuclear counterforce. If I have anything new to add to the debate, it concerns the distinction between ambitious counterforce and modest counterforce.

First quickly a word about conventional war-fighting, which tends to be forgotten in discussions of grand nuclear strategies. At least, if the attack is conventional, the resistance can be conventional, if the defender is prepared for conventional defense. Let me just say here that I would turn the entire budget of SDIO over to the U. S. Army for use in NATO—for tanks, for artillery, for retention of trained personnel, better training, better preparedness, more spare parts and ammunition. The best deterrence against nuclear war would be stronger NATO conventional forces that will *deter* attack and *defer* resort to nuclear counterattack. In order to see the reasons why I would trash SDI, however, we need to work our way through the role of missile defenses in the two alternatives to conventional war-fighting: ambitious nuclear counterforce and modest nuclear counterforce. My main positive suggestion is that the distinction between ambitious counterforce and modest counterforce is crucial, not only for thinking about defenses, but also for thinking about offenses, since after all, as I argued in the beginning, we must in any case think about offenses and defenses together as whole strategic packages.

An advocate, if there were any, of pure assured destruction would target the victims of the enemy government and simply hope that he never had to implement his monstrous plan. The advocate of either kind of counterforce—ambitious or modest—says, quite rightly, I think, that even if your main purpose is to *deter* war, not to *fight* war, you need to have something in mind in case deterrence fails other than "blowing up buildings and killing people." You need to have something that you could be *believed* by your adversary to be willing to do and, unless you are really going to do nothing if your deterrent threats are not heeded, something you would be *willing* to do.

The better thing to do seems to be to fight the attacking forces in some fashion, instead of murdering their families behind them. This leads, roughly speaking, to counterforce targeting and war-fighting strategy. Now, counterforce-warfighting has its own problems, which assured destruction does not have. They too are familiar, and as I did with assured destruction, I will simply list my broad conclusions without the supporting arguments, in order to set the stage for a brief discussion of modest counterforce.

The basic trouble with much counterforce is that, unless the attacker is quite incompetent so that many of his warheads simply fail to destroy their targets, it is always to some degree to one's advantage to attack first, if one can do it reasonably efficiently. (A truly incompetent attack would deplete your own forces by using them up to no effect more than it would deplete the adversary's forces.) The advantage for the attacker is greater, the larger the number of warheads on each missile, since 8 or 10 warheads might destroy 4 or 5 enemy missiles, while 1 or 2 enemy missiles might destroy your missile in its silo with all 8 or 10 warheads.

So why haven't the U. S. and the U. S. S. R. already attacked each other, if there is such an advantage in going first? Well, there are probably a lot of other reasons why no attack has occurred, which have nothing at all to do with deterrence. In terms of deterrence dynamics, however, the reason is that there is an enormous difference between (1) the advantage of going first and (2) what is usually called a first-strike capability. Having a first-strike capability means not only having *some* advantage from going first but having such an overwhelming advantage from going first that the retaliation that the subject of the attack can mount is so inadequate as to constitute only "acceptable damage." Since even one warhead exploded in a metropolis like New York would cause what might reasonably be considered unacceptable damage, a first-strike capability would be constituted only by a virtually perfect attack. So, the advantage of going first does not readily translate into a temptation to launch a first-strike.

At last, however, we have found a conceivable role for SDI: SDI, if highly successful, could eliminate any enemy missiles not destroyed in a first strike. The defense could clean up after the offense. But we do not need to discuss whether this is feasible, because it is clearly not desirable. We do not want a first-strike capability, not only because such a surprise attack would clearly be unethical if launched cold-bloodedly while untried ways of averting nuclear war remained, but because it would be highly dangerous for us if our adversary had any reasonable grounds for believing that we were actually capable of a first-strike. The genuine conviction that we were capable, through coordinated offenses and defenses, of a first-strike would give our adversary the strongest possible reason to preempt if we ever seemed actually to be moving toward an attack by, for example, going into an alert status.

Counterforce which keeps moving toward a first-strike capability, constrained only by our budget and by the adversary's counter-moves, is the clearest example of what I am calling ambitious counterforce: counterforce the ultimate goal of which, however unattainable in the short- and intermediate-term, is to be capable of eliminating the adversary's forces. Ambitious counterforce has a role for SDI, but ambitious counterforce is a bad idea because of the well-known problems about the creation of the temptation to preemption in crises, which I just skimmed across, and the creation of arms race instability, which I have left entirely aside.

These problems of instability are not inherent in counterforce and war-fighting as such, however. They arise only from ambitious counterforce which is moving in the direction of a capability to disarm the opponent. Modest counterforce, counterforce with a strict ceiling on its capability that kept it unarguably incapable of a disarming first-strike, would neither tempt us to strike first or to preempt in a crisis nor tempt the adversary to strike first or to preempt in a crisis. If we cannot come close to disarming him even if we go first, and we have a significant invulnerable second-strike too, he has too much to lose by attacking first and so do we. Modest counterforce, which is itself invulnerable, is then *not* de-stabilizing. Ambitious counterforce *is* de-stabilizing, but modest counterforce is not.

Assured destruction is either grossly irresponsible for having no plans for deterrence failure or monstrous for planning the massacre it threatens. Either way, the role of defenses does not matter, because the offensive part of the package is grossly unethical. Ambitious counterforce has a role for defenses, but the defenses would simply exacerbate the tendencies toward instability inherent in the ambitiousness of ambitious counterforce. Ambitious counterforce is probably ethically objectionable on its own because it raises the probability of nuclear war; the addition of defenses would simply make the tendencies to instability worse. By a process of elimination, then, the only hope for a useful role for missile defenses is as part of modest counterforce, because modest counterforce is the only form of offense that could possibly be morally acceptable. What could the defenses do?

On the one hand, if you actually thought SDI could yield a *population* defense, defenses could protect American civilians from a Soviet attack. Obviously, millions would be lost in any serious nuclear attack, but if other millions could be saved, that would be a wonderful achievement. Since I am arguing about desirability and ethical acceptability, not feasibility, I happily concede that if the defenses would save lives from an attack they had not helped to provoke, they would be to that degree a very good thing. And in fact the defenses could save more lives as part of modest counterforce than as part of ambitious counterforce because there would be many fewer missiles to protect. Even if the priority of the defenses was to destroy incoming missiles aimed at missiles before destroying incoming missiles aimed at cities, any given level of defense could save all the more cities, the fewer missiles it had to save.

The other thing—surely, in fact, the main thing—that defenses could do is to protect missiles: to protect as much as possible of the modest counterforce capability—to, as the advocates of SDI like to say, increase the attacker's uncertainty about how much, and what, he would accomplish. This increase in the uncertainty of success would increase deterrence. And since the modest counterforce capability is already modest *before* being attacked, it can least afford to suffer attrition and could therefore be thought most to be in need of defending (if it is not already invulnerable by other means).

My overall suggestion, then, is that the morality of defenses depends entirely upon the morality of the type of offense they are combined with. The significant possibilities are three. (1) Assured destruction, since it is either a policy of pre-meditated massacre or no policy at all, is already either so monstrous or so irresponsible that the addition of defenses would not affect its abysmal morality one way or the other. The situation with counterforce is quite different. (2) If defenses are combined with ambitious counterforce, they are bad, because they intensify the tendencies toward instability that are inherent in the ambitiousness of ambitious counterforce—inherent, that is, in the endless race for either parity or superiority. (3) If defenses are combined with modest counterforce, they are good, because they might save some lives and they might enhance deterrence by increasing the uncertainties of the attacker. (Whether a significant level of effectiveness is possible at either (a) any price or (b) any reasonable price is a question I leave to others. I am trying to answer only the question: is there something that it would be good for defenses to do, if they could do it at a supportable cost?) Defenses themselves are neither good nor bad but as the offense they complement makes them so. Defenses make a bad offense like ambitious counterforce worse. They make a better offense like modest counterforce better still. On the moral status of a policy of studied indecision or premediated slaughter they have no discernible effect.

So, should SDI go forward or not? If what I have said so far is correct, we can answer the question about defenses if we know what our offense is. Is it clear what the U. S. strategy is? Yes, I think it is very clear: it is ambitious counterforce. We are adding counterforce capability with no ceiling specified. We are racing for counterforce superiority, and the Soviets are racing right along. Thus, in the world in which we actually live—a world of mutual strategies of ambitious counterforce—missile defenses would make things worse. Until our offensive strategy changes, defenses are a bad idea. Consequently, I would close down the SDIO on September 30, 1986, give the furniture to the offices of the members of the Senate Armed Services Committee and give the budget to the Army to strengthen NATO/Europe. Any future acceptability of defenses would be conditional upon a sharp change in offenses.

I have asserted, with virtually none of the supporting argument filled in, but mostly for the usual reasons, that a capability for modest counterforce is the best of a bad lot, the least objectionable of the three general types of deterrence that appear possible. I also claim that the addition of defenses to this offense would make it at least a little better still. For now this means only that we can imagine a strategic world in which defenses would help, but that world is not the real world. But would a strategy of modest counterforce (with or without defenses) really be better than the two alternatives? Two doubts in particular deserve consideration. First, would modest counterforce, if implemented, really produce any less a massacre than assured destruction? Once you consider collateral damage, escalation dangers, and nuclear winter thresholds, would the magnitude of the destruction wrought really be significantly less? Second, would modest counterforce, if implemented, really deter? What if, where ambitious counterforce *provokes* attack through too much capability, modest counterforce *invites* attack through too little?

To the first question I have no confident answer. I am inclined to think that you would kill a somewhat larger number of civilians if you were making a point of killing civilians than if you were making a point of avoiding them, but with monstrous weapons like even precision-guided low-yield nuclear weapons, the relative difference would surely be dwarfed by the absolute magnitudes.

On the second question—wouldn't modest invite attack where ambitious provoked attack—I am a little more confident, but in a way that reinforces my worries about the first question. A true policy of modest counterforce would include a firm resolve *against* attacking cities: a definitive rejection of assured destruction. However, as Robert Jervis has convincingly argued, any significant capability for counterforce is, willy-nilly, a capability for assured destruction. Genuine modest counterforce does not hint at or desire to rely upon a threat of assured destruction. Nevertheless, in fact an adversary is bound not to rely on assurances that cities would never be attacked. Consequently, the deterrent effectiveness of modest counterforce will in fact be no less than the deterrent effectiveness of assured destruction. Objective capabilities are what matter and it is not as if counterforce weapons are incapable of countervalue uses. This is the good news, so to speak, strictly in terms of deterrence: even a modest counterforce capability can have no less credibility than a capability for assured destruction because it *is* a capability for assured destruction, whatever our actual plans for it.

The bad news is moral, if it is indeed bad. Assume that our policy is firmly counterforce and that, whatever the enemy government fears, we would never attack the cities in its territory. Two moral worries still arise.

First, since we know that even if we are unwilling to rely on the threat of assured destruction, we can rely on it because our adversary will surely worry about it no less if it is not our policy than if it were our announced policy, are we still somehow guilty of relying on the threat of the massacre of hostages? I don't think so, but that is a tricky question.

The second question is: what is your moral responsibility for keeping around a capacity for assured destruction even if you are as firmly as is humanly possible committed to preventing the capability's use against cities? Who is the "we" who are firmly committed against assured destruction? What if "we" lose control, and whoever takes control chooses assured destruction instead of modest counterforce? "We" could have prevented that by eliminating the capability.

Would defenses help with our normal dilemma? Yes, *if* they were *population* defenses and *if* they were *Soviet* defenses. The moral problem we are discussing—there are others—is what we might do to powerless and vulnerable Russians, Poles, Hungarians, *et al*. Missile defenses for the U. S. are totally irrelevant to *this* moral problem. Defenses could help insure that our modest counterforce stayed counterforce, but only if those defenses were in the U. S. S. R. Only Soviet defenses can save American souls.

4

A Critique of Pure Defense*

Gregory Kavka

Kavka argues that the presumption that all purely defensive actions are morally acceptable is unwarranted. Pure defense may defend aggressors; pure defense may deflect harm onto the innocent or may provoke harms that otherwise would not have occurred. Such conditions, in which purely defensive actions can be morally criticized, Kavka finds satisfied in the case of strategic defense.

N uclear deterrence, I once suggested, is a parent of moral paradoxes.[1] Perhaps strategic defense is the other parent. One sign of this is that, in the political debate on strategic defense, you cannot tell the players without a scorecard—most conservative "militarists" favor defensive measures, while many liberal "humanists" prefer threats of murderous retaliation. A related aspect of the matter is revealed by extending our genealogical metaphor. In the family of nuclear defense and deterrence, moral paradox is an unwanted child. Security is the intended and desired offspring. But security might be produced asexually (that is, by strategic defense alone) or sexually (that is, by the combination of strategic defense and deterrence by threat of retaliation). Though some may sincerely believe in the former mode of security production, much of the public discussion of strategic defense is Victorian, with a highly sexual reality being hidden beneath a veneer of asexuality.

Gregory Kavka is professor of philosophy at the University of California at Irvine.

This essay was first published in *The Journal of Philosophy* in November 1986 (Vol. 83, No. 11, pp. 625–633). Used with permission of The Journal of Philosophy, Inc., and Gregory Kavka.

*I am grateful to George Draper, Steven Lee, and Christopher Morris for helpful comments on an earlier draft of this paper. My research was supported by a grant from the University of California's Institute on Global Conflict and Cooperation.

[1]"Some Paradoxes of Deterrence," *The Journal of Philosophy*, LXXV, 6 (June 1978): 285–302; to be reprinted in my *Moral Paradoxes of Nuclear Deterrence* (New York: Cambridge, forthcoming).

My purpose here, however, is neither to question the motives of participants in the strategic-defense debate nor to provide a comprehensive moral analysis of strategic defense. Having discussed strategic defense from a consequentialist perspective elsewhere,[2] I wish to explore a different moral approach to the problem. Supporters of strategic defense sometimes appeal (often implicitly) to a simple but highly attractive argument: strategic defense *must* be morally permissible because it is defensive rather than offensive.[3] Since purely defensive acts are never wrong, there can be no decisive moral objection to strategic defense. It is this *pure-defense argument* that I wish to examine and refute.

I. Pure Defense

The pure-defense argument infers the permissibility of strategic defense directly from a general normative principle concerning the moral status of things which are purely defensive. Let us call this principle the *pure-defense principle* and initially formulate it as follows:

> (PD1) If an act, object, institution, or policy is purely defensive, then it is morally permissible.

Though strategic defense is not a single act, but rather a complex policy involving various objects, institutions, and acts, I will—to avoid unnecessary complications—discuss the pure-defense principle largely as it applies to acts. In the absence of arguments to the contrary, I assume that any problems that the principle encounters as regards acts will also arise in the case of policies.

Before the plausibility of PD1 can be assessed, I must say something about when an act is purely defensive. Two distinct criteria are involved: one involving motive, and the other involving the physical nature of the act itself. An act is purely defensive according to the motivational criterion if and only if the predominant motive of the agent is the prevention of possible harm to himself or some other person(s).[4] The intuitive idea behind the physical criterion is that

---

[2]"Space War Ethics," *Ethics,* XCV, 3 (April 1985): 673–691; portions to be reprinted in my *Moral Paradoxes, op. cit.*

[3]Richard Sybert, special assistant to the secretary of defense, provides a typical example of such an appeal when he writes, "SDI [the strategic defense initiative] . . . is . . . ethical—defensive measures kill no one" (*Los Angeles Times,* Jan. 27, 1986, part II, p. 9). Even so vigorous a critic of SDI as Lord Solly Zuckerman seems to endorse this argument when he describes as "fairly unassailable" the proposition that "defense . . . is always a good thing" ("The Wonders of Star Wars," *New York Review of Books,* Jan. 30, 1986, p. 35).

[4]We could strengthen this criterion so that prevention of harm must be the *only* motive of the act, but then—given the complexity of human motives—very few acts would qualify as purely defensive, and strategic defense almost certainly would not. Also, pure defense of valuable objects other than persons (e.g., animals, artworks) is excluded to avoid unnecessary complications.

purely defensive acts work by physically repelling a harmful force or by appearing to be able physically to repel it—they do not involve attacks on, or threats to attack, those who create or direct that force. According to this criterion, an act is purely defensive if and only if it tries to prevent harm by *deflecting* or *redirecting* the potentially harmful force of attack. The notions of "deflection" and "redirection" employed here are technical. "Deflection" means avoiding the harmful effects of a force by changing the path of the objects embodying it, by destroying those objects before they reach the protected objects, or by moving the protected objects out of the way. "Redirection" is short for "redirection by threat of deflection" and refers to changing a potential attacker's target by appearing to have the capacity to deflect an attack on the original target. Both natural forces (e.g., floods) and attacks directed by people can be deflected, but, since natural forces cannot choose their targets, only attacks directed by people can be redirected.

Neither the motivational nor the physical criterion seems restrictive enough, by itself, to capture the notion of a purely defensive action. The motivational criterion would be satisfied, for example, by the act of shooting down a number of poor teenagers in order to prevent the violent crimes that some of them are likely eventually to commit, according to demographic statistics. (More generally, the motivational criterion classifies many preventive attacks as purely defensive.) The physical criterion would allow that one was acting purely defensively if one deliberately constructed a wall to deflect mudslides away from an unused corner of one's property including a flood-control channel, and into a hated neighbor's hot tub.

To avoid these counterexamples, I propose a more restrictive account of pure defense—one that regards the stated motivational and physical criteria as individually necessary, and *jointly* sufficient, conditions of an act being purely defensive. This account has three additional advantages. First, it is plausible to claim that if an act both is defensively motivated and operates by deflecting rather than initiating force, then it is purely defensive. Second, this restrictive account of pure defense is fair to supporters of the pure-defense principle: by narrowing the scope of what they have to justify, I make their job of justification easier and mine of criticism harder. Third, this account is broad enough to allow that strategic defense (and the U. S. Strategic Defense Initiative) is purely defensive, provided we are willing to stipulate (at least for the sake of argument) that the prevention of some of the harms of nuclear attack is the governing motive of those who are planning to create strategic defenses. In the sequel, then, purely defensive acts will be acts that satisfy both the motivational and the physical criteria.

Are all such acts morally permissible, as implied by PD1? Remembering that the guilty can be defended as well as the innocent, we see that this is not so. If one is rightfully convicted of a serious crime, it is not permissible to resist just punishment even if one does so only to avoid harm and by "deflecting" the physical force of arresting officers. So PD1 must be revised. Let us define a technical sense of *innocence* according to which one party is innocent with respect to a harm that might be imposed by another party if and only if it would not be morally proper for the latter to impose that harm on the former. Further, an act (object, etc.) is *purely defensive of an innocent party* when the party is innocent, in the above-defined sense, with respect to the harms he is "purely defended'' against by that act (object, etc.). Then the pure-defense principle may be restated as follows:

> (PD2) If an act, object, institution, or policy is purely defensive of innocent parties, it is morally permissible.

This principle seems, on the surface, quite plausible. How could one criticize an act that tries to protect the innocent from harm by deflecting or redirecting potential attacks on them? We shall see that, surprisingly, there are a number of cogent ways of doing so.

II. Critique

How could an act of pure defense of the innocent be morally defective? There are at least four ways. Such an act could protect the guilty, deflect harm onto other innocents, make aggression by the defended party safer and more likely, or be ineffective as a means of defense. Let us consider these four possibilities in turn.

Protection of the Guilty

Acts or policies that defend the innocent often save some of the guilty from deserved punishment. A nation, for example, may refuse to extradite any of its citizens accused of committing crimes in other countries, in order to protect its nationals from being wrongfully punished by foreign legal systems. It will thereby prevent the just punishment of some citizens who commit crimes elsewhere and flee back to its territory.

Believing that protecting the innocent from undeserved harm is more important than punishing the guilty, we are often willing to endorse such acts or policies. But there are limits to how much punishment of the guilty we are willing to forego to protect the innocent. If the crimes are great enough, we may judge that defense of neither the innocent nor the guilty would be morally preferable to defense of both. Imagine, for example, that an official must decide whether to prosecute or to cover up mass murder by members of a certain battalion, and that he is tempted not to prosecute because he realizes that the reputations and careers of members of the battalion who did nothing wrong would be damaged by prosecution of the wrongdoers. Most of us think that he should prosecute. For the punishment of mass murder is a stronger moral imperative than the protection of some careers and reputations from undeserved tarnishing. In any case, the fact that an act would protect the guilty from deserved punishment can carry considerable weight in the moral assessment of that act, especially if the crime in question is a horrible one.

Deflecting or Redirecting Harm onto the Innocent

Sometimes when we defend against harm, the harm is deflected or redirected onto others who do not deserve to suffer it. The defensive act may still be permissible, as when I surround my home with conspicuous security devices which redirect burglars' attention to my neighbors' less well-guarded homes. But sometimes such deflection (or redirection) of harm is wrong. This would seem to be so, for example, if the new victims are as innocent as those protected, if the harm they suffer is as great or greater, if their suffering this harm is probable enough, and if they are less able to defend themselves by alternative means. Thus I should not protect my yard from mudslides by building a wall that deflects them onto an impoverished orphanage. There is no simple general rule indicating precisely when redirection or deflection of harm is, and is not, permissible. But surely if an act of pure defense would deflect or redirect harm or risk onto other innocent parties, this must, to some degree, count against its permissibility.

Aggression Made Safer

Pure defense can make aggression more probable. The danger of suffering harm from defensive acts during an attack (or retaliatory acts after) is often a deterrent to undertaking aggression. Defense of an agent may, by reducing this danger, make him more likely to commit acts of aggression. Thus, a criminal with a bullet-proof vest may feel safer committing crimes, and therefore commit more of them.

It may be objected that the possibility that defense will make aggression safer cannot count against the morality of pure defense. For purely defensive acts are, by definition, not (predominantly) motivated by aggressive designs, hence are not subject to this criticism. However, even if we ignore the possibility of aggression as a secondary motive, this objection errs by confusing the motives and effects of defensive acts. The criminal's *motive* in obtaining the bullet-proof vest is purely defensive—to protect himself from gunfire while practicing his trade. But the predictable *effect* of his having it may be that he is willing to commit more crimes and is less likely to abandon his trade because of fear. Note also that the offensive acts that defensive measures make more likely need not even be deliberate. For instance, a man may know that he often starts brawls impulsively when drunk and that aversion to the pain of being hit in the stomach sometimes prevents him from doing so. While sober, he may consider strengthening his stomach by exercise so as to lessen his pain when punched there during brawls. The act in question satisfies both criteria for being purely defensive; yet it may be wrong to do if its predictable effect is to make the man likely to start more barroom brawls.

By making aggression safer, pure defense may also make capitulation to unjust demands of aggressors more likely. For some potential victims, perceiving the futility of repelling or retaliating against the well-defended aggressor, will simply give in. Bodyguards, for example, will be less likely to defend their clients against armed kidnappers if the latter are wearing bullet-proof vests. This example, and those of the vested criminal and the barroom brawler, illustrate the same general point: acts of self-protection, even if they work by deflection (or redirection) and are defensively motivated, can lead to aggression (or capitulation) by changing the payoff structure of situations faced by potential aggressors and victims.

Ineffectiveness

A purely defensive act aimed at protecting someone from harm may be ineffective and make it more likely that he will suffer harm. This can happen in at least two ways. Others may not perceive the defensive motive behind the act and may be provoked into aggressive or preemptive action. For example, a drug dealer who wears a bullet-proof vest to all his meetings with other dealers may provoke suspicions that lead to violence against him. Defensive acts may also lead to overconfidence and recklessness on the agent's part. Our vested criminal may undertake one too many dangerous crimes, and our hard-stomached drinker may start a brawl that leaves him with a broken jaw.

But is the ineffectiveness of a defensive act a *moral* failing of that act? There are at least three ways in which it can be. First, if there are duties to oneself, defending oneself from wrongful attack is probably one of them. One may be violating such a duty if one chooses ineffective means of defense when other and better means are available. Second, some agents (e.g., governments) may have duties to defend other agents (e.g., their citizens). If they choose certain means of defense, when available evidence indicates that such means are ineffective or counterproductive, they may be acting irresponsibly. Third, ineffective defensive measures can provoke conflicts in which innocent third parties are harmed. Thus, the ineffectiveness of an act of pure defense, like the other features discussed in this section, can have direct bearing on the moral status of that act.

III. Strategic Defense

We have seen that, from a moral perspective, pure defense is not always as pure as the driven snow (or even as pure as Ivory Snow). Acts of pure defense with one or more of the four features discussed in section II may not be morally permissible, despite what PD2 says. What are the implications of this with respect to strategic defense? That depends upon whether any of these four features characterize strategic defense. If none does, the pure-defense argument for strategic defense can be saved by simply inserting into it a new version of the pure-defense principle which takes account of the four features. One such version is:

> (PD3) If an act is purely defensive of the innocent only, and is effective without deflecting (or redirecting) harm onto other innocent parties and without making aggression by the agent (or other protected parties) more likely, then it is permissible.

But this plausible normative principle fails to apply, and tells us nothing about the moral status of strategic defense, if strategic defense possesses some of our four features, as we now proceed to show that it does.

Consider first protection of the guilty. A strategic defense system that effectively protects nuclear command and control centers, would—in the event of a nuclear war wrongfully started by the nation possessing it—protect the guilty war-starters from retaliation. Furthermore, these people who launched a nuclear first strike out of malice, ambition, or recklessness would be killers on a scale unapproached in human history. Of course, it seems highly unlikely that deploying strategic defenses would lead to a nuclear attack by the side possessing them (especially if that is "our side"). Still, the future is uncertain. And once strategic defenses that protect those whose fingers are on the nuclear trigger are deployed, there will be some risk of some such people committing unpunished mass murder.

Strategic defenses may also redirect some of the danger of nuclear attack onto other innocent parties. If a nation deploys strategic defenses, it may well be rational for its nuclear opponents to retarget some of their strategic weapons in either of two ways. They may aim some weapons once pointed at military targets at cities, to ensure that they maintain a credible second-strike assured-destruction capability.[5] Or opponents may retarget weapons onto allies of the strategically defended nation, either to maximize efficiency in the face of apparently effective defenses, or to use the innocent civilians of these allied nations as nuclear hostages now that the civilians of the strategically defended nation no longer serve that purpose as well as they once did.

Strategic defenses, if those who possess them believe they are effective (or believe that others will so regard them), could lead to aggression. Just as the West's possession of a nuclear monopoly led even Bertrand Russell to contemplate preventive war,[6] unilateral deployment of strategic defenses by a superpower might make its leaders feel safer and more prone to foreign military adventures. Or, if both superpowers deployed strategic defenses, it could well make them more aggressive in their dealings with lesser nuclear powers. It is imaginable, for example, that a strategically defended Soviet Union might launch a strategic strike against China's nuclear arsenal.[7]

Finally, deploying strategic defenses—at least in the foreseeable future—is probably an ineffective, indeed counterproductive, means of a superpower

---

[5]See sec. IV of my "Nuclear Deterrence: Some Moral Perplexities," in Douglas MacLean, ed., *The Security Gamble* (Totowa, N. J.: Rowman & Allanheld, 1984), pp. 123–140; to be reprinted in *Moral Paradoxes*.

[6]See "The Future of Mankind" in his *Unpopular Essays* (New York: Simon & Schuster, 1950), pp. 34–44; and Ronald Clark, *The Life of Bertrand Russell* (London: Jonathan Cape, 1975), chap. 19.

[7]There is some evidence that the Soviets may have seriously contemplated such a strike in the late sixties. See H. R. Haldemann, *The Ends of Power* (New York: Dell, 1978), pp. 128–135; and Marvin Kalb and Bernard Kalb, *Kissinger* (Boston: Little, Brown, 1974), pp. 226–228.

A Critique of Pure Defense

defending itself. As I have argued elsewhere,[8] pursuing strategic defense would be a bad prudential gamble for either superpower because the defense achievable would be highly imperfect, it would produce distrust and dangerous countermeasures by the other side, and it might lead to overconfidence and reckless action on the part of the leaders of the strategically defended nation. Over all, strategic defense would most likely diminish, rather than augment, the security of those whom it was intended to protect. And it would also increase the nuclear risks borne by those living outside the defended area—friends, foes, and neutrals alike.

The upshot of all this is that strategic defense possesses, to some degree at least, each of the four features that render acts of pure defense morally questionable. As a result, the pure-defense argument for strategic defense collapses: that argument must either appeal to a faulty normative premise, PD2, or a defensible normative premise, PD3, that does not apply to strategic defense. This, in itself, does not prove that strategic defense is morally wrong. There may be other and better moral arguments for strategic defense. But such arguments should be considered, and evaluated, on their own merits. Proponents of these arguments, and of strategic defense, should no longer be allowed to maintain the pretense of occupying the moral high ground simply because the programs they favor are purely defensive.

---

[8]See my "Space War Ethics," *op. cit.*

5

How Defensive Is Strategic Defense? A Comment on Kavka

Jefferson McMahan

In the preceding essay, Gregory Kavka developed a "pure defense" principle. Such a principle is what students of ethics call a "deontological permission"—that is, a principle that allegedly provides a moral license to perform a certain kind of act simply because of its righteous nature. Many defenders of strategic defense appeal to such deontological permissions when they argue that defenses are morally permissible simply because they are defensive.

In this paper, Jefferson McMahan takes issue with Kavka's principle and shows, by counterexamples, how difficult it is to justify an act purely on the grounds that it is "defensive." For McMahan, strategic defenses can be morally problematic even if used to protect the innocent.

McMahan is interested not only in how strategic defenses *might* be used but how they *would* be used by the United States. McMahan argues that the most likely use of American strategic defenses would be to foster the aims of an aggressive foreign policy.

I want to begin by asking what the status of Kavka's pure defense principle is.[1] In each of its three variants it asserts the permissibility of certain acts, objects, or policies. Since, at least in its first two formulations, it doesn't refer to consequences, it doesn't have the form of a consequentialist permission (assuming that there could even *be* such a thing as a general consequentialist permission to do an act of a certain type). Instead it asserts the

---

Jefferson McMahan is assistant professor of philosophy at the University of Illinois, Champaign-Urbana.

This essay has not been previously published. Copyright © 1989 Jefferson McMahan. Used by permission of the author.

[1]Gregory Kavka, "A Critique of Pure Defense," this volume, pp. 91–98.

permissibility of a certain type of act on the basis of the *kind* of act it is. It is, in short, a deontological permission. It simply tells us that purely defensive acts or objects are *inherently* innocuous, that there's nothing in the *nature* of purely defensive acts or objects that's objectionable on deontological grounds. (Thus, as applied to SDI, the pure defense principle asserts that there's nothing inherently objectionable about strategic defense, as it might be claimed that there *is* about nuclear deterrence.) It is, however, implausible to suppose that there are *absolute* deontological permissions—permissions to do certain types of act irrespective of the consequences. (There may, of course, be deontological permissions *not* to act in certain ways—e.g., permissions not to do what's absolutely forbidden to do.) So all deontological permissions must be *prima facie* permissions. They assert that certain types of act are permissible, other things being equal—permissible, that is, unless the consequences of doing an act of one of these types on a particular occasion would be so bad as to rule out the act as impermissible.

For this reason I find PD3, which Kavka regards as the most plausible of the three variants, a rather odd moral principle. For it contains within itself certain qualifications that have to do with consequences. There are three objections to this. One is that, since our understanding of nonabsolute deontological permissions is such that we always implicitly concede that the permission may be overridden by considerations of consequences, there's simply *no need* to try to list in the permission itself all the specific ways in which it might be overridden. A second objection is that the qualifications Kavka builds into his principle are incomplete. He hasn't, that is, given an *exhaustive* account of the ways in which purely defensive acts can have bad consequences. Here, for example, is another way that Kavka hasn't considered. Suppose there's some maniac who's on his way to McDonald's in order to secure a place for himself among the ranks of American serial murderers, but who's so amused watching me being attacked by a chihuahua that he's temporarily diverted from his mission. I know that if I continue to allow the chihuahua to snap at my ankles I'll be able to hold the maniac spellbound until the police arrive, whereas if I pick up a garbage can lid to place between my feet and the dog, the maniac will become bored and head on off for McDonald's with his rifle. Here my act of pure defense against the attack by the chihuahua would be wrong, but not because I would be protecting the guilty, or deflecting or redirecting the chihuahua's attack onto other innocents, or making it more likely that I would engage in aggression, or because the garbage can lid would be ineffective or might provoke the dog to even greater heights of viciousness. This case is therefore a counterexample to PD3—though not one, of course, that has any obvious relevance to the case of SDI. What it shows is that there are other ways in which an act of pure defense might have unacceptable consequences than those that Kavka mentions and takes into account in PD3. If the pure defense principle didn't attempt to specify all the various possible qualifications pertaining to consequences, but was instead simply equipped with the standard *certeris paribus* clause that should accompany all nonabsolute permissions, then it couldn't be knocked down in this way.

The third and final objection to including the qualifications in the pure defense principle is that the qualifications don't necessarily rule out acts that fall foul of them, so that it's not clear why they're included in the statement of the principle.

Suppose, for example, that, as Kavka suggests, a purely defensive SDI would cause the Soviets to retarget some of their missiles against the United States's allies who would not be protected by the defenses. As Kavka recognizes, SDI might still be permissible. But now PD3 wouldn't *recognize* it as permissible. I find this curious. If satisfying the qualifications isn't a necessary condition for the permissibility of a purely defensive act, then why are they included as conditions in a principle that asserts a permission? If failure to meet the conditions for permissibility doesn't entail impermissibility, then what work are the conditions doing?

The upshot of these remarks is that Kavka seems to have failed to find the most plausible variant of the pure defense principle. Consider the following alternative principle: *If an act, institution, or policy is intended to be purely defensive of innocent persons only, then it is morally permissible.* Let's call this PD4. PD4 is a purely deontological permission. It asserts that there's nothing *inherently objectionable* about an act that's intended to be purely defensive of innocent persons— innocent, that is, in the technical sense defined by Kavka. Acts that are intended to be purely defensive of *guilty* persons—that is, acts of pure defense intended to protect people from justly deserved harms—are *not* permitted by PD4. This implies, plausibly I think, that there *is* something inherently objectionable about acts of *this* sort. By contrast, acts that are *unintentionally* purely defensive of the guilty are not deemed objectionable by PD4, although this is compatible with their being objectionable on other grounds—the most obvious, of course, being that they have the protection of the guilty among their consequences.

Is PD4 plausible? Is it right to assert that there's no deontological objection to acts or objects that are intended to be purely defensive of the innocent only, and hence that there's a presumption that acts of this sort are morally permissible— that is, that they're permissible if other things are equal? Kavka's arguments don't show that PD4 is unacceptable. What they show is that there are numerous ways in which the presumption set up by PD4 may be overridden by considerations of consequences. Thus he shows that, even if strategic defenses get PD4's seal of approval, that doesn't mean that it's permissible to deploy them, for they're still open to the sorts of objections he cites at the end of his paper.

I want to reinforce Kavka's argument by challenging PD4 directly. I want to argue that even if an act or object is intended to be purely defensive of the innocent only, that's insufficient to show that it's unobjectionable on deontological grounds, or that there is then a presumption in favor of its permissibility. Thus, even if strategic defenses would be permitted by PD4, that's insufficient to show that they would be unobjectionable from a deontological point of view.

The apparent presumption in favor of the permissibility of pure defenses derives from a consideration of both physical and motivational factors. Consider Kavka's example of the bullet-proof vest. The design and function of the vest are such that it can't be used to attack or harm anyone—assuming, of course, that it's used according to its function. (A bullet-proof vest could, of course, be used to smother someone, but that wouldn't be being using it according to its function.) Since the sole function of the vest is defensive, then, again assuming that one's aim in acquiring it is to use it according to its function, one's *immediate* motive in acquiring it must necessarily be defensive. (Again, someone might be motivated to buy and wear a bullet-proof vest by the thought that bullet-proof vests are chic, but such a person wouldn't be acquiring it to use it according to its function.) Thus the acquisition of a bullet-proof vest with the aim of using it to defend oneself against undeserved harms seems necessarily innocuous.

Yet we know that bullet-proof vests aren't always innocuous. To think that they are is to ignore the role that they might have in some larger pattern of activity. If I buy a bullet-proof vest simply to protect myself as I walk home from work through an area that's notorious for random and pointless violence against passersby, then there's nothing inherently objectionable about my wearing it. But if a criminal who owns a gun buys a bullet-proof vest, his wearing the vest will not be innocuous. When he wears it, his physical capabilities will not thereby become more defensively oriented. On the contrary, the vest will enhance his ability to use his gun effectively, thereby increasing both his ability to threaten others and his effectiveness as a criminal.

These effects may be intended or unintended. Kavka focuses on the case in which the criminal's increased tendency to commit crimes is a predictable but *unintended* effect of the acquisition of the vest. He doesn't discuss the possibility that a criminal might desire the protection provided by the vest because it would allow him to commit crimes that would otherwise be too risky. It is, however, this sort of case that Kavka seems to have in mind when he refers parenthetically to "the possibility of aggression as a secondary motive," which suggests that he believes that the bullet-proof vest could satisfy the motivational criterion for being a purely defensive object even when it's intended to facilitate crime. But if it *could* then it would seem that PD4 would sanction the criminal's wearing the vest even though his wearing it would be intended to enable him to act in ways that are immoral. This possibility undermines the plausibility of PD4, for we now see that PD4 counts as permissible acts that are clearly objectionable on deontological grounds.

It might, of course, be objected that PD4 would *not* deem it permissible for the criminal to wear the vest while he's engaged in criminal activities, since the intended function of the vest would then be to protect the guilty. This objection seems right if the vest is intended to enable the criminal to resist arrest. But we can imagine the case of a criminal who's prepared to surrender if he's ever caught by the police but who nevertheless wears the vest to protect himself from the gunfire of vigilantes and irate homeowners. In this case the harms from which the vest would be intended to protect him would not be ones that he would deserve to suffer. Hence the vest would not be intended to protect the guilty in the relevant sense, and PD4 would not condemn his wearing it. But it would still be wrong for him to wear it as long as it was intended to enable him to commit crime more effectively.

What does all this imply about the morality of strategic defense? We should perhaps note at the outset that it's unclear whether SDI will satisfy the physical criterion for being purely defensive. For it *is* clear that the technologies involved in SDI will have many important offensive uses. Thus if having certain offensive functions is sufficient to disqualify an object as purely defensive, then SDI won't be purely defensive and the pure defense argument won't even get off the ground as an argument for SDI. Suppose, on the other hand, that an object can have offensive functions and still qualify as purely defensive if it's *intended* to be used in defensive ways only—that is, if it's intended only to repel or deflect an attack. In that case it would at least be *possible* (however unlikely it might be) that SDI could meet the physical criterion. But then there would be other objections to certain purely defensive objects—namely, ones that have potential offensive uses—that Kavka fails to mention. One is that the possession of a purely defensive object of this sort would always carry a risk that the object would be used for offensive purposes, in spite of its owner's original intentions. Another reinforces Kavka's objection that pure defenses may provoke suspicions among potential adversaries, making them more likely to attack you. For if pure defenses can also have offensive uses, then potential adversaries may be provoked to behave rashly for fear not only that the defenses may be used as a shield for aggression but also that they may be used in an offensive mode.

But let us put this question aside for the moment and assume that the technologies involved in strategic defense will have no offensive uses. The system will then unambiguously satisfy the physical criterion for pure defense. And again, as in the case of the bullet-proof vest, since the sole function of the system will be defensive, the immediate motive for its deployment will necessarily be self-protection, assuming that the point of deploying it is to use it according to its function. Given these assumptions, a strategic defense system will be a purely defensive system. But the lesson of the bullet-proof vest is that the permissibility of deploying such a system can't be assessed in isolation. It must instead be evaluated according to its role in one's overall military strategy.

If strategic defenses of this sort are ever deployed, they will, at least initially, be deployed in conjunction with offensive nuclear forces. None of those persons in positions of power who advocate the deployment of defenses has suggested that they should be deployed only after the United States has disarmed unilaterally at the nuclear level. Moreover, it's extremely unlikely that those who advocate the deployment of defenses would ever countenance the abandonment of offensive nuclear forces as long as the defenses remained imperfect, thus leaving the United States potentially vulnerable. Indeed, it's doubtful that defenses would *ever* entirely replace offensive forces, even if it became possible to deploy defenses that were perfect, or "leak-proof," as the saying is. For even perfect defenses can't be guaranteed to remain perfect, and it will therefore be thought that offensive forces will remain necessary in order to hedge against the possibility of a breakthrough by some adversary that would allow the penetration of the defenses. In short, no one envisages that strategic defenses will completely replace reliance on offensive nuclear forces. Thus in testimony before the Strategic Policy Panel of the House Armed Services Committee in March of 1985, Secretary of Defense Weinberger noted that "once research is completed and a decision to deploy is made, we will still need to deter. . . . Will there ever be a time when we don't need deterrence? No. . . . The SDI is not going to end war. . . . We do not propose to give up deterrence."[2]

---

[2]Quoted in Robert M. Bowman, *Star Wars: Defense or Death Star?* (Chesapeake Beach, MD: Institute for Space and Security Studies, 1985), p. 48.

To say that it's unlikely that the deployment of defenses will lead the United States to abandon offensive nuclear weapons is in fact an understatement. As the Soviets have made clear, they won't agree to reduce their offensive strategic nuclear forces as long as the United States is pursuing the development of strategic defenses. Rather, if the United States deploys defenses, the Soviet Union will increase the number of its offensive arms. This is only rational, given the framework of deterrence theory. For the deployment of American defenses is from the Soviet point of view tantamount to an involuntary reduction of the number of weapons that they can target on the United States. Thus if the United States were to develop a system capable of stopping half of the Soviet Union's missiles, then the Soviets would feel compelled to recover their initial position by doubling the number of their missiles—or, since they would be working on the basis of worst-case estimates of the effectiveness of the American defenses, they would presumably *more* than double the number of their missiles. And, since the Soviet buildup of offensive arms would begin well in advance of the actual deployment of the American defenses, the United States would presumably expand its offensive forces to avoid becoming visibly inferior to the Soviet Union.

In sum, the deployment of defenses is unlikely to cause the United States to abandon its offensive forces, or even to reduce them significantly. But if the United States deploys defenses while retaining its offensive forces, then the deployment of defenses will be unlikely to make its overall posture more defensive in character. Rather, defenses will make it less risky for the United States actually to use its offensive forces and will therefore enhance the United States's offensive strength. This consequence will naturally result in a greater readiness on the part of the United States to act aggressively in the pursuit of its foreign policy.

This effect could be either intended or unintended. Again, Kavka focuses on the case in which the effect is unintended. He objects to the deployment of defenses on the ground that it "might make [the] leaders [of the country that has them] feel safer and more prone to foreign military adventures," implying that increased aggression would be an unintended though perhaps predictable effect of the deployment. It is, however, equally if not more important to consider the possibility that increased aggression would be an intended effect of the deployment of defenses. Indeed, it's hard to believe that it would *not* be an intended effect. For any government that would deploy defenses would almost certainly be influenced by the knowledge that the better protected the United States was, the fewer constraints there would be on the pursuit of its foreign policy. Thus Colin Gray, whose work provides perhaps the most comprehensive articulation of the ideas behind the Reagan administration's strategic policies, has noted that "a United States capable of limiting damage to itself would be a United States that should be perceived by Soviet leaders as far more willing (than may be presumed to be the case today) to take extreme risks on behalf of allies."[3] By implication, it would be willing to take bolder action for the sake of other foreign policy goals as

---

[3]Colin Gray, "Strategic Defense, Deterrence, and the Prospects for Peace," *Ethics* Vol. 95, No. 3 (April 1985), p. 670.

well—many of which would be, as they have always been, nondefensive in nature.

It is, of course, a factual question whether the United States's Strategic Defense Initiative is motivated in part by a desire to facilitate the implementation of an aggressive foreign policy. That there are prominent aspects of American foreign policy that are aggressive in nature I take to be beyond dispute. Current policy in Nicaragua demonstrates that; and an impartial review of the historical record will reveal that American aggression in Nicaragua isn't an isolated occurrence but is instead only one manifestation of a consistent pattern of violent aggression that seems to have its source in certain deep institutional pressures rather than being merely the contingent result of a series of individual choices. I have, moreover, elsewhere collected extensive evidence in the form of quotations from numerous high officials in the Reagan administration that to my mind demonstrates that the SDI is indeed intended in part to free the United States from certain constraints in the implementation of its foreign policy.[4] But obviously there's no space to review that evidence here. So my conclusion will have to be a conditional one. *If* I'm right that SDI is intended in part to facilitate the implementation of an aggressive foreign policy, then it's obviously objectionable from a deontological point of view.

The question now is whether it would be permitted by PD4. If it *would* be permitted then we have here another counterexample to PD4. But perhaps PD4 wouldn't permit it. This depends on whether the defenses could really be said to be intended, at least in part, to protect those responsible for the formulation and implementation of American foreign policy from the consequences of their wrongdoing, and on whether the retribution from which the defenses would be intended to protect them would be just. These aren't easy questions, and I won't even try to answer them. For the important point here is that, if defenses as I have described them would not be permitted by PD4, then what that would mean is that there are *two* deontological objections to them rather than one.

Suppose, however, that SDI *isn't* intended to facilitate aggression, and thus isn't intended to protect the guilty, *and* that it isn't intended to provide the United States with any offensive military options. I think these assumptions are pure fantasy, but if we grant them then SDI would seem to be unobjectionable from a deontological point of view. It would then satisfy what we can now see to be the most plausible version of the pure defense principle. This principle is as follows:

> (PD5) If an act, object, institution, or policy is intended to be purely defensive of the innocent only, and is not intended as a contribution to some scheme of wrongful activity, then it is permissible.

This is of course a *prima facie* deontological permission. Thus even if SDI were able to satisfy the conditions it sets, that wouldn't show that SDI would be permissible all things considered. And I agree with Kavka in his earlier paper on

---

[4]Jefferson McMahan, *Reagan and the World: Imperial Policy in the New Cold War* (New York: Monthly Review Press, 1985). Esp. Chapter 2.

the subject that the consequences of pursuing SDI—or, rather, the consequences of pursuing SDI *without* the United States's first abandoning nuclear weapons— are likely to be far worse than the consequences of not pursuing it.[5] So even under the most favorable assumptions SDI will get little mileage out of the pure defense argument.

---

[5]Gregory S. Kavka, "Space War Ethics," *Ethics* Vol. 95, No. 3 (April 1985).

6

Philosophical Scrutiny of the Strategic Defence Initiatives

Jonathan Schonsheck

In the earlier sections of this essay, not published here, Professor Schonsheck distinguishes between *defensive weapons* and a *strategic posture of defense*. Defensive weapons are mere hardware; a strategic posture of defense is a policy involving the intention to use one's weapons, not to dissuade attack, but to repulse it.

In the sections printed here, Schonsheck argues that most systems of strategic defense are simply refined versions of nuclear deterrence and do not represent a shift to a radically new strategic posture of defense. He observes that even perfect or near perfect defenses would not obviate the need for deterrent responses, or else opponents would have an incentive to continually test the defenses for flaws. Thus envisioned, systems of defense cannot remove the moral flaws inherent in deterrence, whatever these are.

I. The Strategic 'Defence' Initiatives

1. SDI as 'Astrodome'

The SDI proposal that has received the most attention in the popular press—and which was responsible for SDI's being called 'Star Wars'—envisions a multi-layered 'peace shield' protecting the entirety of the United States from attack by Soviet missiles: an 'Astrodome'. The

Jonathan Schonsheck is associate professor of philosophy at Le Moyne College.

This selection consists of parts III and IV of "Philosophical Scrutiny of the Strategic Defence Initiatives," *Journal of Applied Philosophy* 3:2 (1986). Used with permission of the *Journal of Applied Philosophy* and Jonathan Schonsheck.

107

various exotic weapons of Astrodome are envisioned as destroying Soviet missiles at various 'phases' in their journey from launch to target.

Whether the technological obstacles between the present and Astrodome are merely daunting or absolutely prohibitive is a matter of much controversy. One can safely say that what does *not* now exist is an array of weapons capable of intercepting the offensive weapons that *do* now exist. Should the technologies of Astrodome components prove feasible against existing offensive weapons, it can scarcely be believed that countermeasures will not be employed, designed either to attack the Astrodome itself, or to penetrate its defensive weaponry. If decidable at all, the issue of whether the technology of Astrodome could outrace the technology of offensive weapons and their countermeasures is decidable only in the (distant) future. So let us leave these speculations to physicists and weapons technologists, and ask: would Astrodome, if it worked perfectly as envisioned, constitute a 'strategic posture of defence'? The answer is straightforward: it does not. As envisioned, Astrodome offers no defence against, no interception of, cruise missiles, manned bombers, nuclear torpedoes, or Submarine Launched Ballistic Missiles with a 'flattened trajectory' (launched from submarines poised close to the United States). While a perfect Astrodome could intercept *some* nuclear weapons delivery systems, it is by no means an impenetrable shield against *all* delivery systems. Sufficiently many weapons could circumnavigate Astrodome to obliterate the United States. Reliance for safety could not be placed on Astrodome's interception of nuclear weapons; thus it could not justify a transition from deterrence to a 'strategic posture of defence'. Granted, were Astrodome deployed, Soviet military planners might decide that so many of their attacking weapons would be destroyed that no strategic objective could be attained by an attack, and thereby be dissuaded from attacking.[1] But this would be an instance of a deterrable adversary being in fact deterred. Astrodome, in such a case, would have a deterrent effect, be an element of deterrence.

But could Astrodome, while in itself insufficient for a transition to a 'strategic posture of defence', be an *element* of such a defence? Nothing could be easier than enhancing a vision; envision a protective shield able to intercept nuclear weapons delivery systems in space, in the air, in the sea. Envision AstroAtmosOceanDome.

2. SDI as AstroAtmosOceanDome

Although an AstroAtmosOceanDome is logically possible—and can be drawn with a crayon in a pro-SDI television advertisement[2]—its logical possibility is its only possibility. Awesome as are the technological obstacles to Astrodome, the technological obstacles to AstroAtmosOceanDome are orders of magnitude

---

[1]Keith B. Payne and Colin S. Gray, "Star Wars: Pro and Con," *Foreign Affairs*, Spring 1984, p. 823.

[2]U. S. television viewers have seen a pro-SDI commercial in which a child draws a protective shield with a crayon—attacking "Soviet" weapons are unable to penetrate it, and are destroyed.

greater. The exotic weapons imagined for Astrodome, even if completely successful, are ineffective in the atmosphere, and under water. Detection of nuclear
weapons delivery systems that stay in the atmosphere (SLBMs with flattened
trajectories, ground-hugging supersonic bombers, cruise missiles) is far more
difficult than is detection of ICBMs in standard, space trajectories. Underwater
delivery systems are even more difficult to detect and intercept. Bluntly:
Astrodome is envisioned as intercepting the nuclear weapons delivery systems
that are the *easiest* to detect and intercept, and yet whether it could prove
successful even against *existing* delivery systems is in serious technological
doubt. And worse, there exist *today* other delivery systems that are known to be
far more difficult to detect and intercept—these even without the countermeasures that would be the inevitable consequence of AAODome technological
successes.

Would AstroAtmosOceanDome be a 'defence' in the sense of a 'strategic
posture of defence'; would a *transition* from a strategic posture of deterrence to a
strategic posture of defence be justified if the United States were to have deployed
an operational AAODome? Let us consider a series of concerns.

Now it must be noted that *if* what is under consideration is truly a *transition*
from deterrence to defence, then that entails that the U S relies for safety on the
interception of weapons and not on the preclusion of a Soviet decision to attack. If
it is to be a strategic posture of defence *purely,* and not defence conjoined with
deterrence, then the U S relies not at all on dissuading a Soviet decision to attack
by making the threat to retaliate—or possessing weapons of retaliation. That is to
say, if SDI as AAODome is conjoined with the weapons and threats of retaliation,
then the U S strategic posture is not one of defence, but of deterrence plus
defence. So let us subject to philosophical scrutiny—for the moment—the
scenario in which the U S has SDI as AAODome, and no offensive weapons for
retaliation; its strategy is purely defensive, and contains no element of deterrence.

For the U S to be justified in relying for its safety solely on the interception of
Soviet weapons, the AAODome would have to be *incredibly* effective. The claims
of some extremists notwithstanding, I think it reasonable to believe that the
United States could suffer *some* nuclear detonations and persist as a geopolitical
entity. But how many? Even a dozen or so, if 'properly' targeted, could cripple
the United States for decades, and perhaps centuries. Here, as is so often the
case, Einstein's claim about the nuclear age is apt: that everything has changed
except our thinking. In non-nuclear contexts, having some 'defence' is better than
having none; having more 'defence' is better than having less. A boxer unable to
ward off any of an opponent's blows will have a short career; the more he can fend
off, the better. In the context of nuclear exchanges, however, this thinking
commits (what I call) the 'Fallacy of Incrementalism': it just is not the case that,
were the Soviets to launch a serious attack, intercepting, e.g., 30% of the
incoming warheads would be better than intercepting none, or that intercepting
80% would be better than intercepting 30%. Given what we know about the
destructive power of nuclear weapons, and the number of them possessed by the
Soviet Union, were 20% of that arsenal detonated in the United States, the U S
would be obliterated. Not only would tens of millions of people be killed by the
prompt effects of the blasts and radioactive fallout, but that 20% would be more
than sufficient to precipitate the devastating ecological consequences known

Philosophical Scrutiny of the Strategic Defence Initiatives   **109**

collectively as 'Nuclear Winter'.[3] Consequently it is quite specious to claim that defensive measures which intercepted 80% of incoming warheads are better than measures that intercepted half as many. The more porous the defences the more who will die of prompt effects; the less porous, the more who will die of longer-term effects (radiation sickness, hypothermia, starvation, civil disorder, etc.). In either case few of the citizens and nothing of the civilization would 'survive' in any meaningful way; it is silly to suggest that one scenario is 'better' than another, that if one's defence is incrementally more effective, it is incrementally 'better'. Only if AstroAtmosOceanDome could be phenomenally successful, could intercept as incredible percentage of warheads, would the U S be justified in relying for its safety on this 'defence'. (The seriousness of the challenge to AAODome gains support from consideration of the most recent U S weapons system fiasco: the Sgt York Division Air Defence Gun [DIVAD]. Despite the investment of more than a billion dollars, it was unable to 'defend' grounds troops from air attack—it was unable to intercept incoming offensive weapons at a reasonable rate.) Yet virtually any target will be destroyed should even a single nuclear weapon evade AAODome; again, should but a handful evade that shield, the United States would be devastated.

Would the Soviet Union launch an attack against a United States which had AstroAtmosOceanDome but no deterrent weapons? One must approach such issues with more unease than confidence. At the core of the issue is this: precisely what is the deterrent effect of U S retaliatory weapons? No progress on that issue is to be made here. I want merely to observe (I think this uncontroversial) that while no *cardinal* specifications of various deterrent effects can be made, some *ordinal* comparisons can be made with plausibility. Certain weapons configurations have more deterrent effect than other configurations. In particular, to have an array of retaliatory weapons (e.g. the current U S arsenal) has greater deterrent effect than not having any such weapons. Put another way: U S retaliatory weapons have a dissuasive effect, in promising to exact a toll on the Soviet Union in the event of an attack, that would be lost were the U S not to have such weapons. (To deny this is to hold that U S weapons have no dissuasive effect at all—a position that is most implausible.)

Imagine a geopolitical conflict between the superpowers that, in escalating in seriousness, propelled the Soviets to the point of considering a nuclear attack on the United States—a U S that possessed SDI as AAODome, but no deterrent weapons. What *dis*incentives are there to the launching of such an attack? Granted, there are some: for example, the Soviet leadership could face a legitimacy crisis for having launched nuclear weapons against a non-nuclear adversary. Additionally, this action would intensify the efforts of other nations to initiate or expand nuclear weapons programmes.[4] But in a crisis of such magnitude, with perceived national interests in such jeopardy, these disincentives

---

[3] Paul R. Ehrlich, Carl Sagan, Donald Kennedy, and Walter Orr Roberts (1984), *The Cold and the Dark: The World after Nuclear War* (New York, Norton). Cf. the Appendix on the low threshold—how few nuclear detonations might be sufficient—for initiating Nuclear Winter.

[4] I owe this point to Jefferson McMahan.

are likely to prove insignificant. The Soviets would know that they could launch a nuclear attack against the U S from which their civilian population and military forces would emerge unscathed. A plausible scenario: employing a variety of countermeasures—attacking the defensive weapons of AAODome itself, attempting to overwhelm the system with decoys, or evade those defences with novel delivery systems—the Soviets attack. If the attack is fully successful (AAODome is extremely effective, but sufficiently many warheads penetrate and detonate on target to obliterate, or at least intimidate, the U S), the Soviets are victorious. If the attack is less successful, the U S still might be intimidated into making serious concessions. Finally, suppose that SDI is completely effective—every warhead is detected, intercepted and destroyed. The Soviets will have learned of the ineffectiveness of their countermeasures—indispensable in developing its next generation of countermeasures. Worse, it will *still* have no disincentive to launching another attack, since its only military cost has been the weapons expended. In this, or in a subsequent conflict, victory over the U S is still a possibility: that is to say, while possessing defences only, the very best outcome for the U S is that it survive; the worst for the Soviet Union is that it does not succeed. U S survival requires the stunning success of AAODome in every salvo; Soviet victory requires only one successful attack. This asymmetry provides compelling reason for not relying on defensive weapons only, for maintaining deterrent (retaliatory) weapons even if one possesses an effective AstroAtmosOceanDome.

What scrutiny reveals is this: a transition from a strategy of deterrence to a strategy of defence is unthinkable unless one's defensive weapons can be expected to be incredibly successful at intercepting an adversary's weapons—this because so few nuclear weapons are sufficient to eliminate a nation as a geopolitical entity. Thus, only something like AAODome, envisioned as intercepting all the routes a nuclear weapons delivery system might take, has any claim at all to being a (deterrent-less) 'defence'. Further, *even if* a nation possessed such an AAODome, it is not credible that it adopt a pure 'strategic posture of defence'. In exacting no toll on an adversary's military (other than the minor ones noted above), it provides no disincentive to an attack beyond 'deterrence by denial': one might be dissuaded from attacking by the belief that the attack would not succeed. But if perceived vital interests are in jeopardy, and there is so low a cost to making the attempt—*and there is the prospect of military success*—launching an attack becomes a plausible option.

AstroAtmosOceanDome lies far in the technological future—if it is technologically feasible at all. Yet *only* AAODome has even the *prospect* of warranting a transition from nuclear deterrence to defence. But even *with* AAODome, the dismantling of one's retaliatory weapons—the dismantling of one's deterrent—is strategically unjustified.

Earlier I described the bedrock horror-frustration of the nuclear age—that an adversary can kill one if he so chooses. AstroAtmosOceanDome offers the prospect of escape from that horror-frustration. But two important points must be noted. First, that prospect can be fulfilled *only if* AAODome is amazingly successful—more successful than can justifiably be believed. Second, no set of defensive weapons less encompassing than AAODome—e.g. Astrodome, or SDI as Defence of Military Installations (discussed below) has any prospect at all of offering escape from that horror-frustration. Defensive measures less than AAODome—i.e. 'warfighting defences'—may dissuade a strike. But that is only to say that such measures are elements of deterrence, and succeed only against a deterrable adversary continuously deterred. Against an undeterrable adversary, or against an adversary who is in some instance undeterred, only AAODome might offer sanctuary. Permeable defences result in the destruction of individual targets, and would be likely to result in the elimination of the United States as a geopolitical entity.

In my judgement, much of the popularity of the Strategic 'Defence' Initiative arises from an equivocation of 'defence', a failure to distinguish 'defence' as 'warfighting defence' from 'defence' as 'strategic posture of defence'. When President Reagan announced the programme, its proclaimed goal was to make nuclear weapons 'impotent and obsolete'.[5] The profound attractiveness of this is undeniable. But Astrodome would not make nuclear weapons *per se* 'impotent and obsolete', but only certain nuclear weapons delivery system—and those easiest to detect and intercept at that! Only a fully successful AstroAtmosOcean-Dome has a *chance* of making nuclear weapons impotent and obsolete (there is still the continuous challenge of offensive weapons countermeasures, and of delivery systems not yet conceived). A significant portion of the U S citizenry believes that support of SDI is support of 'defence', 'defence' as a contrary of 'deterrence', 'defence' against undeterrable or undeterred adversaries, 'defence' that makes nuclear weapons impotent and obsolete, 'defence' as in a 'strategic posture of defence'. This belief is mistaken. Little is being done to dispel this confusion, confusion that serves well the interests of the many individuals and institutions that will prosper from continued SDI funding.

3. SDI as Defence of Military Installations

Another of the Strategic Defence Initiatives envisages the protection of militarily significant targets—ICBM silos, nuclear submarine and bomber bases—from 'terminal phase' Soviet warheads, from warheads as they near their targets. This proposal is variously called 'point defence' or 'defence of military installations' [DMI]. SDI as DMI would employ 'defensive' weapons, and would, loosely speaking, 'defend' against a Soviet attack, protecting a military installation. But it is clear that SDI as DMI is not a 'strategic posture of defence'; there could be no shift from deterring a Soviet attack (preclusion) to the *interception* of Soviet warheads as the basis of people's safety. For under SDI as DMI, U S population centres are completely vulnerable to Soviet nuclear weapons. Were SDI as DMI to work perfectly, a Soviet attack could result in military installations' remaining intact, while virtually the entire population of the U S is killed by the prompt effects of nuclear blasts. SDI as BMD (Ballistic Missile Defence) has even less claim to being a 'strategic posture of defence' than does Astrodome—which, as I have argued, has no claim at all. Reliance for safety of U S citizens is placed *not*

---

[5]Widely recorded; cf. e.g. Daniel Graham and Gregory A. Fossedal (1983), *A Defense That Defends* (Old Greenwich, Connecticut, Devin-Adair), Appendix C., p. 145.

on intercepting incoming Soviet warheads, but on precluding the decision to launch an attack—i.e. on deterrence. Indeed, what DMI would protect are the retaliatory weapons themselves, the *sine qua non* of deterrence by retaliation. The function of SDI as DMI is to introduce doubt into the minds of Soviet planners about the possibility of achieving any strategic objective by launching a preemptive strike against U S military installations (i.e. a 'counterforce' strike). The function of DMI is to provide a factor for calculation of costs and benefits made by rational minds seeking to advance certain ends (and *avoid* certain eventualities taken to be evils). DMI can succeed only against a deterrable adversary; at best it functions to continue (or enhance) his being deterred. Against an undeterrable or undeterred adversary, SDI as DMI offers no 'protection' to the civilian population.

Despite the proposal's having no pretensions to 'defence' (in the sense of a strategic posture), it is characteristic of the literature promoting DMI that the language of 'defence' is invoked incessantly. Payne and Gray, in the *Foreign Affairs* article mentioned above, argue in favour of 'limited defence for U S retaliatory forces',[6] specifically for ICBMs, bomber bases, and 'selected critical command, control and communication facilities'.[7] At the conclusion of the article they argue that such a defensive system would be an *enhancement* of deterrence, and not an alternative to it.

> But strategic defense, embracing a wide range of near-term and far-term weaponry, promises to strengthen the stability of deterrence by imposing major new uncertainties upon any potential attack. In the long run, it holds out the possibility of transforming, though not transcending, the Soviet–American deterrence relationship.[8]

So Payne and Gray see defence of military installations as 'not transcending' deterrence. However, the above-quoted passage begins with the expression 'strategic defense'. Consider too these expressions: "[d]uring the initial phase of a defensive transition. . . ."[9] "A defensive transition. . . ."[10] ". . . if America is defended. . . ."[11] The list could be continued. We have here the rhetoric of defence in support of deterrence. It is difficult to escape the conclusion that the comforting language of 'defence' is being used to garner support for a proposal— Defence of Military Installations—that is clearly a strategic posture of deterrence. Deterrence by denial is being added to deterrence by retaliation, to be sure; nonetheless, the strategic posture is one of deterrence.

---

[6]Payne, op. cit., p. 823.

[7]Ibid.

[8]Ibid., p. 842.

[9]Ibid., p. 827.

[10]Ibid., p. 830.

[11]Ibid., p. 831.

A paradigmatic case of the language of 'defence' and 'deterrence' being garbled, in an attempt to advance a political agenda, appears in a paper by one of SDI's most vocal supporters, Robert Jastrow. In the opening paragraphs he discusses the strategy of deterrence by retaliation, noting that population centres are not to be protected by a defensive weapons system.

> If, however, either side acquires an effective defense against enemy missiles, it can attack the other side with impunity, secure in the knowledge that this defense will protect it from retaliation. Therefore, runs the reasoning, the best way to avoid war is for both sides to leave themselves entirely undefended.[12]

And two paragraphs later, he writes, "In this way it became the official policy of the United States to keep its people undefended against nuclear attack".[13] Does deterrence leave cities "undefended against nuclear attack"? Well, yes and no. If taken as 'defence (broadly conceived)', cities are indeed 'defended'; the measure taken to preserve their safety is just the making of the deterrent threat; *deterrence* is the 'defence (broadly conceived)'. In contrast, cities are *un*defended, if 'defence' is taken as 'warfighting defences', and if 'defence' means protection by a system of 'defensive weapons', e.g. an anti-ballistic missile system [ABM]. It is at least misleading, and arguably just false, to say that cities are 'undefended' in the strategic posture of deterrence.

The bulk of Jastrow's article is an expression of concern about the 'survivability' of U S nuclear weapons (and thus their capability as a deterrent), and an urging of the defence of military installations. He writes:

> If our missile silos were defended, Soviet leaders could not eliminate this threat to their existence by knocking out American ICBM's in a preemptive first strike. If nothing else deterred the Soviet leadership from an attack on the United States, that circumstance would certainly do so.[14]

In this passage it is clear that Jastrow contemplates such a 'point defence' as part of a strategic posture of deterrence; its effectiveness requires a deterrable adversary. Jastrow catalogues other ways in which defending military installations will enhance deterrence,[15] and sums up by saying that "All these measures improve our chance of being able to retaliate against a Soviet attack, and therefore make an attack less likely".[16] Jastrow argues that an 'area' defence of cities would

---

[12]Robert Jastrow (1984), "Reagan vs. the Scientists: Why the President Is Right About Missile Defense," *Commentary,* January 1984, p. 23.

[13]Ibid.

[14]Ibid., p. 28.

[15]Ibid., p. 30.

[16]Ibid.

be better than just a 'point' defence of military targets[17]—but we ought not to neglect the benefits of the latter. Then this startling passage:

> The problem facing us in the short run, between now and the end of the 1980's, is the vulnerability of American ICBM's and other military installations to a Soviet surprise attack. The smart mini-missile, with its TNT and keg of nails technology, is less exotic than a laser defense, but it is already state-of-the-art, and can be available on short notice for the protection of our missile silos, submarine and bomber bases, and command posts. In doing that, the mini-missile will strengthen and preserve the American deterrent to a Soviet attack. *By strengthening our deterrent, this simple defense will also protect our cities.*[18] [emphasis added]

In earlier passages Jastrow claimed that, under deterrence, cities are left 'undefended'. The shock value of this claim is undeniable (and its use can hardly be accidental). In the current passage Jastrow claims that, under deterrence, our cities will be 'protected'. That that is comforting is undeniable (and its use can hardly be accidental). Would the adoption of SDI as Defence of Military Installations result in this marvellous transition, from cities undefended to cities protected? As I remarked above, it is at least misleading, and as exploited by Jastrow, just *wrong* to say that cities are 'undefended' in the strategic posture of deterrence. An accurate reconstruction of Jastrow's argument is this: Under deterrence by retaliation cities are defended in that the Soviet Union is loath to attack them for fear of a retaliatory nuclear strike by the U S. Were the U S to adopt, in addition to deterrence by retaliation, deterrence by denial (by adopting SDI as DMI), the probability of a Soviet attack against cities is even lower, since they would know that they could not destroy the U S retaliatory nuclear weapons that imperil their cities. That is to say, the most that SDI as DMI *could* do is *not* 'protect' previously 'undefended' cities, but rather to lower the probability of a Soviet pre-emptive strike, or a general nuclear war, by strengthening the deterrent effect of the U S nuclear arsenal (by 'defending' it against a Soviet attack). Whether it would in fact do this, whether the United States would be more secure, whether deterrence would be strengthened to any *significant* degree (and in a cost-effective way) by adding deterrence by denial (Defence of Military Installations), to existing deterrence by retaliation, is outside the scope of this paper.[19] My goal in offering this critique of Jastrow is to provide evidence that 'defence' and 'deterrence' are indeed used in ways that are confused and misleading—and evidence of the need for philosophical scrutiny of these crucial issues.

Of the three SDI proposals, then—Astrodome, AstroAtmosOceanDome, Defence of Military Installations—only AAODome *might* justify a 'strategic posture of defence'. Despite the prolific use of the language of 'defence' in support of

---

[17]Ibid., pp. 30–31.

[18]Ibid., p. 31.

[19]Cf. Jonathan Schonsheck (1986), "Confusion and False Advertising of the Strategic 'Defense' Initiatives," *International Journal on World Peace* (forthcoming).

them, the other SDI proposals would be variants of the strategic posture of deterrence.

II. On the Purported
Moral Superiority
of the Strategic
'Defence' Initiative

The essence of deterrence by threat of retaliation is the threatening of harm, and conditionally intending to do harm to (i.e. to kill) millions of people. The vast majority of these victims would be non-combatants, and (in the terms of just war theory) would be 'innocents'.[20] Many philosophers subscribe to the 'Wrongful Threats Principle' [WTP]: "It is wrong to threaten to do what it would be wrong to do", and the 'Wrongful Intentions Principle' [WIP]: "It is wrong to intend to do what it would be wrong to do." It is argued on many grounds that massive nuclear retaliation upon suffering a nuclear first strike would be wrong, and nuclear deterrence is then rejected on moral grounds. If it would be wrong to launch a retaliatory nuclear strike, then it is wrong (by the WTP and WIP) to threaten to launch, or intend to launch such a strike—but making that threat, having that intention, is the *essence* of deterrence. Anthony Kenny, in an early paper, invokes both these nonconsequentialist moral principles in rejecting deterrence:

> NATO defence policy, therefore, can be justified only on the plea that these [deterrent] threats are not seriously meant. For if they are seriously meant, then NATO defence policy involves a readiness to commit murder on a gigantic scale. The intention to do so is admittedly a conditional one. But one may not intend even conditionally to do what is forbidden absolutely. . . . We must give up our nuclear deterrent not because by so doing we shall achieve some desirable aim, but because to retain it is wicked.[21]

More recent philosophical interest in issues of nuclear deterrence was inspired by Gregory Kavka's 'Some Paradoxes of Deterrence'.[22] Kavka agonises about the

---

[20]This is called into question by Christopher W. Morris on the basis of Hobbesian metaethics. Cf. Christopher W. Morris (1985), "A Contractarian Defense of Nuclear Deterrence," *Ethics,* 95, pp. 479–496. Cf. also Jonathan Schonsheck (1985), "The End of Innocents: An Array of Arguments for the Moral Permissibility of a Retaliatory Nuclear Strike," *Journal of Social Philosophy* (forthcoming).

[21]Anthony Kenny (1965), "Postscript: Counterforce and Countervalue," in G. E. M. Anscombe (ed.), *Nuclear Weapons and Christian Conscience,* pp. 162, 165. (London, Merlin Press). This essay is reprinted in Anthony Kenny (1985), *The Ivory Tower: Essays in Philosophy and Public Policy,* pp. 65–75 (Oxford, Blackwell).

[22]Gregory Kavka (1978), "Some Paradoxes of Deterrence," *Journal of Philosophy,* 75, pp. 285–302.

(apparent) conflict between the Wrongful Intentions Principle and nuclear deterrence (ultimately supporting deterrence, having argued that the WIP is 'inapplicable' to a class of situations of which nuclear deterrence is an element). Two very recent collections of essays contain several articles rejecting deterrence on account of its threatening or intending to harm innocents. In one, Gerald Dworkin writes that "One can believe that neither the actual use of nor the threat to use nuclear weapons is morally permissible. This is the view that I shall be defending in this essay".[23] In another, David A. Hoekema claims that "the threat of nuclear attack *or counterattack* is unavoidably immoral".[24] Sadly, it is characteristic of these essays that they *end*, having reached the conclusion that deterrence ought to be rejected on moral grounds; rarely does one encounter the suggestion, much less argument for, a morally superior nuclear weapons policy.[25] (Elsewhere I argue that this results from an incorrect theory of the role of moral principles in moral arguments, and that this has been to the detriment of both philosophy and policy.[26]

Should philosophers see an obligation to go beyond the rejection of deterrence, and argue the merits (on moral grounds) of some alternative strategic posture, could that alternative be the Strategic Defence Initiative? Certainly some SDI proponents think so. Richard V. Allen, former National Security Advisor to President Reagan, speaks of the "obvious *moral* and military merits of such a strategy".[27] Reagan himself has claimed that space defences would be morally superior to deterrence:

> Our research into an anti-nuclear defense system is not only the moral way. How long, after all, can the American people hold to a strategy that threatens innocent lives? That's just not the American way.[28]

And U S Navy Commander Bruce L. Valley sees SDI as possibly offering "an opportunity to end the decades-old balance of terror"; he continues,

> SDI challenges both the old traditionalists and the new moralists to break out of the thinking into which they've been locked for forty years—thinking which says

---

[23]Gerald Dworkin (1985), "Nuclear Intentions," *Ethics*, 95, p. 445: special issue on ethics and nuclear deterrence. This volume has now been published as a book.

[24]David A. Hoekema (1985), "The Moral Status of Nuclear Deterrent Threats," *Social Philosophy and Policy*, 3, p. 117 [italics added].

[25]Having dismissed nuclear deterrence as "wicked," and claimed that NATO ought to give up its deterrent weapons, Kenny says: "What will then follow is not in our hands" (Kenny, op. cit.). In my judgement this is a paradigmatic case of moral irresponsibility.

[26]Jonathan Schonsheck (1986), "Wrongful Threats, Wrongful Intentions, and Moral Judgements about Nuclear Weapons Policies," mss.

[27]Cf. Graham, op. cit., p. xiii [italics added].

[28]*The New York Times*, 10 October 1985, p. A 10.

that there are only two alternatives—a threat of horrible revenge or complete disarmament. The first of these alternatives is at best of dubious morality—the second has never been politically and practically feasible. Now, perhaps, there may be a third way—a way consistent not only with morality but with the practical political requirements of maintaining the security of America and her allies. In that light, SDI is not only a potential key to our nation's future security—it is as well a moral quest which America must undertake.[29]

Finally, at least one philosopher—while expressing deep reservations about the *feasibility* of SDI—claims that such defensive measures "deserve careful consideration from a moral standpoint, since they are motivated at least in part by recognition of the immoral character of nuclear threats".[30]

SDI is morally superior to nuclear deterrence, it is claimed, because deterrence violates a number of attractive nonconsequentialist moral principles—e.g. the Wrongful Intentions Principle and the Wrongful Threats Principle—and SDI does not. True enough, a strategic posture that was purely *defensive,* that relied solely upon the ability to intercept an adversary's weapons, and issued no threats, harboured no intentions to retaliate, would not violate these nonconsequentialist principles. But once again philosophical scrutiny is in order: what would it be like to adopt such a strategic posture? As consideration of the various SDI proposals has shown, only a fantastically effective AstroAtmosOceanDome has even the potential to justify relying for safety solely on the interception of weapons rather than precluding the decision to attack. Thus, this sort of moral superiority of the SDI can be claimed only with respect to SDI as AAODome. SDI as Astrodome and SDI as Defence of Military Installations, to make any strategic sense at all, must be *conjoined with* nuclear deterrence. As such, both make deterrent threats, and harbour deterrent intentions—i.e., violate the WTP and the WIP. SDI as Astrodome and as DMI cannot coherently be claimed morally superior to nuclear deterrence, for both *include* nuclear deterrence (with its violation of nonconsequentialist principles). Thus, only SDI as AAODome—technologically the most dubious SDI proposal—has any pretence to moral superiority over nuclear deterrence.

But as I argued above, when considering SDI as AAODome, it makes little strategic sense to dismantle one's retaliatory nuclear weapons *even if* one had successfully deployed AAODome. Since SDI would exact no significant penalty on an adversary, it provides, in times of geopolitical crisis, very little disincentive to an adversary considering an attack. Even with an effective AAODome, preserving one's retaliatory weapons as a deterrent to attack is strategically smarter than depending for safety upon successfully intercepting every attack. If this is correct—that even with SDI as AAODome one strategically ought to maintain one's retaliatory weapons (and threaten, and conditionally intend, to use them)—then claims of SDI's moral superiority over nuclear deterrence (in that SDI does not violate the nonconsequentialist moral principles that deterrence

---

[29]Bruce L. Valley (1985), "The Morality and Psychology of Science," *Vital Speeches of the Day,* 51, p. 735, 15 September.

[30]David A. Hoekema (1985), op. cit., p. 114, n. 28.

118   Jonathan Schonsheck

does violate) are baldly false, or incoherent. SDI violates precisely those principles violated by deterrence, since deterrence continues to be an essential element of one's strategic posture.

A (significantly) lesser claim to the moral superiority of SDI over nuclear deterrence might be made. One might argue that SDI *conjoined with* nuclear deterrence is morally superior to naked deterrence e.g. because SDI would offer some protection in case deterrence fails (and an attack is launched). Two replies are in order. First, whether the protection offered by SDI would be *significant* is highly controversial. Recall my earlier discussion of the Fallacy of Incrementalism; it just isn't the case that intercepting some Soviets weapons is always 'better' than intercepting none. It might merely reduce the number of times the rubble is bounced, or kill immediately (blast, etc.) people who would inevitably die somewhat later anyway (radiation, ecological collapse, etc.). Secondly, and more important to this discussion: to adopt this position is to shift grounds dramatically as regards the (purported) moral superiority of SDI. The proclamations of Allen, Reagan and Valley, and the suggestion of Hoekema, based the moral superiority of SDI on its not violating nonconsequentialist moral principles that are in fact violated by nuclear deterrence. On the new grounds, it must be conceded that all the moral liabilities that accrue to deterrence for violating the Wrongful Intentions Principle and the Wrongful Threats Principle accrue to SDI also.

Alternatively, one might argue that deterrence plus SDI is morally superior to naked nuclear deterrence in that SDI strengthens the deterrent threat, thereby enhancing the stability of deterrence, thereby better protecting U S citizens. (Note that in this position, the violation of the WTP and the WIP is even more blatant.) Whether deterrence is in need of enhancing (or current forces are adequate), whether SDI would indeed enhance deterrence (or in contrast be provocative and destabilising), whether SDI is the most cost-effective way of enhancing deterrence (or some other weapons system would be more efficient)— all these issues would have to be addressed before one could conclude that nuclear deterrence with SDI is morally superior to bare nuclear deterrence. And once again, even if true, this superiority is much less dramatic, and is based on wildly different considerations than those proclaimed by Reagan, Allen *et al.*[31]

---

[31]I have benefited greatly from conversations with colleagues J. Barron Boyd, Jr., Janet A. Coy, and Patrick J. Keane, and from comments by Jefferson McMahan.

7

Understanding and Evaluating
Strategic Defense

David B. Myers

Professor Myers sets forth five criteria for the evaluation of public policies, including strategic weapons policies. Two of these criteria, the coherence criterion and the moral acceptability criterion, provide tests that, in his view, philosophers are specially trained to conduct.

Myers argues that strategic defenses do not constitute a coherent policy since they can be construed both as moves toward pure defense and as moves towared a first-strike capability. Furthermore, they may not constitute a morally acceptable policy, since by themselves they would provide no means of just retribution for an unjust attack on the United States.

This question of "nuclear retribution" is not often raised, and Myers's discussion of it introduces an original element into discussions of strategic defense. At some points, defenders of counterforce doctrines justify precise nuclear counterattacks on the grounds that they provide for morally acceptable nuclear retribution on behalf of those who have suffered a nuclear first strike. But for Myers, the problem is that such retribution, even if morally acceptable, cannot be combined with nuclear defenses without producing a provocative first-strike posture.

N uclear policy analysis, conceived as a critical and normative enterprise, is concerned with the problem of choosing the most rational and morally defensible objective, strategy, and force system—in response to the Soviet nuclear threat. For decades the only real question for the

David B. Myers is associate professor of philosophy at Moorhead State University in Minnesota.

This essay was first published in *Public Affairs Quarterly* in January 1987. Used with permission of *Public Affairs Quarterly* and David B. Myers.

makers of nuclear policy was: What and how much do we need to deter a Soviet first strike? The objective of deterrence was never seriously questioned—at least in public—by those in power. Nuclear strategy and nuclear forces were unquestioningly designed to fulfill the objective of deterrence. The existence of nuclear warheads on both sides was taken for granted: the only problem was how we should organize them to prevent their use.

Now, with the Reagan Administration's proposal for research on a comprehensive missile defense system (SDI), deterrence based on nuclear terror has been officially called into question. In March 1983 President Reagan presented a vision of a world in which United States security would no longer rely on the threat of nuclear retaliation.[1] The future of nuclear policy is now cloudier than it has been since the creation of nuclear weapons—a healthy crisis in so far as it requires that all previous policy assumptions be challenged.

The choice of deterrence as a policy objective was not the result of a public, democratic process. Michael Walzer observes that the policy of deterrence

> has been worked out and implemented by small groups of politically powerful or scientifically expert men and women. The most important arguments have been unpublicized; the key decisions have been made in secret or on the basis of information fully available, or fully comprehensible, only to an inner circle of scientists, soldiers, and political leaders.[2]

Walzer points out the paradox that the policy of deterrence, which is meant to defend democracy, is the product of an undemocratic, secretive nuclear autocracy. Despite the technicalities, Walzer contends that the arguments about nuclear policy "must be carried out in the open" and that "ordinary citizens must listen and join in."[3]

If there is to be a public debate over competing policy objectives, the contending options must be made accessible to ordinary citizens. But how can the public cut through the technicalities and jargon to grasp the fundamental differences between policies?

I suggest that one way policy options can be made intelligible to a broad public is to frame them in terms of an analogy, one which allows citizens to see the nuclear debate in more familiar terms. Walzer's philosophical contribution is to provide us with such an analogy—one which I will expand to provide a basis for understanding and evaluating strategic defense. According to Walzer, the legitimate response of a nation to the threat of armed aggression can be fit within what he calls the *legalist paradigm,* an analogy that conceives military aggression by

---

[1]Ronald Reagan, "Peace and National Security: A New Defense" (March 1983 Speech), in *Moral Dilemmas,* Richard L. Purtrill (ed.) (Belmont, CA: Wadsworth Publishing Company, 1985), pp. 22–29.

[2]Michael Walzer, "Deterrence and Democracy," *The New Republic,* July 2, 1984, p. 16.

[3]Ibid., p. 21.

Understanding and Evaluating Strategic Defense

one nation against another as parallel to domestic crime and the morally justified response to such aggression as parallel to state criminal correction procedures:

> The comparison of international to civil order is crucial to the theory of aggression. Every reference to aggression as the international equivalent of robbery or murder relies upon what is called the domestic analogy. Our primary perceptions and judgments of aggression are products of analogical reasoning. When the analogy is made explicit . . . the world of states takes on the shape of a political society the character of which is entirely accessible through such notions as crime and punishment, self-defense, law enforcement, etc.[4]

Although Walzer's reference is to conventional aggression, I believe that public discussion of nuclear weapons policy can be illuminated by conceiving the foreign policy decision we face (in dealing with the threat of Soviet nuclear aggression) as analogous to the domestic policy decision we confront in dealing with criminal threats to society.

Prima facie what makes a criminal correction theory an appropriate analogue for nuclear defense policy is that the former tries to provide a practical and morally justifiable response to violent threats to the social order. In both the domestic and the international spheres the problem is how best to deal with aggression against society—in the former the threat is internal, in the latter external.

I will return to this analogy when I begin to discuss strategic defense. As a background to that, I want first to discuss more specifically how nuclear policy has been shaped in the United States.

The Formation of Nuclear Policy

In the past there were really two questions which nuclear policy makers had to answer:

1. How should we publicly say we will respond to nuclear aggression?

2. How should we actually respond to nuclear aggression?

These are logically distinct questions because a government's *announced* plan for dealing with the *threat* of nuclear aggression might differ from its *operational* plan for dealing with the *act* of nuclear aggression. This is, of course, the distinction between *declaratory* and *action* policies. As long as policy is under the control of a few individuals, the distinction remains real because the policy the government articulates for public consumption may not coincide with what it really plans to

---

[4]Michael Walzer, *Just and Unjust Wars* (New York: Basic Books, 1977), p. 58.

do. The difference between declaratory and action policy dissolves only if nuclear policy is democratically decided—that is, only if policy is made in public by the public (or its elected representatives.) Hence, one aim of the democratization of policy would be the abolition of this distinction.

If nuclear policy were democratized, the declared/action policy objective would be a product of substantial public debate. Once the public had deliberately chosen a policy objective, a strategy and supporting force system could then be worked out to achieve the objective. A logical policy sequence would, therefore, involve the formulation of a policy objective, followed by the development of an appropriate strategy which, in turn, would call for an implementing force system.

What is current American nuclear policy and specifically how has it been determined? Although my primary aim is to critically analyze strategic defense—a proposal for the future—a few remarks about the formulation of existing policy are relevant. Walzer is correct when he states that American nuclear policy has not been the result of democratic discussion, but I think his analysis is misleading to the extent it implies the existence of special, unified elite who have secretly deliberated and carefully worked out the policy objectives which have generated our enormous and varied collection of nuclear weapons.

"Decisions" about nuclear policy appear in fact to be the result of an undemocratic and uncoordinated plurality of converging forces: defense industry lobbying, defense science, interservice rivalry, intelligence reports (sometimes inaccurate) on Soviet strategy and weapons, the given administrations preferences (as guided by advisors from strategic think tanks), congressional interests, acceptance of worst case scenarios, and, to a minor degree, public opinion.[5] To the question, Who is in charge?, no one group can be identified and held accountable. This, then, is the problem for those who seek to democratize nuclear policy: it is not merely a matter of making defense options intelligible to the public, but also a matter of breaking the grip of the competing special interests at the top.

The present *declared* (although not widely publicized) nuclear weapons policy involves a *countervailing strategy* which seeks first to deter a Soviet nuclear attack and second, in the event of an attack, to be able to fight a limited nuclear war in such a way as to deny Soviet objectives at any level of nuclear aggression, with the aim of bringing the conflict to a rapid end on terms favorable to the United States. It is a flexible strategy whose primary objective is deterrence: it claims a war-fighting capability as insurance in case deterrence should fail (and, of course, as a psychological strategy designed to make deterrence more credible).[6]

The current (limited war-fighting) strategy does not seem to be the result of years of careful deliberation and debate about competing policy objectives. Again, it appears to be the product of the plurality of forces mentioned above. Perhaps

---

[5]Sheila Tobias et al., *The People's Guide to National Defense* (New York: William Morrow and Company, 1982), pp. 236–285.

[6]Office of Technology Assessment, *Strategic Defenses* (Princeton: Princeton University Press, 1986), pp. 76–81. Caspar Weinberger, "U. S. Defense Strategy," *Foreign Affairs,* vol. 64, no. 4 (Spring, 1986), pp. 678–679.

the most powerful determinant of the current policy is emerging weapons technology (the yield of defense science). Freeman Dyson observes that

> as strategic weapons became more numerous and more accurate the mission of assured destruction no longer provided enough targets for available warheads. The professional targeters were compelled, whether they believed in limited nuclear war or not, to assign warheads to missions of a more limited character than assured destruction. In this fashion the concept of limited nuclear war became unofficially embodied in the targeting lists long before it was officially acknowledged as a determining factor in strategic policy.[7]

In other words, what "decided" policy was the evolving quantity and quality of nuclear weapons. Thus, the idea of a rational, deliberate sequence in which a broad policy objective produced a strategy, which in turn determined weaponry, appears to be a reverse image of historical practice in which the proliferation of new weapons created a justifying policy objective. Solly Zuckerman reflects: "During the twenty years or so that I was professionally involved in these matters weapons came first and rationalizations and policies followed."[8] Technological advances in weapons seem to have shaped strategy in such a way as to yield ad hoc policy making.

If ordinary citizens are not to allow the defense establishment to "make up" policy as it goes along—to wing it—then practice must be turned right side up so that strategy and weaponry conform to a policy objective that is democratically and deliberately decided in advance. If SDI turns into official and operational policy, then, perhaps for the first time, a policy objective will precede weapons technology. The public needs, however, some clear idea of what is being proposed and some specific criteria for evaluating the proposal. What follows is an attempt to provide these prerequisites so that a public debate on strategic defense can be facilitated.

Evaluating Strategic Defense

The intelligent democratization of nuclear policy requires not just an open debate which the public joins in—as Walzer rightly recommends—but a public debate structured by at least the following five questions which could serve, in effect, as fundamental tests for any policy proposal.

1. Is the policy coherent? That is, does it involve any contradictions or significant ambiguities? I use the term *coherence* in its double sense—as referring to both *consistency* and *clarity*. The test of consistency can be applied to the policy objective by itself or in relationship to a proposed supporting strategy and

---

[7]Freeman Dyson, *Weapons and Hope* (New York: Harper Colophon, 1985), p. 229.

[8]Solly Zuckerman, "Nuclear Fantasies," *New York Review of Books,* June 14, 1984, p. 7.

force system. (For example, MAD deterrence is often criticized as characterized by a central contradiction: the intention behind the construction of nuclear weapons is their nonuse—yet each side must convince the other side that—if attacked—it intends to use its nuclear weapons. Moreover, even if the objective of MAD could pass the coherence test, any strategy which involved protecting the homeland—e.g., civil defense—would be inconsistent with that objective.) What is prima facie a contradiction may turn out to be no contradiction at all, but only an ambiguity in the formulation of the doctrine. Public assessment of any policy requires its clear communication so that citizens have a clear concept of what is being proposed. The use of specialized language can insulate policy makers from criticism and give them considerable control over the nuclear debate, keeping it confined to an inner circle of policy experts. The *private,* technical, language of nuclear strategists (e.g., *countervalue*) may, of course, be designed to conceal from the public the real intention (e.g., indiscriminate killing of civilians).

2. Is the policy morally defensible? This is a question not only about the objective (end), but about the means (strategies and force system). It is conceivable that an objective (e.g., deterrence) is morally defensible while its supporting strategy (e.g., terroristic nuclear threats) is morally reprehensible. Those who have previously made nuclear policy seem not to have been very interested in this question. How one morally judges a policy will, of course, turn on one's normative perspective—with teleologists and deontologists representing the standard opposition. (The relevance of this normative debate to strategic defense will be shown below.)

3. Is the policy technically feasible? If a policy appears to pass the logical and moral tests but is technically unworkable, then its coherence and moral appeal are irrelevant. (Many critics of strategic defense, for example, grant that its objective and proposed means are morally laudable while objecting that it is technically utopian.)

4. How much will it cost to implement the policy? A policy proposal may be coherent, morally defensible, technically workable, but so economically burdensome as to be impractical. The public must ask itself what it is willing to pay—including reduction in spending in other areas of need—to achieve the objective. (This, of course, is for many critics a major objection to strategic defense: that it will bankrupt the nation.)

5. How will the proposed policy fit with Soviet plans (assuming we can discover Soviet perceptions and operational strategy)? Does the policy require Soviet cooperation (e.g., *mutual* homeland vulnerability) or can we go it alone (e.g., *unilateral* disarmament)? Is it probable that the proposed policy, if put into effect, will produce a Soviet response that enhances international security? (This, of course, is the standard question about whether it is likely to be stabilizing or destabilizing.)

Can philosophy contribute to assessing the extent to which strategic defense or any policy option satisfies the above tests? On the face of it, philosophical analysis is most appropriate in dealing with the questions of coherence and moral defensibility—that is, with a logical and moral assessment of a proposal. This does not mean that philosophy has nothing to contribute in the other areas—only that its contribution cannot be as substantial and direct. For example, although philosophers are not competent judges of technical feasibility, philosophers of science can say something significant about the epistemological status of conclusions reached by scientific supporters of a particular policy; scientific advocates of a policy sometimes make claims to a certainty which exceed what any science can achieve. Social philosophers can offer an analysis of the place of experts in a democracy, suggesting how citizens can make rational judgments in the face of disagreement among specialists.[9] Although economists must calculate the costs of a proposal, philosophers might insist on supplementing cost-effectiveness accounting with moral considerations, or suggest ways of integrating economic and moral analysis.

One thing is clear: the empirical and the philosophical issues cannot be easily separated in discussing nuclear policy. It is difficult to engage in a philosophical examination of the morality of a policy without referring to weapons systems and their projected effects. Although the critical analysis of moral concepts is the proper activity for a philosopher, such analytic work may prove irrelevant if it is not informed about existing and possible force systems (including those in the Soviet Union). On the other hand, those who know and deal with force systems as professional strategists are dealing with a normative enterprise, whether they like it or not. In making strategic judgments, strategists necessarily make moral judgments—for example, about what risks are worth taking to preserve a free society and about who or what should be nuclear targets. An important achievement of a public debate in this area would be—as Joseph Nye demands–to open up communication between strategists and moralists.[10]

Working with Walzer's domestic analogy and applying the criteria of coherence and moral defensibility, I will illustrate the kind of contribution philosophy can make to the evaluation of strategic defense. A critical analysis of the concept of strategic defense must proceed comparatively, because its supporters want us to see it as the most rational and morally defensible of existing nuclear policy options. I will analyze it as an alternative to two major strategic options: the countercity strategy of MAD and the counterforce strategy of the nuclear war-fighting doctrine.

The logic of MAD is well known. What is important for our purpose is to recognize that it is a punitive theory guided by a purely deterrent objective. It seeks to prevent nuclear aggression by threatening to destroy the society of the attacker. Like the domestic theory of criminal deterrence it assumes the rationality of the potential agressor—that is, it assumes that the potential offender calculates before acting and that he fears the threatened punishment. Of course, unlike domestic deterrence, under MAD deterrence, use (nuclear punishment) constitutes failure: MAD requires perfection.

War-fighting strategy is also guided by a punitive objective, but it does not stand or fall on the deterrence value of the threat of nuclear punishment. It contains a retributive component in so far as it requires a force system which allows for a flexible response—a response which, on analogy with domestic retribution,

---

[9]See, for example, Rosemarie Tong, *Ethics in Policy Analysis* (Princeton: Princeton University Press, 1986), chap. 3.

[10]Joseph Nye, *Nuclear Ethics* (New York: The Free Press, 1986), p. 11.

proportions retaliation to the nature of the (nuclear) offense and which attempts to restrict retaliation to those who are most culpable, those involved in the act of aggression. Thus, it seeks to retain the concept of *jus in bello*.

Strategic defense—unlike the above two strategies—is (as originally formulated by Reagan) grounded in a nonpunitive objective. Its guiding aim is the same as that of the domestic theory of social defense: the equal protection of all citizens. As a theory of how best to deal with domestic crime—internal aggression against the social order—domestic social defense asserts the protection of society should be the end and incapacitation of the criminal the means. The point is to find ways to render criminal offenders harmless. The concern is not to punish criminals but to protect citizens. So long as dangerous individuals are prevented from inflicting harm, the objective of social defense is satisfied, whether it involves incarceration, exile, or execution.[11]

Applied to nuclear defense policy social defense means that our primary goal should be protection of society from nuclear attack. It calls for a strategy which can achieve the opposite of mutual assured destruction: military forces must be organized for the purpose of making the homeland as invulnerable as possible. The means to achieve national nuclear social defense are to be the same as those used by domestic social defense: techniques designed to render the aggressor harmless. In President Reagan's language, we must find "the means of rendering these nuclear weapons impotent and obsolete."[12] A comprehensive defensive strategy of the kind originally proposed by the President calls for active and passive components. Active defense seeks to neutralize or destroy attacking weapons before they hit: it is to be a layered defensive system which targets ballistic missiles during different phases of flight.[13] Passive defense—the evacuation of cities and construction of fall-out shelters—attempts to limit the damage resulting from the aggressor's penetration of the active defense. If protection from the threat of nuclear aggression is considered as much of a right as protection from criminal violence, then shelters must—as Freeman Dyson argues—be made universally available to all citizens—thus guaranteeing equal protection, regardless of economic class.[14]

Coherence

Does the concept of strategic defense pass the coherence test? Although its objective—unlike MAD—does not seem to be paradoxical, its proposed

---

[11]Marc Ancel, "New Social Defense," in J. Gerber and P. McAnnany (eds.), *Contemporary Punishment: Views, Explanations, and Justifications* (Notre Dame: University of Notre Dame, 1972), pp. 132–139.

[12]Ronald Reagan, "Peace and National Security," op. cit., p. 29.

[13]Keith Payne and Colin Gray, "Nuclear Policy and the Defensive Transition," in *The Nuclear Reader,* C. Kegley and E. Wittkopf (eds.) (New York: Saint Martin's Press, 1985), pp. 202–205.

[14]Freeman Dyson, *Weapons and Hope*, p. 90.

means—the incapacitation of the aggressor—is profoundly ambiguous. The problem is that the notion of incapacitation can be applied to potential as well as actual aggressors. Does social defense theory require that the act of incapacitation occur only after an act of aggression has been initiated, or could it justify preemptive "defensive" incapacitation on the grounds that preventive action is the best way to protect society?

The domestic version of social defense is itself ambiguous: it could and has been used to justify the preventive incapacitation of individuals who, although they have committed no crime, are judged to be dangerous.[15] If criminal correction authorities see it as their primary responsibility to protect society from potentially dangerous individuals, then, unlike those committed to the theory of retribution, they may—on the grounds of a potential threat to society—authorize incapacitation, even in the absence of an actual offense.

Analogically extending the concept of preventive defense to the nuclear context would mean that, in the name of protecting American society, social defense strategists could justify a preemptive counterforce first strike which would render impotent the nuclear capacity of the Soviet Union. Those who deny that *declaratory* strategic defense is a deceptive part of a secret *operational* war winning plan must clear up this substantial ambiguity. If the advocates of strategic defense insist that their objective is purely defensive-retaliatory (against attacking weapons)—as opposed to preemptive-offensive (against sitting weapons)—then they must somehow show that operational policy reflects this. The ambiguity must be cleared up in order to convince two groups: the public, assuming it democratically approves a purely defensive strategy, and the Soviet authorities who may be driven to preemption if they come to believe that we are developing a strategy of preventive incapacitation. The coincidence of declaratory and operational policy should be transparent to American citizens and Soviet strategists.

Philosophy can expose the serious ambiguity at the heart of the concept of social defense, but the required clarification cannot ultimately be achieved by philosophical theory: it is a practical, strategic matter of developing the appropriate force system.

Moral Defensibility

If the advocates of strategic defense could somehow convince critics that their aim is purely defensive, then I think—while they may have satisfied the coherence test—they will face two serious moral problems. One problem involves the moral incompleteness of a purely defensive objective; the other problem has to do with the question of the appropriate transitional strategy—that is, with the question of what interim doctrine would best fit with a morally complete ethic of strategic defense.

---

[15]R. Gerber and P. McAnnany, op. cit., pp. 129–130.

The Morality of the Objective

It might appear that there could be nothing morally objectionable about the goal of strategic defense: the protection of citizens from nuclear attack. After all, it does not involve targeting noncombatants or even combatants, but only weapons. Many critics seem to have conceded this, focusing their moral attacks on the human costs of paying for what they judge to be a technically unfeasible project and on the likelihood that strategic defense will extend the arms race into space, making nuclear war more probable.

Assuming that the aim of the policy is purely defensive, what possible objection could anyone have to it? Even restricting ourselves to the moral standpoint of those (in the Reagan Administration) who endorse strategic defense, I believe that the objective of this policy proposal is open to serious criticism. That is, I will give an internal critique of a purely defensive policy.

Administration proponents of strategic defense like to point out that supporters of MAD have no morally defensible answer to the question of *what happens if deterrence fails,* that MAD leaves us with an unacceptable moral dilemma: suicide or surrender.[16] Strategic defense advocates assume that one advantage of their policy will be deliverance from such moral dilemmas.

On the contrary, I think it can be argued that even an effective defensive system would leave its supporters in an equally serious moral dilemma. Let us, for the sake of argument, assume that a comprehensive defensive strategy is possible—that the United States can build an almost perfect shield of the homeland supported by a system of comprehensive civil defense. This means that if the Soviet Union launches a nuclear attack it will not devastate American society; any destruction which takes place will be largely that of attacking Soviet missiles. But do advocates of this policy have a morally defensible answer to the question: *What happens if strategic defense succeeds?* Success, to repeat, means that the aggressing weapons are destroyed, without destroying the aggressing humans (the agents who ordered and were involved in the nuclear attack). If we apply the domestic analogy, the moral logic is this: we are only concerned with protecting American society from harmful criminal behavior, not with punishing criminals. If, however, we hold individuals *culpable* for their *attempted* harm of innocent citizens—don't these *culprits* deserve some form of punishment for their criminal behavior? Isn't a purely defensive strategy analogous to a criminal justice system in which the police shoot the deadly weapons from attempted murderers' hands and then allow the culprits to walk away with impunity?

I think it is safe to say that conservative political morality, of the kind espoused by the Reagan Administration, favors retribution in criminal justice—holding even failed criminals responsible and making them pay for their attempted crimes. We can, then, logically infer that this Administration would apply the same retributive principle to Soviet aggression against the United States. Granting that, with a successful strategic defense system, the United States would no longer possess the nuclear weapons that Reagan has declared unacceptable (in the long

---

[16]Caspar Weinberger, op. cit., p. 680.

run)[17]—punishment of the Soviet aggressor could only take the form of conventional retaliation. Hence, if the Soviet Union committed nuclear aggression against us—even if the attack was rendered ineffective—a belief in retributive justice would seem to require punishment of the aggressor and, in effect, a conventional war with the Soviet Union.

Either the advocates of SDI have no answer to the question of how we *should* militarily respond to the Soviet Union if strategic defense were to succeed (i.e., operated effectively in defending the homeland against a Soviet attack)—in which case they seem to be assuming that it will function as a perfect deterrent (the very assumption they questioned in rejecting MAD)—or they must, it would appear, endorse a supplemental (conventional) retributive strategy (to be used in case the defensive system does not deter a Soviet nuclear attack), in which case they must admit: (1) the moral inadequacy of a purely defensive strategy, and (2) the inability of even a perfect defensive system to prevent World War III. The point is that the *objective* of social defense is morally problematic even within the normative framework endorsed by its advocates. Its purely defensive objective is not—as both its advocates and critics have assumed—morally beyond question. Unless its proponents are operating on the dubious assumption that it will be a perfect deterrent, it requires (at least from their moral viewpoint) supplementation by a retributive objective, along with an adequate supporting retaliatory conventional force system which could implement this backup response. This, then, is the moral dilemma: if strategic defense fails to deter a Soviet attack, even if it succeeds in defending the nation, those in power must either allow this attempted act of mass murder to go unanswered—thus violating the requirements of retributive justice—or they must respond in a fashion proportional to the attack, targeting only the culpable Soviet leaders, commanders, and military forces—thus engaging in a (conventional) third world war in which the devastation on both sides—given the enormous power of modern conventional weapons—is likely to approach that of a limited nuclear conflict.

A Morally Defensible Interim Strategy

This brings me to a second moral problem created by the strategic defense proposal. Assuming the American public commits itself to a policy of strategic defense, what transitional *nuclear* strategy should serve in the interim while the United States builds such a system? Between the nuclear dominated present and a (nonnuclear) defense dominated future, what kind of transitional nuclear (deterrent) forces should we have: countercity or counterforce? It should be pointed out that public commitment to a policy of defense dominance (as a future goal) does not necessarily mean presupposing that strategic defense will achieve a near perfect astrodome—only that commitment is made to build the best defensive system possible (no matter how leaky).

Reagan's call for a defensive system was prefaced by a condemnation of nuclear

---

[17]Ronald Reagan, "Arms Control Policy: A Plea for Patience," in *Moral Dilemmas,* op. cit., p. 30.

revenge. Does this mean that MAD is ruled out as an interim strategy? In order to determine the moral defensibility of MAD as a transitional doctrine, an understanding of the nature of this condemnation is crucial. If the objection to MAD is consequentialist—if it is based on the view that MAD, while morally defensible in terms of its past and near future deterrent value, ought to be replaced simply because "no offensive deterrent, no matter how fearsome, is likely to work forever, and the consequences of its failure would be intolerable for civilization"[18] then there is no essential incompatibility between the morality behind strategic defense and MAD as an interim doctrine.

If, on the other hand, the objection to MAD is not based on its fallibility but on its inherent immorality (in, for example, targeting civilians), then MAD is essentially incompatible with the ethic of the advocates of strategic defense. The objection would be a deontological one—a matter of principle; indeed, it would be grounded in the very principle which, we noted above, is missing in a purely defensive objective: the principle of retribution. It should be recalled that this principle, in affirming the need to punish criminal aggressors, at the same time restricts retaliation to the culpable, thereby ruling out the intentional killing of the innocent—or even threats to kill the innocent as a method of deterring crime. Applied to war, commitment to retributive justice requires adherence to the *jus in bello* prohibition on targeting noncombatants. If the call to move toward (no matter how imperfect) a defensive strategy is grounded in a moral condemnation of targeting civilians—in the view that we should not punish (or even threaten to punish) Soviet society indiscriminately in response to the crimes of Soviet leaders, but should try to limit our retaliation to military forces, including the human agents who have ordered or are participating in nuclear aggression—then some form of (interim) nuclear counterforce strategy seems required.

Given what Caspar Weinberger has said about the immorality of retaliating against the Soviet people for "an attack launched by the Soviet leadership—a leadership for which the Soviet people are not responsible and cannot control"[19]—the deontological interpretation seems to be the one most consistent with the Reagan Administration's normative perspective. Considering what was said above about the need for a retributive supplement to the objective of social defense and what we have just said about the need for a retributive restriction on targeting—it would appear that an interim limited nuclear war-fighting (counterforce) strategy fits best with the moral philosophy of this Administration. This, of course, *is* the current declared nuclear weapons policy.

Although a counterforce doctrine seems to be morally required as an interim *nuclear* strategy in the transition toward a *nonnuclear* strategy, the problem with this as a transitional doctrine is that it reintroduces the ambiguity into social defense which, we saw earlier, allows—from the Soviet perspective—for preemption and thus communicates the message of a victory plan. In his speech announcing SDI, Reagan showed awareness of, and a concern to avoid, this

---

[18]Keith Payne and Colin Gray, op. cit., p. 201.

[19]Caspar Weinberger, op. cit., p. 681.

ambiguity: "If paired with offensive systems, [defensive systems] can be viewed as fostering an aggressive policy, and no one wants that."[20] On the other hand, although MAD violates a fundamental principle behind a morally justification of strategic defense—to wit, retributive justice (as opposed to MAD's massive revenge)—MAD might prove more stabilizing as an interim policy: its countercity forces do not threaten Soviet retaliatory weapons. Its inaccurate force system cannot be misread as a victory strategy.

The moral dilemma generated by the choice of an interim doctrine should now be clear. If their objection to MAD is a matter of principle, how can advocates of strategic defense compromise themselves by living with an immoral strategy on the way to a morally justifiable policy? But how can they risk adopting an interim doctrine—countervailing/counterforce strategy—which may send the wrong (destabilizing) message (victory strategy) to Moscow? Is it morally defensible to adhere to a moral principle—whose aim is to avoid harm to civilians—which could make nuclear war—and thus the destruction of millions of civilians—more probable?

Without solving the moral dilemma, Michael Walzer suggests a way of provisionally justifying MAD deterrence. He contends that MAD

> for all its criminality, falls or may fall for the moment under the standard of necessity. But as with terror bombing, so here with the threat of (nuclear) terrorism: supreme emergency is never a stable position . . . we are under an obligation to seize upon opportunities of escape, even to take risks for the sake of such opportunities. So the readiness to murder is balanced, or should be, by a readiness not to murder, not to threaten murder, as soon as alternative ways to peace can be found.[21]

Proponents of strategic defense could, therefore, justify MAD provisionally by arguing that they are working to overcome the need to threaten mass murder. Given doubts about whether limited nuclear war is a meaningful concept, and the likelihood that if a nuclear war began, the result of a countervailing strategy would not look different from the result of a failed MAD (either because of escalation to all-out nuclear war or because of the nuclear winter effects of even a limited war)—advocates of strategic defense could justify MAD as transitional strategy under the heading of *supreme emergency*.

Still, the willingness to target civilians seems to be a clear violation of an important principle behind strategic defense: the protection of innocent civilians, which, if interpreted in Weinberger's morally comprehensive way, would include Soviet noncombatants. Thus, Walzer's notion of a conditional commitment to MAD is morally dubious, given the moral viewpoint of the Administration, at least as stated by the Secretary of Defense

The point is that the problem SDI supporters face in choosing a transitional strategy is not merely a technical one: it is a profoundly moral choice. Perhaps

---

[20]Ronald Reagan, "Peace and National Security: A New Defense," op. cit., p. 29.

[21]Michael Walzer, *Just and Unjust Wars,* op. cit., p. 283.

creative strategic thinkers who are also sensitive to the moral issues can provide a way out of this dilemma. For example, in his book *Nuclear Ethics* Joseph Nye—a former Under Secretary of State and a political scientist with an unusual appreciation of the moral dimension of nuclear strategy—suggests a way of going around the horns of the dilemma. He recommends an alternative targeting doctrine that would avoid the problems of large-scale assured destruction while also avoiding the problems of counterforce targeting. Nye points out that counterforce strategies have generally focused on missile silos. Denying that this is necessary, Nye asks us to consider a limited counterforce strategy which targets soft military forces—Soviet armies—thus avoiding "the excesses of prompt hard-target (silo) counterforce versus counter-city choices."[22] Counter-combatant targeting has, according to Nye, the virtue of reducing harm to civilians and promoting stability. Although innocent people would be killed in such attacks, there would be fewer deaths than under MAD. It would, in addition, supposedly reduce a Soviet temptation which exists under counter-silo strategy: to launch weapons they might otherwise lose. Although the proposed strategy would require more modernization than MAD allows, "it would establish somewhat clearer and lower limits than the current emphasis on counter-silo and counter-industrial targeting does."[23]

It is not clear whether the Nye proposal can provide a morally defensible interim strategy. Nye is honest about its problematic status:

> Perhaps less harm would be done by the counter-combatant approach . . . questions about consequences are difficult to answer. In situations where consequential analysis is so uncertain, we might make a choice by invoking our sense of integrity about reducing harm to innocents, preferring a counter-combatant targeting doctrine. . . . The injunction to minimize harm to innocents . . . should encourage us to explore new approaches to strategic doctrine that will be morally defensible in democratic societies.[24]

SDI is an attempt to explore a new approach to strategic doctrine—one guided in part by the Nye imperative: to protect the innocent, to minimize harm to civilians (on both sides). Supporters of strategic defense need to find—for the transitional period—something like the Nye strategy, an interim doctrine which would be morally compatible with the principle of countercity avoidance and strategically compatible with the requirements of stability. Nye himself does not see his recommendation as part of an interim strategy on the way to strategic

---

[22]Joseph Nye, *Nuclear Ethics*, op. cit., p. 112. I should point out that Nye's alternative was not formulated as a solution to the moral dilemma which the need for an interim strategy generates. He simply presents it as a third way between the countersilo and countercity strategies. His recommendation is, however, one that supporters of strategic defense might find helpful in overcoming their dilemma. Nye himself is not a supporter of strategic defense.

[23]Ibid, p. 113.

[24]Ibid, p. 114.

defense, but as an attempt to find a way to live with nuclear weapons while preserving a concept of "just deterrence." Indeed, he doubts that strategic defense can realize his moral imperative; he suggests that the attempt to seek a comprehensive defensive system may increase the risk of nuclear conflict while missing opportunities for arms control and for improving our relationship with the Soviet Union.[25]

---

[25]Ibid, pp. 125–131.

8

"Star Wars": Step toward a First Strike

Michio Kaku and Daniel Axelrod

Kaku and Axelrod contend that the real purpose of the Strategic Defense Initiative is to provide the United States with a first-strike capability against the Soviet Union, restoring the United States to the position of global military dominance it enjoyed in the early 1950s. Even if strategic defenses cannot satisfactorily absorb a Soviet *first* strike, they may be effective enough to absorb a Soviet *second* strike, a counterattack launched with the few Soviet weapons that survived an American surprise attack. Even if the United States never used such first-strike capability, the possession of such an ability would enable the United States to dominate confrontations with the Soviet Union on any level, by threatening escalation to levels at which the United States, assisted by Star Wars, would win.

I f 5% of the Soviet arsenal—400 warheads—slipped past a U. S. Star Wars shield, it would still inflict unacceptable damage, crippling the U. S. as an industrial nation. Yet even if Star Wars can never function as an effective defensive system, there is another application to which even a partial, leaky shield has vast military potential. If a nation possessed a leaky shield, that nation could launch a first strike, destroy most of its adversary's missiles on the ground, and use the shield to absorb a weakened second strike. In this scenario, the sword (the MX, the Trident, the Pershing) would strike first, disabling the enemy's missiles in their silos, and then the shield (Star Wars) would be raised to intercept any Soviet missiles that might have escaped the first strike.

As Kissinger has candidly noted, "A country with a full ABM defense might imagine it could strike first and then use its ABMs to intercept the weakened

---

Michio Kaku is professor of physics at The Graduate Center and City College, City University of New York. Daniel Axelrod is associate professor of physics at the University of Michigan.

This selection is excerpted from Kaku and Axelrod's *To Win a Nuclear War* (Boston: South End Press, 1987). Used with permission of South End Press.

retaliatory blow."[1] In other words, even a primitive ABM would prove effective as a backup to a first strike.

The arithmetic is simple. If an ABM system is 80% effective (probably the best that can be attained by the 1990s) then 1,600 Soviet warheads would still manage to evade the system if the Soviets struck first. However, if the United States were to strike first, and if that first strike was 95% successful, then only 400 Soviet warheads would survive. Then the ABM system would target the remaining warheads, letting perhaps 80 warheads reach the U. S. Eighty warheads would still cause tremendous damage to the U. S., but with civil defense measures in place, this blow could be consistent with "acceptable loss" and with a reasonable "post-attack recovery period," according to the war-fighters.

From the war-fighters' perspective, even a primitive ABM system is sufficiently effective in a first strike. In fact, a primitive ABM system attains maximum effectiveness only as a cleanup weapon after an offensive first strike. Even a partially effective ABM system, therefore, has "threat value" and can be used in a "policy of calculated and gradual coercion." Lt. Col. Robert Bowman, who directed the U. S. Air Force version of Star Wars during the Carter years, even called the system "the missing link to a first strike."[2]

It was precisely the lack of such a nuclear shield which contributed to Eisenhower and Kennedy's decision to overrule recommendations for a surprise attack on the Soviet Union made by members of the National Security Council. The shield was the missing link.

Like the MX system, a Star Wars system has "threat value" because it is specifically designed to prevent retaliation. In a conflict, any nation armed with such a system can always threaten another nation with perhaps a 99% confidence kill. In fact, any system designed to prevent retaliation can be considered a part of a first strike system. This means that Star Wars, anti-sub warfare, and even a civil defense all have "threat value" because they are designed to prevent the other side from successfully retaliating after a first strike. A nation with effective Star Wars and civil defense systems could strike at other nations with impunity. Even a leaky Star Wars system, in concert with other first strike systems, can have tremendous "threat value."

The Pentagon is systematically building weapons which are designed to nullify every possible avenue of Soviet retaliation. These weapons will target every possibility of coordinating a second strike: ASATs to destroy the early warning system, Pershing IIs to kill the leadership*, MXs and Tridents to destroy Soviet missiles, ASW to sink Soviet subs, and Star Wars to prevent retaliation.

The Soviets, of course, are well aware of this. Former Premier Andropov stated on March 26, 1983, just three days after Reagan's Star Wars speech, that a U. S.

---

[1] Henry Kissinger, *White House Years* (Boston: Little Brown, 1979), p. 205.

[2] Rosmarie Reed, *Arming the Heavens*. Radio broadcast, WBAI-FM (New York), 1985.

*If the Senate approves the Intermediate Nuclear Forces treaty between the United States and the U. S. R., the Pershing II will be removed from the American arsenal. Many of the strategic functions of the Pershing II, however, can be picked up by the new American Trident D-5. *Ed.*

ABM system would secure "the possibility of destroying, with the help of ABM defenses, the corresponding strategic systems of the other side; that is, of rendering it incapable of dealing a retaliatory strike." This would be tantamount to "a bid to disarm the Soviet Union in the face of the U. S. nuclear threat."

Of course, the Reagan administration has gone to great lengths to emphasize the peaceful intentions behind the Star Wars shield. Intentions, however, account for little in the calculus of counterforce. No matter how sincere are the assertions of the Reagan administration that the system is purely defensive, the Soviets are still left facing a formidable adversary that is systematically building weapons which threaten to destroy them with impunity if the U. S. strikes first. No nation is likely to gamble its national survival on verbal assurances of a self-declared enemy. What will determine the Soviet response is how the Soviets perceive Star Wars, and they have already said that they see it as a means to achieving first strike capability.

Before such a system can be built, however, there are formidable technical obstacles that must be overcome. Because of this, even with a crash program, the deployment of a leaky (though effective) "shield" is not likely to come until the early 1990s.

9

Is Nuclear Deterrence Rational, and Will Star Wars Help?

Steven Brams and D. Marc Kilgour*

Brams and Kilgour analyze nuclear deterrence in terms of the game of
Chicken, the precise structure of which is provided by the theory of
games. On their view, nuclear deterrence without strategic defenses
can deter war if threats to retaliate are perceived as such by
opponents. Furthermore, deterrence can be made maximally robust by
assuring substantial responses to small provocations and relatively
smaller responses to large provocations. The introduction of strategic
defenses need not destabilize deterrence, but the threat of instability
grows as the defenses become more effective. The threat of instability
is greatest when both sides deploy defenses and the defenses of one
side are superior to the defenses of the other.

Steven Brams is professor of politics at New York University. D. Marc Kilgour is professor
of mathematics at Wilfred Laurier University.

This essay was first published in *Analyse & Kritik* 9.1&2 (Frankfurt, October 1987). Used
with permission of *Analyse & Kritik* and Steven Brams.

*The first part of this paper on deterrence is a slightly revised version of Brams and Kilgour
(1986b), but the second part on Star Wars is new. The material on deterrence is based in part
on Brams (1985, chap. 1) and the several papers on deterrence and threats cited in the text.
The models in these papers and others on escalation in an arms race, crisis stability,
verification of arms-control agreements, and winding down if deterrence fails are developed
within a common framework in Brams and Kilgour (1988). Brams gratefully acknowledges
the financial support of the National Science Foundation under Grant No. SES 84-08505.
Kilgour gratefully acknowledges the financial support of the Natural Sciences and
Engineering Research Council of Canada under Grant No. A8974.

Nuclear deterrence is the cornerstone of the national-security policies of not only the superpowers but other nations as well. By threatening untoward action against an opponent who initiates conflict, even at great potential cost to oneself, one seeks to deter the opponent from committing aggression in the first place.

The controversy over the viability of nuclear deterrence has largely concerned the rationality of adhering to a policy that can lead to enormous destruction—perhaps even mutual annihilation—if the policy fails. The party attacked would seem foolhardy to bring upon itself a disastrous outcome if, by compromising or—heaven forbid!—capitulating, it could do better. On the other hand, by fighting (irrationally?) to the bitter end, it would seem to violate the very canons of rationality on which deterrence rests. Yet by caving in, or indicating that it might, it would seem to invite attack.

A number of different nuclear doctrines to support deterrence have been proposed, perhaps the most notable being MAD, or 'mutual assured destruction'. The inclusion of mutual in the MAD doctrine implies that each side can destroy the other, even if attacked first; this reciprocal vulnerability is presumed to make deterrence stable, at least as long as the mutual destruction is 'assured'.

Sometimes MAD is used to denote 'mutual assured deterrence', with the means for assuring deterrence not necessarily assumed to be the destruction of society. Other terminology is less lurid than MAD. 'Countervalue', which is stressed in the doctrine of mutual assured destruction, refers to the destruction of cities and industries, whereas 'counterforce' stresses the destruction of military forces, particularly missile sites, and command and control facilities. Still different strategies such as 'damage-limitation' and 'war-fighting' defenses after a limited nuclear attack—should deterrence fail—are also discussed in the national-security literature and are now part of the nuclear vernacular.

The rather arcane debate about nuclear deterrence and its alternatives is generally not about whether one should respond to attack, but how. Here our concern is broader—with the nature of deterrence itself: the conditions under which one should respond to an attack, with what degree of certainty, and at what level. Our purpose is not so much to describe optimal threats to deter an opponent—though such prescriptions will come out of the models we describe—but rather to show that deterrence is amenable to rational analysis. The foundation of this analysis is the mathematical theory of games, whose application to the problem of deterrence helps to clarify the main strategic issues.

Before attempting to apply this theory directly, consider what general argument can be used to justify deterrence, assuming that it is costly for a threatener to carry out a threat if attacked. While conceding that it is irrational to carry out a threat in a single play of a game, one might argue that it may well be rational in repeated play (Brams and Hessel, 1984). The reason is that a carried-out threat enhances one's credibility—in doing the apparently irrational thing in a single play—so that, over the long run, one can develop a sufficiently fearsome reputation to deter future opponents. Thereby, although losing on occasion in the short run, one can gain over time.

British Prime Minister Margaret Thatcher evidently made this calculation when she responded to Argentina's invasion of the Falkland Islands in 1982 by dispatching the British fleet. The conflict was very damaging to both sides, but

Is Nuclear Deterrence Rational, and Will Star Wars Help?

Britain's successful invasion left little doubt about that country's resolve in future territorial disputes, such as might occur over Gibraltar.

This is not a satisfactory argument, however, if carrying out a threat leads to something as unthinkable and irredeemable as nuclear war between the super-powers, which probably would occur only once. Unlike deterrence in a conventional conflict—between, say, a superpower and a smaller country without nuclear weapons, in which one's willingness to carry out a threat will affect one's reputation in future conflicts—credibility in a game without a sequel is purely academic.

To model deterrence between two nuclear powers, we begin with the two-person game of Chicken, in which each player can choose between two strategies: cooperate (C) and do not cooperate ($\bar{C}$), which in the context of deterrence may be thought of as 'do not attack' and 'attack', respectively. These strategies lead to four possible outcomes, which the players are assumed to rank from best (4) to worst (1). These rankings are shown as ordered pairs in the outcome matrix of Figure 1, with the first number indicating the rank assigned by the row player (called "Row"), and the second number indicating the rank assigned by the column player (called "Column"). Chicken is defined by the following outcome rankings of the two players:

1. Both players cooperate (CC)—next-best outcome for both players: (3,3).

2. One player cooperates and the other does not (C$\bar{C}$ and $\bar{C}$C)—best outcome for the player who does not cooperate and next-worst for the player who does: (2,4) and (4,2).

3. Both players do not cooperate ($\bar{C}\bar{C}$)—worst outcome for both players: (1,1).

Outcomes (2,4) and (4,2) in Figure 1 are circled to indicate that they are *Nash equilibria:* neither player (Row or Column) would have an incentive unilaterally to depart from these outcomes because he would do worse if he did. For example, from (2,4) Row would do worse if he moved to (1,1), and Column would do worse if he moved to (3,3). By contrast, from (3,3) Row would do better if he moved to (4,2), and Column would do better if he moved to (2,4).

The shorthand verbal descriptions given for each outcome in Figure 1 suggest the vexing problem the players face in choosing between C and $\bar{C}$: by choosing $\bar{C}$, each can 'win' but risks disaster; by choosing C, each might benefit from compromise but could also 'lose'. Each Nash equilibrium shown in Figure 1 favors one player over the other, but the stability of these equilibria as such says nothing about which of the two—if either—will be chosen.

Although the (3,3) compromise outcome is the obvious candidate for the players to agree on, its instability would seem to rule it out as a durable solution. At some point each player might be tempted to depart from it to 'win', or at least threaten the other player with preemption.

One effect of threats in Chicken is not hard to grasp. If, say, Row threatens Column with the choice of $\bar{C}$, and this threat is regarded as credible, Column's best response is C, leading to (4,2), an apparent win for Row and loss for Column.

FIGURE 1

Column

	Cooperate (C)	Do not cooperate (C̄)
Cooperate (C)	(3,3) Compromise A ↓	(2,4) Column "wins," Row "loses"
Row	(4,2) ————————→ (1,1) B	
Do not cooperate (C̄)	Row "wins," Column "loses"	Disaster

Clearly, the player with the credible threat—if there is one—can force the other player to back down in order to avoid (1,1). Although Row would 'win' in this case by getting his best outcome, Column would not 'lose' in the usual sense by getting his worst outcome but rather his next-worst.

This fact illustrates that Chicken is not a *constant-sum* game, in which what one player wins the other loses. That is why we have put 'win' and 'lose' in quotation marks here and in Figure 1. In *variable-sum* games like Chicken, the sum of the players' payoffs at each outcome (if measured cardinally by utilities rather than ordinally by ranks) is not constant but variable. This means that *both* players may do better at some outcomes (for example, (3,3)) than at others (for example, (1,1)).

The *Deterrence Game* is based on Chicken but adds two refinements: (i) the players can make quantitative choices of *levels* of cooperation (or noncooperation), not just qualitative choices of C or C̄; (ii) once these initial choices, which can be interpreted as levels of nonpreemption (or preemption), are made, the less preemptive player may choose a subsequent level or *retaliation* (Brams and Kilgour, 1985a, 1985b).

To illustrate play in this game, consider the extreme case in which Row chooses maximum preemption and Column chooses no preemption initially. Thus, if the game starts out at (3,3), Row's preemption moves it to (4,2), as shown by arrow A in Figure 1. If we assume that the players have complete information about each other's initial choices, there would be no doubt that Row preempted; Column could then retaliate.

Now here comes the rub for Column, the player who cooperated initially. If he responds to Row's preemption and moves the game to (1,1), as illustrated by arrow B, he succeeds not only in punishing Row but also himself. This is precisely what makes retaliation in the Deterrence Game problematic: it would be better for Column to capitulate, accepting his next-worst outcome (4,2), than avenge Row's preemption by moving the game to (1,1), the disastrous outcome for both players.

True, if revenge in this situation is valued more highly than defeat by Column, there is nothing irrational about Column's choosing retribution against Row. But this choice is incompatible with the Figure 1 payoffs; moreover, revenge might be especially hard for a superpower to justify after suffering a limited nuclear attack that the vast majority of its population survives or, more realistically, a large-scale conventional attack, such as by the Soviet Union in Western Europe. Nuclear reprisal, after all, would almost surely result in a full-scale nuclear exchange, whose consequence might well be a nuclear winter in which everybody perishes.

If the rankings of outcomes in Figure 1 accurately describe the problem of retaliation in a nuclear confrontation between the superpowers, how can a policy of deterrence be justified that poses the threat of nuclear war and perhaps mutual annihilation? The superpowers in effect circumvent the problem of rationally responding to a first strike by irrevocably precommitting themselves to retaliate if attacked (Brams, 1985). Thereby they preclude themselves from making conciliatory choices at the very point at which it might be prudent to step back from the precipice.

In fact, command and control procedures that both superpowers now have in place specify preselected targets that will be hit once a first strike of a particular magnitude is detected. Even if the president is incapacitated, authority for the launching of a retaliatory strike devolves (to lower levels of command) to ensure that such a strike will actually be carried out (Bracken, 1983; Blair, 1985; Ford, 1985; Lebow, 1987; Carter, Steinbruner, and Zraket, 1987).

All this smacks of a 'doomsday machine', which responds independently of human decisionmakers. This is an exaggeration, of course, but it probably is accurate to speak of a 'probabilistic doomsday machine' (PDM)—one with built-in uncertainties due to possible failures in C^3I (command, communication, control, and intelligence), including the lack of will of political decisionmakers to order a second strike as well as a variety of technical problems that might arise.

Is a PDM sufficient to deter a first strike by an opponent? In principle, this will depend on whether the opponent thinks he can do better by attacking or by not attacking. Assume, for illustration, that the ranks in Figure 1 are cardinal utilities, or actual values, that each player associates with the four outcomes. If p is the probability that the PDM will function properly when one player—say, Row—attacks the other, then Column can deter Row if the payoff that Row obtains from not attacking, 3, is greater than the expected payoff he obtains from attacking. In this case, Row will obtain 4 with probability $1-p$ (PDM does not work so Column will not retaliate) and 1 with probability p (Column will retaliate). This calculation can be expressed by inequality $3 > 1p + 4(1-p)$, which is equivalent to $p > \frac{1}{3}$.

In other words, Row will be well advised not to attack if Column's PDM has a greater than $\frac{1}{3}$ chance of triggering retaliation. If the consequences of retaliation were much worse than 1 (for example, some large negative value, which might be the case in a nuclear conflict), only a very small probability p of retaliation would be required to make a first strike unprofitable if not perilous for the attacker.

Patently, certain retaliation is not necessary to deter an opponent in the Deterrence Game, at least one who makes the kind of expected-payoff calculation we have illustrated. In international conflicts, especially those that might involve nuclear weapons, there is abundant evidence that national decisionmakers are not reckless but, in fact, rather conservative in their choice of means to satisfy their goals.

Of course, we may not share their goals or even sympathize with them. This fact, however, is not consequential if we have a fairly good idea of what their goals are and, specifically, how they evaluate the possible outcomes that may occur.

Given that they rank outcomes as in Figure 1, there will be some p less than 1 that will render the expected payoff obtained from attack (and subsequent retaliation) less than that obtained from not attacking.

This calculus, nevertheless, does not gainsay that retaliation is always costly to the player attacked in the Deterrence Game. This is why, to make his threat of retaliation credible, he must *precommit* himself to retaliate with a p above the threshold value we have illustrated.

The superpowers have made themselves credible by, in effect, constructing PDMs—somewhat beyond the control even if their top leaders—who might, conceivably, prefer to surrender in a crisis rather than retaliate against a first strike. The fact that they may not be able to countermand the PDM ensures that precommitments to retaliate are credible.

Probabilistic threats of retaliation that deter an attack will presumably depend on the level of the attack. As the level increases and the first strike brings the attacker closer to his highest payoff (before retaliation), the retaliator will have to increase his level of retaliation in order to reduce the attacker's payoff to an amount below what the attacker would get if he had not attacked in the first place.

Visually, one might think of the Deterrence Game as played on a square board, whose four corners give the payoffs shown for Chicken in Figure 1. If Row attacks by moving the outcome vertically from (3,3) toward—but not necessarily reaching—(4,2), Column can respond by moving horizontally from left to right, closer to (1,1). This will decrease Row's payoff, so that given Row's level of attack, at some point on the board defined by Column's level of response, Row will be indifferent between attacking and not attacking. Retaliation that carries the outcome to the right of this point, closer to (1,1), will definitely be worse for Row than staying at (3,3).

We assume in the Deterrence Game that the players' payoffs vary continuously as a function of the distances from the four corners of the board. Each can deter his opponent by threatening retaliation at some level greater than that which causes indifference.

We have calculated, in a variation of the Deterrence Game called the Threat Game, the minimal levels of retaliation that are required to deter attacks and have discovered that a policy of tit-for-tat reprisals may not be the best deterrent (Brams and Kilgour, 1987). In many cases, a more-than-proportionate response is optimal against relatively minor aggression, a less-than-proportionate response against relatively major aggression. The precise levels—and the threshold at which 'more' becomes 'less'—depend on the payoffs of the underlying game of Chicken.

Historically, we will never know whether a strong policy of resistance against Hitler's early incursions would have prevented World War II. Nor can we predict that, after a limited nuclear first strike by one superpower, a diminished response on the part of the other will prevent World War III. There are, nonetheless, good rational reasons to believe that an effective deterrent may be one in which the level of retaliation is tailored more or less—but not strictly—to the level of aggression. By hitting relatively hard when the provocation is small, and backing off somewhat when large-scale conflict might prove catastrophic, one may at the same time discourage 'salami tactics' and defuse all-out escalation should deterrence fail.

Is Nuclear Deterrence Rational, and Will Star Wars Help?

These results support a modified tit-for-tat policy or, in the parlance of the U. S. Defense Department, "flexible response" or "graduated deterrence". But our results are more precise than these qualitative doctrines; they provide quantitative guidelines of the punishment that should be threatened in relation to the level of attack (Brams and Kilgour, 1987). Specifically, as aggression increases, retaliation should also increase, but at a decreasing rate. Whether the threshold retaliation need be more than the aggression at low levels depends on the specific payoffs in the game, but at high levels one need never threaten retaliation commensurate with the provocation to deter it. The reason is simple: such a policy will move the game toward the mutually worst (1,1) outcome, which may be far worse than the (3,3) outcome; rational deterrence can always be acheived without the threat of such 'overkill'.

The (3,3) outcome is in fact a Nash equilibrium in the Deterrence Game and Threat Game when backed up by threats above the minimum level necessary to deter. In other words, the cooperative outcome in Chicken, which is not in equilibrium, can be stabilized by threats—at least if they are considered credible by an opponent.

What helps make them credible is that the threatener does not suffer unnecessarily great damage in carrying them out, making his precommitment to such retaliation more plausible. Although the threatened retaliation probably should be somewhat above the minimum level to guard against possible misperceptions or miscalculations by an opponent, it should never lead to complete devastation of the threatener. Otherwise it would appear incredible; the potential aggressor, suspecting such retaliation would never be carried out, might attack on this very presumption.

It is unfortunate, perhaps, that the palpable fear of annihilation rather than simple good will has prevented nuclear war for forty years. Yet good will alone is insufficient to sustain (3,3) in Chicken precisely because it is rational to defect from this cooperative outcome. Threats in the Threat Game—sometimes entailing retaliation greater than small-scale aggression, but always diminishing in proportion to increasing aggression—can, however, render deterrence rational.

The superpowers have flirted with their own extinction to make deterrence work. Ronald Reagan's SDI (Strategic Defense Initiative, or 'Star Wars'), which purports to provide a defense against nuclear weapons and avert an apocalypse, may eventually replace PDMs, which he finds unsavory.

Unsavory as nuclear deterrence may seem, we have argued that it can be grounded in game-theoretic rationality, given threats of retaliation that have a sufficiently high probability of being carried out. We are not, by the way, suggesting that the throw of dice or the spin of a roulette wheel should determine whether an American president or a Soviet general secretary will retaliate against a first strike but rather that the uncertainties of retaliation are already inherent in C^3I—and its possible breakdown.

Thus, a PDM, in substantial part devoid of human intervention, would appear to be a rational mechanism for stabilizing deterrence. But when it is shorn of its human element and rests so heavily on impersonal detection devices, computers, and the like, there would appear to be something inhumane and even morally repugnant in threatening horrendous destruction in order to deter a first strike.

Should millions of innocent civilians be held hostage to maintain the proverbial 'delicate balance of terror'?

Star Wars holds out the promise of forestalling a preemptive strike by preventing many first-strike weapons from getting through, using one or more shields. If this attack can be stopped or largely blunted, then presumably the potential preemptor will think twice about attacking in the first place. Moreover, even if he does attack, his attack will not be nearly so effective as it would in the absence of a missile defense, thereby decreasing the value of striking first.

This argument for a strategic defense does not hinge on its being totally impenetrable, or 'leakproof', but instead on its lowering the expected payoff to an attacker of a first strike. Consequently, deterrence will be enhanced, which is today the primary justification the Reagan administration uses for Star Wars in light of the apparent impossibility of building a leakproof defense, at least in the foreseeable future.

However, the other side of the coin is that, with a Star Wars defense, each side will be able to degrade the effectiveness of a (retaliatory) second strike. This degradation will be especially upsetting if each side can be crippled or seriously damaged by a first strike, diminishing greatly its capacity to retaliate and thereby undermining deterrence. If a Star Wars defense is in fact possible, the key question is: Will the enhancement of deterrence, by making a first strike more uncertain, be offset by the undermining of deterrence because one's capability to retaliate, particularly after a devastating first strike, will be undercut?

We ignore here the enormous costs of building a Star Wars system. Our focus is solely on the strategic effects of Star Wars on deterrence, assuming that deterrence in some form will not be abandoned, at least until Star Wars is perfected. Yet the perfection of Star Wars, to the point that it becomes a leakproof system, is surely an extremely remote possibility.

To analyze the deterrence-enhancing versus the deterrence-undermining effects of Star Wars, we assume that Star Wars puts limits on the maximum first and second strikes of each player in the Deterrence Game (Brams and Kilgour, 1986). That is, we introduce as new parameters in this game constraints on how far, say, Row can shift the outcome from (3,3) to (4,2) in a maximal first strike, and, in turn, how far Column, after suffering a first strike, can shift the outcome from (4,2)—or wherever the game is after the first strike—toward (1,1) and full retaliation.

We posit three different scenarios that assume different functional relationships between each side's first and second strike defense. Then we let these defenses vary from no defense to perfect defense, subject to these relationships. We will not try to describe the different scenarios here but instead will summarize our principal results, based on all the scenarios.

Generally, we find that, for low levels of strategic defense, deterrence can be maintained. The reason is that each side's threat of retaliation is still sufficient to deter an opponent from preemption, but as defenses improve this threat loses its force and the stability of (3,3) in the Deterrence Game is jeopardized.

At a calculable threshold value of defense, deterrence breaks down and it becomes rational for each side to attack the other. Not only can neither side be deterred by the threat of retaliation when its defense is sufficiently strong, but it also does better attacking preemptively than retaliating after being attacked.

This is a disturbing development, for it renders *mutual* preemption a Nash equilibrium in the Deterrence Game with Star Wars or simply the Star Wars Game; this outcome is never stable in the absence of Star Wars. (True, *unilateral* preemption to (4,2) and (2,4) are also Nash equilibria in the Deterrence Game, but given precommitted threats by both sides above the threshold level calculated earlier, they are dominated by the choice of (3,3).) In the Star Wars Game, by contrast, both sides may find it advantageous to attack each other simultaneously because, if each has a strong enough defense, neither side's threats of retaliation will be sufficient to deter an opponent.

Actually, an equality or near equality in the defenses of the two sides retards mutual preemption, whereas an imbalance in defenses aggravates it. For if one side has a much stronger Star Wars defense than the other, by attacking first it might be able to so weaken its opponent that it can effectively stop whatever retaliation the opponent can throw back. But the opponent can make this calculation, too, and realize that it would do better attacking itself—given it is about to be preempted—resulting in mutual preemption. Such preemption may be arrested either by credible threats of retaliation or, if less than credible, a mutual realization by the players that not attacking is still better than attacking with strong but not necessarily impenetrable defenses.

In our different scenarios, both mutual preemption and deterrence, as well as unilateral preemption, are Nash equilibria for certain levels of defense; conditions under which one equilibrium may dominate another when they coexist are investigated. Perhaps the greatest peril occurs when there is no deterrence equilibrium. Then an extreme form of crisis instability may grip the players and lead them to an abyss. More probable in superpower relations, though, is that deterrence will remain reasonably secure, mainly because both sides have largely invulnerable second-strike capabilities (principally, submarine-launched ballistic missiles and cruise missiles) that Star Wars will have no effect on, at least presently.

At some point, however, perhaps in a severe crisis, crisis stability could be upset and preemption, perhaps even mutual preemption, might appear attractive. This has occurred at lower levels of superpower conflict, usually through surrogates, in different parts of the world. If we are to steer clear of *nuclear* preemption as a rational option, it is imperative that the superpowers recognize that they must carefully chart a course of balanced development of Star Wars defenses—if these ever become feasible—to avoid creating major instabilities, particularly in the period of transition from deterrence to defense.

The replacement of a deterrent policy depending on PDMs by a defensive posture grounded in Star Wars is not imminent. Until it occurs, it behooves us to understand the logic of nuclear deterrence and to improve upon it through calculations that make it as robust as possible. Star Wars, as we have modeled it, seems mostly an assault on this strategic logic.

References

Blair, Bruce G. (1985). *Strategic Command and Control: Redefining the Nuclear Threat.* Washington, DC: Brookings.

Bracken, Paul (1983). *The Command and Control of Nuclear Forces.* New Haven, CT: Yale University Press.

Brams, Steven J. (1985). *Superpower Games: Applying Game Theory to Superpower Conflict.* New Haven, CT: Yale University Press.

Brams, Steven J., and Marek P. Hessel (1984). "Threat Power in Sequential Games." *International Studies Quarterly* 28, no. 1 (March): 15–36.

Brams, Steven J., and D. Marc Kilgour (1985a). "Optimal Deterrence." *Social Philosophy & Policy* 3, no. 1 (Autumn): 118–135. Reprinted in Ellen Frankel Paul *et al.* (eds.) (1986), *Nuclear Rights/Nuclear Wrongs.* London: Basic Blackwell, pp. 118–135; and Newton Garver and Peter H. Hare (eds.) (1986), *Naturalism and Rationality.* Buffalo, NY: Prometheus, pp. 241–262.

Brams, Steven J., and D. Marc Kilgour (1985b). "The Path to Stable Deterrence." In Urs Luterbacher and Michael D. Ward (eds.), *Dynamic Models of International Conflict.* Boulder, CO: Lynne Rienner, pp. 11–25.

Brams, Steven J., and D. Marc Kilgour (1986a). "Deterrence versus Defense: A Game-Theoretic Model of Star Wars." Mimeographed.

Brams, Steven J., and D. Marc Kilgour (1986b). "Is Nuclear Deterrence Rational?" *PS* 19, no. 3 (Summer): 645–651.

Brams, Steven J., and D. Marc Kilgour (1987). "Optimal Threats." *Operations Research* 35.

Brams, Steven J., and D. Marc Kilgour (1988). *Game Theory and National Security.*

Carter, A. B., J. D. Steinbruner, and C. A. Zraket (eds.) (1987). *Managing Nuclear Operations.* Washington, D C.

Ford, D. (1985). *The Button: The Pentagon's Command and Control System.* New York.

Lebow, R. N. (1987). *Nuclear Crisis Management: A Dangerous Illusion.* Ithaca, N Y.

10

Building Peace: A Pastoral Reflection on the Response to the Challenge of Peace*

The Ad Hoc Committee on the Moral Evaluation of Deterrence, National Conference of Catholic Bishops

In 1983, the National Conference of Catholic Bishops issued a celebrated Pastoral Letter on morality and nuclear weapons entitled *The Challenge of Peace*. The pastoral letter argued that nuclear deterrence was neither morally permissible nor morally condemnable. Instead, the bishops stated, "Considerations of concrete elements of nuclear weapons policy . . . lead us to a strictly conditioned moral acceptance of nuclear deterrence. We cannot consider it adequate as a long-term basis for peace." The "strict conditions" for the acceptability of elements of deterrence were (1) that changes in deterrence are acceptable only to the extent that they move toward peace, disarmament, and the elimination of nuclear deterrence, and (2) that the elements of a deterrence policy must conform to the moral standards of just war, including the principles of noncombatant immunity, proportionality, and "last resort." On this basis the bishops rejected the quest for nuclear superiority, condemned plans for long-term nuclear war, opposed "first strike" weapons systems, supported a freeze on nuclear weapons production, called for a comprehensive test-ban treaty, requested the removal of short-range nuclear weapons, and called for deep cuts in strategic arsenals.

The bishops made no statement concerning strategic defenses, and the announcement of the Strategic Defense Initiative came two weeks after *The Challenge of Peace* was adopted. In November 1985, the National Conference commissioned a special study to assess whether the moral conditions set forth in *The Challenge of Peace* were being met by changes in the nuclear arms competition since 1983, especially the Strategic Defense Initiative of the Reagan Administration. The report, prepared by the ad hoc Committee on the Moral Evaluation of Deterrence, chaired by Joseph Cardinal Bernardin of Chicago, was released on April 14, 1988, for consideration, revision, and adoption

*Excerpts from a draft.
© United States Catholic Conference. Reprinted with permission of the United States Catholic Conference.

One of the characteristics of the nuclear debate of the 1980s, fostered in part by *The Challenge of Peace*, has been a growing dissatisfaction with the theory and policy of deterrence. The standard doctrine has come under critique from the left and right of the political spectrum and both have resorted to moral as well as political-strategic arguments to stress the shortcomings of deterrence. . . . Supporters of SDI pick up this theme, joining a critique of Mutual Assured Destruction theories to an argument about the moral stability which will accompany a defense dominated nuclear relationship.

As bishops, we are interested in the scientific and strategic dimensions of the SDI policy debate, but we are not in a position to contribute to them. It is precisely the visible role which the moral argument has assumed in the policy area which draws us into more specific commentary here. The SDI is proposed by some of its supporters as a superior moral answer to the moral dilemmas of the nuclear age analyzed in *The Challenge of Peace*. . . .

The case made for the moral superiority of SDI is primarily an "ethic of intention"; using the just-war ethic, supporters of SDI review the nuclear age, pointing out how classical deterrence doctrine has been willing to abide or endorse threats against innocent populations. In contrast to this posture, a case is made describing the *intended* objective of SDI: either the transition to a world where the nuclear threat has been negated or at least to a world where the principal targets shift from populations to weapons, from targeting societies to targets in space. Stated at the level of intentionality, the SDI case seeks to capture the high moral ground, undoubtedly contributing to the popularity of the program with the general public.

But the complexity and the stakes of the policy debate on SDI require that the moral argument be pressed beyond an ethic of intention. The SDI debate is less a dispute about objectives or motives than it is about means and consequences. Hence an "ethic of consequences" should be used to test the "ethic of intention." To probe the moral content of the consequences of the SDI is to raise issues about the risks, costs, and benefits of pursuing the SDI proposal. . . . The point here is to assert that the moral character of SDI cannot be determined apart from these other elements precisely because consequences count in a moral assessment. . . .

There are risks associated with pursuing some technological paths: risks to the existing arms control regime; risks of introducing dimensions of uncertainty into the already delicate political-psychological fabric of deterrence; risks that defensive systems can have real or perceived offensive uses; finally, risks that some forms of SDI would be ineffective against an adversary's first strike, but more effective against a retaliatory second strike, thereby eroding crisis stability. Assessing these risks—evaluating which are prudent to pursue, which are too high to tolerate—involves a moral as well as a technological judgment. . . .

Assessment in light of its impact on strategic stability will force the moral argument onto the path of examining the contrasting views of whether the "transition" from assured destruction to common security can be carried off with acceptable risk. Supporters of the SDI argue from the moral and the strategic perspective about the opportunities it provides to transform the nuclear dilemma—to break free from the continuing hostage relationship inherent in deterrence. These arguments stress the goal of the transition.

While this goal is undoubtedly attractive, the more compelling moral case presently rests with those who specify the likely consequences of an aggressive SDI program at this time: (1) the obstacle it poses to effective movement on arms control; (2) the possible shift toward offensive use of this defensive system; (3) the further "tilt" of the deterrence relationship toward preemptive strategies during the transition period. No one of these results is a certain consequence of pursuing SDI development, but the collective danger they pose to the dynamic of deterrence leaves us unconvinced of the merits of proceeding toward deployment of the system. The combination of the technological and strategic evaluations of the present status of SDI appears to us to promise serious risks and very hypothetical benefits at this time.

The feasibility and strategic stability argument are central to policy debate about SDI. The economic argument—the escalating cost of SDI in a time of continuing budget deficits and in a decade which has seen deep cuts in programs for the poor at home and abroad—has particular moral relevance. . . . A program which fails to attract a clear consensus on technological-strategic grounds should not be allowed to command resources at a time when other human needs go unfulfilled.

Our judgment about SDI can be summarized:

1. Some of the officially stated objectives of the SDI program—to move away from a long-term reliance on deterrence and to protect civilians and society as a whole—correspond to key themes in the pastoral letter.

2. The pursuit of these objectives must be carried out within limits which protect other principles of the pastoral letter:

   a. that the framework of arms control agreements and negotiations not be eroded or made more difficult;
   b. that a new surge of offensive competition not be stimulated as a consequence of introducing defensive proposals;
   c. that the stability of deterrence not be weakened in an untested attempt to transcend or enhance it;
   d. that defense spending as a whole not absorb a morally disproportionate percentage of the federal budget.

3. Observing these limits in the immediate future requires that:

   a. SDI be maintained as a research and development program, within the restrictions of the ABM treaty, not pressed to deployment;
   b. the ABM treaty should not be cast aside or overridden;
   c. a specific test of each new step in SDI be an assessment of its consequences in the offensive-defensive interaction of the arms competition;
   d. clear criteria be established about spending for SDI in relationship to other needs in legitimate defense expenditures (e.g., conventional forces) and particularly in relationship to the basic human needs of the poor in our country and in other nations.

A Bibliography of Books and Articles on Strategic Defense

1. Collections

Binnendijk, Hans. *Strategic Defense in the 21st Century* (Washington, DC: Center for the Study of Foreign Affairs, Foreign Service Institute, U.S. Department of State, August 1986).

Brzezinski, Zbigniew, ed. *Promise or Peril: The Strategic Defense Initiative* (Washington, DC.: Ethics and Public Policy Center, 1986).

Carter, Ashton B., and **David N. Schwartz,** eds. *Ballistic Missile Defense* (Washington, DC: Brookings, 1984).

Cimbala, Stephen J., ed. *The Technology, Strategy, and Politics of SDI* (Boulder, CO: Westview, 1987).

Dallmeyer, Dorinda G., ed. *The Strategic Defense Initiative: New Perspectives on Deterrence* (Boulder, CO: Westview, 1987).

Haley, P. Edward, and **Jack Merritt,** eds. *Strategic Defense Initiative: Folly or Future?* (Boulder, CO: Westview, 1986).

Howe, E. L., ed. [Ten articles on strategic defense] *Journal of Social, Political, and Economic Studies* 9.2 (Summer 1984).

Miller, Steven E., and **Stephen Van Evera,** eds. *The Star Wars Controversy: An International Security Reader* (Princeton, NJ: Princeton University Press, 1986).

Schneider, William, Jr., ed. *U.S. Strategic Nuclear Policy and Ballistic Missile Defense* (Cambridge, MA: Institute for Foreign Policy Analysis, 1980).

Snyder, Craig, ed. *The Strategic Defense Debate: Can "Star Wars" Make Us Safe?* (Philadelphia: University of Pennsylvania Press, 1986).

Thompson, E. P., ed. *Star Wars* (New York: Pantheon Books, 1985).

Tirman, John, ed. *The Fallacy of Star Wars* (New York: Vintage, 1984).

Tirman, John, ed. *Empty Promise: The Growing Case against Star Wars* (Boston: Beacon Press, 1986).

Velikhov, Yevgeni, ed. *Weaponry in Space: The Dilemma of Security* (Chicago: Imported Publications, 1986).

2. Books, Articles, Official Statements

Abrahamson, James A. "The Strategic Defense Initiative," *Defense 84* (August 1984).

Abrahamson, James A. "SDI: A Program Update," *Defense 86* (January/February 1986).

Adams, Benson D. "In Defense of the Homeland," *U.S. Naval Institute Proceedings* 109.6 (June 1983).

Adelman, Kenneth. The Impact of Space on Arms Control," *Defense Science 2003+* (April/May 1985).

Aftergood, S. "Nuclear Space Mishaps and Star Wars," *Bulletin of the Atomic Scientists* 42.8 (October 1986).

Aspen Strategy Group. *The Strategic Defense Initiative and American Security* (Lanham, MD: University Press of America, 1987).

Arbess, Daniel. "Star Wars and Outer Space Law," *Bulletin of the Atomic Scientists* (October 1985).

Ball, George. "The War for Star Wars," *New York Review of Books* (11 April 1985).

Bethe, Hans, Richard L. Garwin, Kurt Gottfried, and **Henry W. Kendall.** "Space Based Missile Defense," *Scientific American* (October 1984).

Blechman, Barry M., and **Victor Utgoff.** *Fiscal and Economic Implications of Strategic Defenses* (Boulder, CO: Westview, 1986).

Bova, Ben. *Assured Survival: Putting the Star Wars Defense in Perspective* (Boston: Houghton Mifflin, 1984).

Bowman, Robert M. *Star Wars: An Insider's Case against the Strategic Defense Initiative* (Los Angeles: Jeremy Tarcher, 1986).

Broad, William J. *Star Warriors* (New York: Simon and Schuster, 1985).

Brown, Harold. "The Strategic Defense Initiative: Defense Systems and Strategic Debate," *Survival* (March/April 1985).

Brzezinski, Zbigniew. "The Political Implications of 'Thou Shalt Not Kill'," *America* (31 May 1986).

Bundy, McGeorge, George F. Kennan, Robert S. McNamara, and **Gerard Smith.** "The President's Choice: Star Wars or Arms Control," *Foreign Affairs* 63.2 (Winter 1984–85).

Burrows, William F. "Ballistic Missile Defense: The Illusion of Security," *Foreign Affairs* (62.2 (Spring 1984).

Carter, Ashton. *Directed Energy Missile Defense in Space* (Washington, DC: U.S. Congress, Office of Technology Assessment, April 1984).

Chalfont, Alan. *SDI: The Case for the Defense* (London: Institute for Strategic Studies, 1985).

Chalfont, Alan. *Star Wars: Suicide or Survival?* (Boston: Little, Brown, 1986).

Chayes, Chayes, and **Antonia Handler Chayes.** "Testing and Development of 'Exotic' Systems under the ABM Treaty: The Great Reinterpretation Caper," *Harvard Law Review* 99.8 (June 1986).

Council on Economic Priorities. *Star Wars: The Economic Fallout* (Cambridge, MA: Ballinger, 1987).

Deudney, Daniel. "Forging Weapons into Spaceships," *World Policy Journal* (Spring 1985).

Douglass, Joseph D., Jr., and **Samuel T. Cohen.** "SDI: The Hidden Opportunity," *Defense Science 2003+* (August/September 1985).

Drell, Sidney D., Philip J. Farley, and **David Holloway.** *The Reagan Strategic Defense Initiative: A Technical Political and Arms Control Assessment* (Stanford, CA: Center for International Security and Arms Control, 1984).

Drell, Sidney, and **Wolfgang Panofsky,** "The Case against Strategic Defense: Technical and Strategic Realities," *Issues in Science and Technology* (Fall 1984).

Durch, William J. *The ABM Treaty and Western Security* (Cambridge, MA: Ballinger, 1987).

Dyson, Freeman. *Weapons and Hope* (New York: Harper and Row, 1984).

Dyson, Freeman. "The Case for Star Wars," *The Economist.* 3 August 1985.

Fletcher, James C. *The Strategic Defense Initiative: Defensive Technologies Study* (Washington, DC: Department of Defense, March 1984).

Garthoff, Raymond L. *Policy vs. the Law: The Reinterpretation of the ABM Treaty* (Washington, DC: Brookings, 1987).

Garwin, Richard. "Star Wars: Shield or Threat?" *Journal of International Affairs* (Summer 1985).

Glaser, Charles L. "Why Even Good Defenses May Be Bad," *International Security* (Fall 1984).

Glaser, Charles L. "Do We Want the Defenses We Can Build?" *International Security* (Summer 1985).

Graham, Gen. Daniel O. "Toward a New U.S. Strategy: Bold Strokes Rather Than Increments," *Strategic Review* IX.2 (Spring 1981).

Graham, Gen. Daniel O. *High Frontier: A New National Strategy* (Washington, DC: High Frontier, 1982).

Graham, Gen. Daniel O. *The Non-Nuclear Defense of Cities* (Cambridge, MA: Abt Books, 1983).

Graham, Gen. Daniel O. *We Must Defend America—And Put an End to MADness* (Chicago: Regnery Gateway, 1983).

Gray, Colin. "A Case for Strategic Defense," *Survival* (March/April 1985).

Gray, Colin. "Strategic Defense, Deterrence, and the Prospects for Peace," *Ethics* (April 1985).

Gray, Colin S., and **Keith Payne.** "Nuclear Policy and the Defensive Transition," *Foreign Affairs* 62.2 (Spring 1984) 820–42.

Graybosch, Anthony J. "Star Wars: Close Encounters of the Worst Kind," *Cogito* (December 1985) 1–20.

Graybosch, Anthony J. "SDI: Tactics and Ethics," *Philosophy in Context* 15 (1986) 62–72.

Guerrier, Steven, and **Wayne C. Thompson.** *Perspective on Strategic Defense* (Boulder, CO: Westview, 1987).

Hartung, William D. et al. *The Strategic Defense Initiative: Costs, Contractors, and Consequences* (New York: Council on Economic Priorities, 1985).

Hoffman, Fred. *Ballistic Missile Defenses and U.S. National Security, Summary Report* (Washington, DC: Institute for Defense Analysis, October 1983) [The Future Security Strategy Study].

Hoffman, Fred. "The SDI in U.S. Nuclear Strategy," *International Security* (Summer 1985).

Jacky, Jonathan. "The 'Star Wars' Defense Won't Compute," *The Atlantic* (June 1985) 18.

Jastrow, Robert. "Reagan vs. the Scientists: Why the President Is Right about Missile Defense," *Commentary* (January 1984).

Jastrow, Robert. *How to Make Nuclear Weapons Obsolete* (Boston: Little, Brown, 1985).

Kass, Ilana, ed. *People in Space: Policy Perspectives for a Star Wars Century* (New Brunswick, NJ: Transaction Books, 1985).

Keyworth, George, II. "The Case for Strategic Defense: An Option for a Disarmed World," *Issues in Science and Technology* (Fall 1984).

Kogut, John, and **Michael Weissman.** "Taking the Pledge against Star Wars," *Bulletin of the Atomic Scientists* (January 1986).

Krauthammer, Charles. "Will Star Wars Kill Arms Control?" *The New Republic* (21 January 1985).

Lawrence, Robert M. *Strategic Defense Initiative: Bibliography and Research Guide* (Boulder, CO: Westview, 1986).

Lehrman, Lewis E. "The Case for Strategic Defense," *Policy Review* (Winter 1985).

Lin, Herbert. "The Software for Star Wars: An Achilles Heel?" *Technology Review* (July 1985).

Lodal, Jan. "Deterrence and Nuclear Strategy," *Daedalus* (Fall 1980).

Longstreth, Thomas K., John E. Pike, and **John B. Rhinelander,** *The Impact of U.S. and Soviet Ballistic Missile Defense Programs on the ABM Treaty* (Third Edition) Report for the National Campaign to Save the ABM Treaty (March 1985).

Marsh, Gerald E. "SDI: The Stability Question," *Bulletin of the Atomic Scientists* 41.9 (October 1985) 23–24.

Meinel, Carolyn. "Fighting MAD," *Technology Review* (April 1984).

Meyer, Stephen H. "Soviet Military Programs and the New High Ground," *Survival* (September 1983).

Military Publishing House (Moscow). *Star Wars: Delusions and Dangers* (Moscow: Progress Publishing, 1985).

Mische, Patricia M. *Star Wars and the State of Our Souls* (Minneapolis, MN: Winston Press, 1985).

Nelson, Greg, and **David Rudell.** "SDI and the ABM Treaty," *Department of State Bulletin* (August 1985).

Nelson, Greg, and **David Rudell.** "SDI: Its Nature and Rationale," *Current Policy* [U.S. Department of State No. 751] (24 October 1985).

Parnas, David L. "Why Star Wars Software Won't Work," *Harper's* (March 1985).

Patel, C., Kumar N., and **Nicolaas Bloembergen.** "Strategic Defense and Directed Energy Weapons," *Scientific American* (September 1987).

Payne, Keith. *Strategic Defense: Star Wars in Perspective* (Lanham, MD: Hamilton Press, 1986).

Pike, John. "The Strategic Defense Initiative: A Debate [with Daniel Graham]," *Policy Forum* 2.17 (October 1985).

Pournelle, Jerry, and **Dean Ing.** *Mutual Assured Survival* (New York: Baen Books, 1984).

Pressler, Larry. *Star Wars: Debating the Strategic Defense Initiative* (New York: Praeger, 1986).

Ralston, A. "Star Wars: What Is the Professional Responsibility of Computer Scientists?" *Abacus* 3.1 (1985).

Rathjens, George, and **Jack Ruina.** "BMD and Strategic Stability," *Daedalus* (Summer 1985).

Reagan, Ronald. "President's Speech on Military Spending and a New Defense," New York *Times* (24 March 1983) A20; Official text, *Department of State Bulletin* 83.2073 (Washington, DC: GPO, 1983).

Reagan, Ronald. "President Reagan on the Strategic Defense Initiative," *Defense Science 2003+* (April/May 1985).

Reagan, Ronald. "Strategic Defense Initiative," radio address 13 July 1985.

Schlesinger, James R. "Rhetoric and Realities in the Star Wars Debate," *International Security* (Summer 1985).

Sherr, Alan B. "Sound Legal Reasoning or Policy Expedient? The 'New Interpretation' of the ABM Treaty," *International Security* 11.3 (Winter 1986–87).

Shue, Henry. "Is Strategic Defense Morally Superior?" *QQ—Report from the Center for Philosophy and Public Policy* (Spring 1985).

Smith, Maj. Milton. "Legal Implications of a Space Based Missile Defense," *California Western International Law Journal* 15.1 (Winter 1985) 52–75.

Sofaer, Abraham D. "The ABM Treaty and the Strategic Defense Initiative," *Harvard Law Review* 99.8 (June 1986).

Teller, Edward. *Better a Shield than a Sword: Perspectives on Defense and Technology* (New York: Free Press, 1987).

Vlahos, Michael. *Strategic Defense and the American Ethos: Can the Nuclear World Be Changed?* (Boulder, CO: Westview, 1986).

Webster, Alexander F. C. "Towards a Morally Credible Deterrent," *Catholicism in Crisis* (April 1985).

Wieseltier, Leon. "Nuclear Idealism; Nuclear Realism: What's Really Wrong with Star Wars," *New Republic* (11 March 1985).

Wieseltier, Leon. "Madder than MAD," *New Republic* (12 May 1986).

York, Herbert. *Does Strategic Defense Breed Offense?* (Lanham, MD: University Press of America, 1987).

Zuckerman, Solly. *Star Wars in a Nuclear World* (London: William Kimber, 1986).